CORPORATE MANAGEMENT

CORPORATE MANAGEMENT

PROF. RAMESH CHANDRA

KALPAZ PUBLICATIONS
DELHI–110052

CORPORATE MANAGEMENT
(Management)

Rs. 890

ISBN: 81-7835-141-2

Published in 2002 in India by
Kalpaz Publications
C-30, Satyawati Nagar
Delhi-110052
E-mail: kalpaz@hotmail.com

Laser Typesetting at: A.S. Printers
Printed at: Mehra Offset Printers, New Delhi

Contents

Preface

Corporate management is one area in which the concerned managers have to be updated now and then. Hence in this book an effort has been made to give comprehensive idea of varied aspects of the subject. It presents the concept of corporate management in a completely dynamic and novel way.

In the days of global competition, the corporate managers have to know how to face it and go global. The book gives a detailed description of the changing facets of corporate management and is aimed at any person who wants to understand the changes taking place. It explains what are the various corporate strategies and management issues are. Within the limitations and constraints, an attempt has been made to cover almost all areas of the corporate management.

It will be a very useful handbook for the managers and a source of knowledge to the educationists, besides students, scholars, teachers, policy planners, administrators, etc.

Editor

1

Basics of Corporate Management

The purpose of this chapter is to introduce the scale and scope of corporate strategy as it applies to all commercial business and public sectors, and not-for-profit activities. The strategy of an organisation is the definition and implementation of its purpose. For this to be successful, there are elements which must be present; there are rules that must be followed; and sources of strategy to be found.

Everything about any organization stems from the purpose for its existence. If this is not clear, everything else is clouded also. The plans and policies that are devised, the activities related to strategic development and implementation and the operations, work methods and practices devised in pursuit of this will also lack focus, direction and therefore purpose.

Vision

Organization and strategic vision is a necessary precursor for organization success. The vision of an organization is its shining light, the star by which to steer, the illuminator of the path. It is a combination of visualisation, enthusiasm, ambition, and a commitment to work.

It is usually articulated by the creator of the organization, or by those who are energising or championing particular initiatives and projects. It is often their all-consuming passion, their professional and operational reason for being. As with all visions and visionaries, the matter is approached with zeal, fervour, dynamism and energy; it is the impact of this on those who are to be caught up in the initiative or project that determines its success.

Commitment

Effective organization strategies carry a 'commitment to achieve', in whatever terms this is to be measured: financial gains and profits; effectiveness and quality of service, or a combination of the two. This is also reflected in the volume, quality and nature of resources used; the ways of working adopted; the shared values, management and operational styles drawn up in support of this; and any distinctive moral or ethical stance that is also taken up.

All effective organization strategies place customers and clients at their core: without customers and clients there is no need for the organization or its activities (this also applies to internal strategies and organization systems, subsystems and procedures). The following must be addressed:

- the nature, locations, volume of the customer and customer bases;

- their needs and wants in regard to the organization's range of offerings;
- where this range exists on the scale of a customer's priorities;
- the distinctive advantages held by these offerings in relation to those of competitors;
- reputation, confidence and loyalty to the organization among its customers;
- financial elements.

This can be summarised as: let us commit ourselves to long term service and satisfaction of our customers, remembering that if we do not they will go elsewhere.

A clear recognition and evaluation is required of what is truly to be achieved over different periods of time. This has to be measured in terms of steadiness, permanence and transience. It is a function of the nature and type of investment in which the organization is engaged. It also reflects the nature of returns required by the organization's different stakeholders, and the conflicts inherent in these that must be recognised and reconciled (for example, the capacity to reconcile demand for high wages on the part of the staff, high levels of dividend demanded by shareholders, high share price demanded by stock market investors).

Clarity (or otherwise) of purpose is reflected in the actual words used in the articulation of strategy. The greater the clarity of articulation, the greater the likely clarity of purpose. The converse is also true: where the strategic purpose is not easy to read, follow or understand, because the organization has not fully grasped its own purpose.

This clarity of language is needed across the board in dealings with staff, customers, clients, the wider public and community. It is reinforced by the standpoint adopted to each of these groups, of openness or otherwise, of honesty and directness or otherwise, or of commitment or abdication. Language must also be seen in general terms as the oil of the business processes and systems used, both in the internal operating and staff management systems, and in the external marketing activities, public relations and customer and commercial interfaces.

Flexibility

Strategy is a continuous and dynamic process, not a single event; neither is it cast in tablets of stone. Part of the true clarity of purpose is the reconciliation of the ability to respond to customer demand with the capacity for recognising and evaluating the opportunities that exist. It is therefore necessary to establish a permanent organization which can accommodate this flexibility. Peters calls this the 'simultaneous loose-tight properties.' This is the capacity for allowing latitude to staff departments and divisions to seek out commercial opportunities without deflecting from the absolute standards, qualities, focus and direction of the organization. It is the capacity to include a measure of dynamism within this stated direction.

This is the recognition of the standards and quality of treatment expected on the part of the staff and customers of the organization and its communities. These elements are general standards of honesty, openness, forthrightness, trust and decency.

This is the profit motive. The case is absolute that profitable business is only possible if the soft elements referred to above are in place. Customers will not deal with organizations that are found to be dishonest, closed and untrustworthy. This also applies to the complete range of public services. Where it is impossible to avoid dealing with such bodies they will be approached with trepidation and with the certainty on the part of customers that they are to receive a less than full service or to be treated with duplicity. Business strategies are only successful if profit is made as the result.

A core obligation to all the stakeholders of the organization is to remain in business, to continue and to improve. In public service terms the equivalent is effectiveness. This again is a reflection of the core obligation to stakeholders (in this case to provide high quality and effective services to those demanding them). In the 'not-for-profit' sector the equivalent is effectiveness again: in resource-gathering and utilisation; and also in the generation of commitment to the cause or the matter in hand.

Strategies change and evolve according to the need to remain competitive, according to changes in people's perceptions, needs and wants; and as the result of technological advances. Strategy is therefore a multi-dimensional process, not a linear function.

The rules of strategy

From this, a set of rules may be identified. The golden rule is the placing of a customer at the centre of all activities and the recognition of this on the part of all those who work in the organization, in whatever function.

The others are:

- continuity, permanence and sustenance (investment) that reflect the commitment of the organization to its purpose;
- replacement and re-investment elements, technology, marketing, staff, expertise, premises, capital and consumables;
- the setting of absolute standards of policy, ethics and morality and the creation of shared values and common beliefs in support of this;
- the devising of a suitable culture, style and way of working that both reflects and harmonises the nature of the staff, the nature of the markets the necessary ways of working and the nature of the actual offerings;
- the capacity to quantify and qualify the returns that are made for success, failure, areas carried out by imperfect people;
- recognition that qualities of enthusiasm, commitment, energy, vitality, drive and ambition are required by everybody concerned;
- recognition that loyalty is required by staff, markets and communities to the organization, and by the organization to its customers, staff and communities;
- continuous reference to distinctive expertise, competence and technology;
- continuous reference to reputation and confidence;
- constant attention to improvements in all areas and activities;
- the theme of doing unto others as you would have them do unto you; an absolute regard and respect for all the stakeholders involved.

Sources of strategy

These are the distinctive competence, expertise and technology possessed by the organization, together with its ability to combine these in ways that are suitable for the production of outputs that the public wishes to buy, use or consume (or, in public service terms, that public groups require). It is necessary to identify opportunities, customer bases, market sectors and niches where the outputs produced can be successfully, effectively and profitably offered.

More generally, there is a combination of the identification of gaps in the market, and the demands of the community and society in general that have to be considered. These must then be brought together in ways that allow for success and effectiveness to continue over a sufficient period of time.

In simple markets and one-product or simple product range offerings there is an absolute time factor. There has to be a sufficient absolute time span available to render the exercise meaningful: it is exceedingly rare to be able to carry out a single operation on a short-run timescale in isolation. It is clearly possible to do this as part of a more complex or sophisticated portfolio of offerings, however. Fast moving consumer goods, foodstuffs, electrical clothing, fashion and seasonal goods mixes are all produced on this basis.

It is also necessary to identify the levels of returns desired or necessary to support this on the timescales and frequency with which these returns are required.

The rationale outlined above is then tempered and limited by the human activities that go with it. This may at its most extreme be the whim of the entrepreneur or the chief person of the company ('I want to be a shipping tycoon', for example). This will clearly only be successful in commercial terms if the person in question then goes on to hire others of this distinctive expertise to work for him; however, the initial choice remains just that: choice. A similar position may be taken up around preferred location, technology used, or the desire to work with other particular individuals.

Opportunity

In practice, this occurs frequently. It happens either because the organization in question is approached with an overtly viable proposition or because another sphere of activity opens up as the result of current involvement elsewhere. It may also occur because of pioneering and entrepreneuring/intrapreneuring on the part of those currently active. The opportunity becomes the starting point for another commercial route or journey. It may—and does—also occur from scratch. The Japanese presence in the car and electrical goods sectors of the West was originally founded on the opportunity afforded by the lack of quality or reliability in the local outputs in these areas. This has now been fully developed by the other countries of the Pacific Rim.

Non-rational elements

Having spent the previous pages taking the view that there is a rational approach to the formulation and development of strategy that should be adopted, it is now necessary to recognise that this does not always happen in practice. Many students of strategy go a stage further, holding the view that non-rational elements are essential in the march of progress of the business sphere. The inspirational and creative elements are essential in the development of new products and services.

Any organization that wishes to create new products and services must invest in these activities and qualities if it is to be successful. This is almost a rational approach to the realm of creativity, and explains why organizations sponsor and encourage champions, experimenters, tryers and trialists, suggestion schemes, work improvement groups and quality circles. Similar approaches are taken to procedures, processes and structures, and to management development-type project work.

The best organizations are capable of accommodating, assimilating and evaluating these elements in order to give them life and resources for as long as they merit. Other facts must also be considered. The very nature of work, management, organization and direction all have to be energised by irrational human beings. Translation of strategy, policy and direction into operations and actions may go right, or wrong, or differently for entirely human reasons. All organizations have their own life and the sub-currents, secondary and hidden agenda, and *realpolitik* that occur within them as a matter of course, and all affect operations, activities and performance. There are also resource and time constraints, opportunity costs, opportunity gains, the prevailing wider and economic factors, the state of the markets served, actual (and invariably imperfect) levels of understanding of those markets. Apart from these aspects there are factors present in all organizations that limit, corrupt, dilute, dissipate and destroy (and sometimes enhance) the rational approach. The pressure for quick results is a major factor, and is often at odds with the long-term nature of strategy and direction formulation and implementation.

These come from a variety of directions and include trade unions, professional bodies, professional and trade associations, other lobbies and action groups. Their influence varies in different situations. However, it may be necessary to gain their support (or at least acquiescence) and, in order to do this, the ideal outcome of the proposed initiative may have to be diluted.

Differences with trade unions have come about in the introduction of new technology and some have resisted this because they saw job, status or influence losses as the consequence. This also occurs when difficulties with experts and professionals arise. Again, the result is likely to be a dilution of the strategy in order to engage the support or acquiescence of these groups.

Akin to this is the resistance of internal organization functions, divisions and departments, invariably in response to changes in activities which are (or are see to be) threatening to their own particular well-being. This may lead to the dilution of the ideal in order to gain the required acquiescence.

These exist in sprawling and sophisticated organizations where there may not be the corporate will or structure to control them. This may go a stage further, to the point where the organization actively depends on overmighty subjects to control these departments and divisions. Particular current personal, professional, organizational and occupational expertise also often commands this level of influence.

The ability to block or negate progress is also important. It is found in individuals who carry influence, especially in boards, groups and committees, through expertise, by weight of personality or an aura of decisiveness. The secondary or sub-agenda of those who attach themselves to projects and strategies is also important. Top managers, directors and politicians often need triumphs: something that can be written up and broadcast in glowing terms in the global, national or sectoral media.

At lower and operational levels, individuals require successes for their career resumes in the interests of their own advancement. They also need to be successful in terms of organizational and operational politics. They therefore pursue what is right in these terms, whether or not this is in the organization's best interests. Favouritism and departmental, divisional and functional pecking order in the organization (by accident or design) leads to resources and priorities following the requests and initiatives for these reasons rather than operational necessity. In such circumstances, it is impossible for all departments and functions to have any commonality of purpose. They become too busy fighting their own particular corner.

It follows from this that other departments use their valuable time, effort, energy and resources in building up their own capacities to survive in the organizational *realpolitik*, rather than concentrating on their own core purposes. Ultimately, organizations create an atmosphere and structure of discrete departments surrounded on the one hand by their own defensive walls, and on the other using networks, the canteen culture and extramural relations when anything does need to be done. In such cases, no truly effective strategy is ever going to take place and much effort and resource is dissipated in the structural malfunction.

This is often overlooked, especially in public services and charitable activities. A lack of clear direction is often also to be found in niche offerings and departmental, divisional and individual initiatives in larger organizations. To avoid this, strategic and directional standpoints are much better seen in terms of the following:

- the products, services or offerings that are to be made and the volume and quality in which they are to be made;
- the total level of investment required;
- the market segments and niches to be served;
- the activities in which the organization is to be engaged in their promotion;
- the style of operations and ways of working that are envisaged;
- the desired culture of the organization;
- the means, methods and technology that are to be used to produce the offerings;
- the nature and quality of staff to be employed; the qualities required of them; the ways in which work is to be divided and jobs defined; the management structure and style chosen; the operational ways of working; systems and procedures adopted;
- the need to bring new offerings into the markets served;
- ethical considerations, defined in the widest terms, and including consideration of the ways in which the organization interacts with staff, customers, community and the wider global business sphere;

- the profit motive in whatever terms this is defined (including high levels of effectiveness for public services).

If this is done then likely or certain areas of difficulty can be assessed at the strategy formulation (or pre-formulation) stage. For example, any proposed entry into high-tech market niches cannot be done on a shoestring, either in terms of production technology or staff. Operations in a public transport niche cannot be carried out without adequate reference to technology, replacement, maintenance and surface considerations, skills, qualities, and, above all, a mission to serve those requiring the transport services. Lessons should also be learned from cases and examples of best and worst practice. Extensive studies have been carried out in recent years, concentrating especially on the following areas.

1. Emergent sectors, especially the Pacific Rim car and electrical goods industries that have a phenomenal track record of commercial success in their dealings with the West over the medium to long term and in taking market share from established and familiar organizations that hitherto produced, marketed and sold these items both successfully and profitably in their own countries.

2. Distinctive companies of high local profitability, reputation and regard. In the UK examples of these are The Body Shop, the Virgin Group, Marks & Spencer and Co-Steel Sheerness. In the USA examples quoted extensively include Stew Leonard (supermarket), Millikens (textiles), WalMart (supermarket and department store chain), and Bethlehem Steel Inc.

3. Distinctive generic sectors—such as food retailing, cars, travel, media—in which many companies operate extremely successfully. The purpose of these studies is the identification of those properties present in organizations that compete in these areas, and the relationship between these and the success of their operations.
4. Segmentation and specialisation and the extent to which these are viable as organization (rather than secondary or subsidiary) strategies, and other elements such as timescale and duration of these niches and the activities that are required to maintain and sustain them.
5. Permanence/transience: the extent to which the certainty of the state of the sector can be predicted. It is seen both in terms of the other elements indicated here, and where the priority to use or consume the particular offerings lies. This has particular importance on the one hand when deciding whether or not to invest in an experience, production/output technology and resources required. It also requires consideration when getting into fashionable and faddish sectors.

The absolute volumes of market sectors. Normally these are measured in terms of,

(a) money: for example, this is an ? million sector/ industry and so on;

(b) volume: for example this sector consumers by tonnes of particular products per annum;

(c) levels of investment required to become a sectoral player;

(d) rates or return: for example, investors in this sector get z per cent return on their investment; or shares in this sector may be expected to rise by z per cent;

(e) numbers of customers available.

These can then be measured in relation to the number and size of other players in the given sector and the nature of the precise rate of return that they get. Analysis of the key players, especially the major players in terms of size, market share, volume of business contracted, profitability, rates and speed of returns, can also then be analysed.

7. Competitors: the extent, nature and prevalence of these and the nature of their offerings, whether absolute alternatives, close substitutes or part of the more general substitution processes discussed elsewhere; the extent to which differentiation is a major part of playing in the sector.

8. The state of the market itself: whether expanding, contracting, declining, young mature, old; in need of rejuvenation; capable of being rejuvenated or re-energised; and the implications of this for the organization concerned.

9. Analysis of public sector services against models of political drive, service creation and client demand.

10. Analysis of distinctive models of operation that exist at the public/national/critical sector crossroads. Two main models of this area nationalisation and privatisation. In addition, there are the beginnings of public/private cooperation in public services provision and in the putting out to contract of particular public activities.

11. Establishing specific criteria upon which to base the analysis and evaluation of strategy. While these clearly vary in detail between sectors, certain common and universal elements may be drawn out. Above all, these are elements relating to cost, price, quality, value, timescales, continuity confidence and expectation to which constant reference is made throughout this book.

12. Questioning existing and traditional approaches to both direction and organization. This includes the questioning of the format and structure of organizations, their ways of working, their targets and outputs.

A great volume of information and literature has emerged from this particularly over the period of the 1980s and 1990s. There are, however, few absolutes. No simple or distinctive sets of traits are found to exist in all organizations or sectors that are successful. No absolute performance targets can be created; they have to be seen in their own particular context. No absolute measures of price, quality, volume, value, cost, confidence, expectation or understanding exist. Again, these all have to be seen in particular contexts, and the nature and balance of these varies between sectors.

Manufacturing and Production Management

While basic principles of strategy formulation and development are universal, they must be applied in particular ways in different sectors. The purpose of this chapter is to identify the aspects of different sectors that affect and influence the strategies adopted. Three sectors are distinguished:

- manufacturing, using the classical model of scales of production, of unit, batch, mass and flow;
- commercial services, including retail, distribution, banking and leisure;
- public service, and the limitations placed on these by the special factors and circumstances included in the facts of political life.

There are also notes on capital and infrastructure projects, and on the activities of the voluntary/not-for-profit sectors. At the core of any manufacturing organization is the strategy that determines the nature, volume, quality and regularity of the product or product range. There are elements of successful-manufacturing strategies that are universal; and also elements that are specific to particular sectors and to the scale of production adopted.

Classically four archetype manufacturing standpoints are identified:

- unit production;
- batch production;
- mass production;
- flow production.

Organizations may operate in one or more of these ways or in all of them. Unit production is normally highly specialised and highly customer-focused. Unit producers manufacture their items in response to specific or near-specific orders. Unit output is usually for highly specific and clearly defined market niches. In some cases the quality and exclusivity of the offering overrides any consideration of timescale, deadline or price. In others there will be a price, deadline and quality balance to be struck. The relationship between manufacturer and client is likely to be close so that customers receive satisfaction and a full understanding of their requirements is achieved. There are vagaries of operating in this way. A balance of quality and exclusivity is essential, as is the ability to charge an economic rent for the output.

The production technology of unit manufacturing is a combination of high levels of personal, technical and often artistic skill with generic, flexible and high-quality equipment. Customers of unit producers have strong and distinctive requirements. In the commissioning and/or purchasing of an exclusive item, exclusivity is sought. Successful unit production requires complete adaptability and flexibility of technology, staff, approach and attitudes, and work methods and patterns. This is likely to include the ability to call upon specialists as and when required.

Batch production

Batch manufacturing is the name given to the production-of small to medium-sized volumes or batches of items. Effective batch production is achieved through a combination of the following:

- high-quality, up-to-date and flexible technology which can easily be reconfigured or rejigged to meet particular demands;
- flexible multi-skilled regular work force, working to both standard and flexible patterns of work;
- flexibility and dynamism in response to orders, balanced with a regular customer base;
- a distinctive, well-recognised and well-received range

of offerings that is nevertheless capable of variation, modification and change, often at short notice;

- a distinctive, well-recognized and well-received way of working, suitable both to the given production efforts and the demands and expectations of the customer base;
- a distinctive price, value, quality and deadline mixture which is well understood, and which can be varied when required.

Batch production is a combination of high output and short (or shortish) production runs. It requires a combination of the ability to respond to orders with the capacity to anticipate likely demand for the products. Batch production activity is therefore concerned with both dealing with orders and producing stocks ready for sale as the orders come in.

Effective batch manufacturing strategies are founded in a full understanding of the capacities of the technology that is used and the staff using it, together with the imagination and creativity to envisage the full range of outputs that is could produce, and to which this expertise could be turned.

Continuous investment in production technology and the ability to maximise its use is therefore critical to the continued success of batch manufacturers. Competitive advantage and organizational reputation is gained through speed of production and response, quality and reliability.

Mass production and manufacturing takes place in order to satisfy mass, even global, markets and their demands for consumer goods and the components. Effective mass manufacturing is dependent upon heavy and continuing levels of capital investment in the production technology used, and in the capacities of the staff involved to operate it effectively. The main differences between this and the production of batches are the sheer scale of activities and the steadier and more stable nature of the outputs. Thus, for example, while a batch production run may result in a batch output in hours or days, the mass producer's aim is likely to be the continuity of production over a period of weeks, months or even years. In car and consumer durable production the main reason for changing the nature of the item is design improvement. Only then, therefore, are the production activities altered.

Mass production activities are driven by maximisation of production technology, economies of scale and the universality of the product, design, appearance, quality and performance. In mass production, competitive advantage is only to be sustained in long production runs. Products are supplied on the basis that there is a continuing general demand for them. While there is a general relationship between orders placed and output, mass production is not order-specific or directly order-responsive. Opportunities and causes for concern are indicated by general trends in product consumption. Whether upward or downward. The mass producer works to satisfy markets often months, sometimes years, in advance.

It is therefore necessary to be concerned with identifying and assessing future trends in the sectors and markets served, those which could potentially be served, and the means by which they are served. Lead times and investment levels, together with elements relating to the commissioning, design, development and ordering of installation of new product technology, are all integral to mass manufacturing success, and should all therefore be considered as part of the mass production strategy.

Flow production takes place in response to universal and continuous demand for a unique (or nearly unique) product or commodity. The technology used is extremely capital-intensive, designed and installed for the precise stated purpose. It is not normally flexible or transferable. The process used is normally continuous; there are huge costs incurred in switching it off and restarting it. The competitive advantage of involvement in flow manufacturing and the sectors that lend themselves to it stem from the very nature of the products: oil and petrol, chemicals, steel, glass and plastic.

Operating in these sectors depends on the continued ability to command and maintain sufficiently high levels of capital for investment in this scale of technology. The level of capital required is a high barrier to entry. Other barriers also exist in the form of, and access to, technology and expertise. The ability to transform and replace existing technology is also dependent upon the command of high levels of capital.

However, the variable costs incurred in operating are low as a percentage of total cost. The processes indicated all simply transform raw materials into commodities with a universal demand. The absolute charge necessary for a litre of petrol at the refinery gate or glass bottle at the factory gate in order to cover variable costs is negligible. The ability to charge commercial and economic rents for these commodities is dependent on the sheer volume of demand, and this ensures high and continuing levels of returns on total capital employed.

Supply and demand

The supply and demand balance has to be assessed because it creates stresses and strains, especially where the emphasis is on responsiveness. There are also matters of concern relating to the length of time that finished goods remain on the shelf awaiting purchase and order. In flow processes, where the emphasis is almost entirely on the supply side it is necessary to open up product storage facilities during periods of low demand. If such periods persist, this may lead to stockpiling and in some cases to product-dumping activities by the organization concerned.

Production environment

There is overwhelming evidence that the quality of working environment has a direct impact on the quality of work and the motivation of the staff. The necessity is therefore (in whatever situation) to make the work environment as comfortable as possible within any operational constraints. In extreme cases—such as those of extreme noise, dirt or temperature—there are legal minima to be observed in the provision of protection and clothing and in the length of time to be spent on activities in any given situation. Above and beyond these minimum requirements there is an increasing perception of the business value and profitability and effectiveness of performance that can be gained through adherence to the golden rule of Mary Kay Ash: 'Do unto others as you would have them do unto you.' This is in turn reinforced by current notions of egalitarianism and the setting of distinctive, high and precise standards of operation, and behaviour at work. It is impossible to do this in an inherently bad working environment.

It is necessary to consider the different service sectors as entities with separate and distinctive identities. This is in spite of the fact that many outputs of the service sectors are clearly highly tangible. Retail, for example, is classified as a service activity, yet the items purchased from outlets are clearly highly tangible. Travel, tourism, sports and leisure pursuits, health care and the outputs of bars, cafes and restaurants all offer a product service mix in fact.

The general concept of service is developed most sharply and distinctively in Western Europe, Australia, New Zealand and above all, North America. The hub of this is intangible: the expectation and satisfaction of the customer. Where this occurs, a mutually satisfactory business relationship is established. Otherwise, the customer may seek redress; if this is not forthcoming, the customer seeks better service elsewhere. If satisfaction is continually not afforded, the customer will in any case seek alternatives. If expectations are consistently exceeded, this eventually becomes the normal level of satisfaction, and to fall back to levels of what was previously quite adequate will then be perceived as a decline.

The product service mix is also important. The purchase of a new car normally carries a commitment to maintenance, service and repair on the part of the manufacturer through a recognised and approved outlet. The purchase of a sandwich has clear service implications in relation to the freshness of the product. The purchase of a public transport ticket carries with it implications for the timing, speed and quality of that service.

Service Nature

	People services: services:	*Goods and possessions*
Tangible:	health care	freight transportation
	passenger transportation	industrial equipment
	beauty salons	repair and maintenance
	exercise clinics	laundry and dry cleaning
	restaurants	landscaping
Intangible:	education	banking
	broadcasting	legal services
	information services	accounting
	theatres	securities
	museums	insurance

The components of service

Features of customer service

- Frequency of delivery
- Time from order to delivery
- Reliability of delivery
- Emergency deliveries when required
- Stock availability and continuity of supply
- Orders filled completely
- Advice on non-availability
- Convenience of placing order

- Acknowledgement of order
- Accuracy of invoices
- Quality of sales presentation
- Regular calls by sales representatives
- Manufacture monitoring of retail stock levels
- Credit terms offered, other financial arrangements
- Dates of payment
- Dates of service delivery
- After sales and service support
- Replacements/alternatives
- Customer query handling
- Quality of outer packaging
- Easy-to-read packaging, brochures, literature
- In store handling and display
- New product/package development
- Reviews product range regularly
- Coordination between production, distribution and marketing
- Meeting expectations
- Constant improvement
- Politeness
- Honesty
- Trust
- Confidence

These are dependent upon the following factors.

1. The nature of service itself.
2. The nature of the benefits, expectations and satisfaction required by the customer.
3. The nature of the relationship between the service organization and its customers.

This includes the frequency or regularity of visits by the customer, the length of each visit, the nature of the transactions entered into, and the nature of the personal and profitable elements of the relationships that are to be developed.

4. The mode of service delivery.
5. The nature of service demanded and supplied. This includes seasonal and weekend factors, and the ways in which demand for the service may be varied up and down. This is heavily affected, above all, by levels of unemployment (in local terms, the higher this goes the greater the decline in demand for all commercial services). It may also be affected by the availability of a substitute; conversely, demand for one service is likely to rise if a substitute closes down or becomes unavailable.
6. The extent to which the service is standardised, universally and equally offered of tailored and customised to the requirements of individual consumers or consumer groups.
7. The technology and equipment required to produce the service. In the restaurant example this is the equipment necessary to store, prepare, cook and serve the food. In the travel agency sector this is the

equipment necessary to gain access to the data bases of tour operators, package companies, and transport services and to make quick and effective bookings. In the personal finance sector it is the technology that enables instant withdrawals and credit to be made (the debit/switchcard system, cashpoints and front of branch database technology).

8. Information requirements, both in the presentation of the services on offer and to illustrate the benefits and satisfaction to be gained on the part of customers. For example, the travel agency books the holiday—the service—on the basis of the brochure presentation, which shows the benefits and potential satisfaction to the customer. The bank offers free and accessible banking to its customers—the service—and also its invulnerability and confidence.

9. The general cost, price, quality, volume and volume mix. For example, if all banks offer free personal banking to individual customers, any bank that then decides that it will make charges must have a range of benefits to offer which outweigh and override this particular benefit.

10. Quality, maintenance and control. This is often extremely difficult to define. On the one hand, the service is being instigated or delivered by a human (and therefore an imperfect being whose performance will vary); on the other, it is being delivered to human beings whose expectations vary. The best organizations get over this to a great extent at least by instilling particular attitudes, values, beliefs and modes of service delivery that are successful, effective and profitable.

Storage and preservation

Some services cannot be stored at all; for example, travel tickets can only be sold up to the point of departure of the train, plane or boat. Theatre, concert and cinema tickets are also sold for particular performances: customers do not buy tickets and then turn up to see what is being put on. Package holidays have a longer shelf-life equivalent: summer packages are sold from the previous. December onwards, and winter packages from September onwards; in both cases there are early booking advantages (to give business an initial boost) and last-minute offers (at the point at which the package sale would otherwise be lost). Restaurant services are subject to the perishability or durability of the food and drink stocks.

Some financial services are relatively durable and universal: for instance, bank branches and insurance companies do not normally limit the number of accounts or clients that they take on. However, the nature of some of the services offered and the implications for the customers may change out of all recognition due to variations in charge and fee levels, interest rates and dependency on cash points rather than over-the-counter provision.

Inseparability is the term used to describe the fact that a critical part of the service takes place at the point of transaction between producer and customer. Both are therefore involved in the service production: the producer in the demonstration of the range of offerings and permutations that are available, and the customer in the articulation of the precise requirement. Customer satisfaction and profitable and effective business occurs where there is a sufficient measure of overlap between the two.

The environment in which the service is offered is also important. There are two major reasons for this: that staff have to work in it, and the customer has to come into it. There are also aspects specific to the nature of the particular service to be addressed. Kwik-Fit, the UK car tyre and exhaust replacement service company, offers hot and cold drinks and newspapers in a waiting room area (akin to that of a doctor or dentist) while the work is carried out. Boots offers chairs for immobile and disabled people to sit and wait while their prescriptions are being made up. Banks and post office counter services now ask customers to wait in a single queue (rather than one at each desk) so that people are served strictly on a first-come-first-served basis. This is perceived by all to be much better than suffering the vagaries of the queue in which one happened to find oneself.

Where the service is not conducted on a face-to-face basis (as, for example, with telephone or mail-order arrangements), the total environment of the service provider has to be substituted by the quality of the telephone transaction and thus created by it to a degree sufficient to ensure both immediate satisfaction and repeat business.

New products, research and development

New products, innovations and developments are continually required by all organizations because of the competitive nature of business, the drive for advantages and the resultant increased expectations and demands of consumers. All organizations therefore do this in some shape or from. Public social security and health services are developed to meet the changing needs of the population, the changes in the population mix and in response to economic factors and circumstances. Education services must constantly be developed and updated through technological advance, the ever-changing history and geography of the world, scientific advances and changes in the general state of understanding enlightenment. It consists of the following.

1. The invention of something that is radically new or different. This does not happen truly very often. Recent inventions (that is, since the Second World War) include the television, computer and space satellite.
2. The application of new technology to existing production processes causing cost and quality improvements and therefore price and value advantages to the customer.
3. The re-presentation of existing products in new forms and to new sectors. Much of this is carried out by some process or other of differentiation, and includes repackaging, redesign, new advertising and promotion campaigns, and new names for existing products.

Products new to the market sectors or niches are introduced following market research, buying patterns and habits, purchasing power, and current levels and density of activity. The organization brings its existing levels of corporate image and expectation together with the amount of precise and targeted interest it has managed to generate by virtue of the proposed new activities.

This is where the company adopts or introduces a distinctly new product to its range. Supermarkets and department stores go into (and come out of) fashion ranges, furniture, furnishings, books and magazines. Most new products do not get to the start of commercial production. Commitment to new product development in spite of this is essential. Lessons and information are drawn from the whole process so that successful innovation takes place eventually.

Organizations clearly strives for as high a success rate as possible in the bringing on of new products. The failure of new products is exacerbated by the following.

This is the anticipation and expectation of instant or near-instant results. When this is not achieved the organization questions its whole commitment to the research, development and new product processes undertaken, rather than the timescale.

Failure of new product strategies and activities is accelerated through resource lack or starvation. In some sectors there is an expedient short-term cash flow advantage to be gained by cutting research and development budgets. The inevitable result of this is a reduction in the quality and effectiveness of the total research and development effort.

The ability of the organization to get its new products on to the market quickly enough is also critical to success. Brilliant inventions have still to be marketed and sold. If an equivalent substitute quickly produce and effectively presented is offered by a competitor, the original organisation is likely to lose market share, and may indeed lose their entire competitive position (as, for example with IBM in the personal computer market).

This is an organization's concern with itself and its own brilliance and expertise (which may be extremely high) without adequate reference to its markets. In such circumstances neither concepts and ideas nor products are truly market tested. Organizations further confuse prevailing attitudes to them, especially if these are favourable, with the behaviour buyers. (A general feeling on the part of consumers towards a particular organization does not mean that they will buy from it; conversely buyers may loathe an organization but buy its products nevertheless.) These matters will be compounded by internal organizational politics, in-fighting and jockeying for position.

Product champions, think-tanks and other overmighty subjects need triumphs; their internal opponents need them to fail. These matters are also likely to be compounded by the faddishness of approaches to new products and initiative. This is extremely prevalent in public policy initiatives, especially in health, social services and education, where such developments (given neither the time nor the resources to work anyway) are superseded at short-term intervals by the next idea. This becomes infinitely worse where the structure and management style (and also the minister and director) are themselves short term and transient.

Public services are provided to support the qualities of life and standards of living that society requires and expects. They reflect the political, social, economic and ethical values and stances of the given society. Societies with strong political ideologies and priorities reflect these in the nature of the services that are provided. (For example, the former USSR concentrated its resources and expertise on defence and military activities, reflecting both its authoritarian and expansionist political drives). Conversely, where there is no clear sense of public purpose, this also is reflected in the lack of clarity and direction of the services offered. In extreme cases this is likely to lead to a collapse of services. This is especially acute where there is a lack of direction compounded by conflicting demands for resources overtly based on the need to satisfy and fulfil them all. If the quality of life is to be supported effectively, there is an absolute necessity to give stability, order, clarity of purpose and resources. There is a large degree of professionalism and professionalisation.

2

Corporate Management: Growth Strategies

The growth strategies of corporate management take one or more of the following forms.

1. Expansion and growth of market share. This is related either to expansion of the total market size, or else takes place at the expense of other operators in the sector.

2. Expansion and growth of turnover, volume, income of profit. This may relate to market share also, or to a drive for efficiencies within the organisation, or in the seeking of greater levels and volumes of business with the existing customer base.

3. The achievement of economies of scale; the command of technology and distribution.

4. The command of the means of gaining and maintaining customer and consumer confidence.

5. Expansion into new market areas and niches. This is where the existing product ranges are priced or

differentiated in ways designed to appeal to different niches. Additionally, in a highly competitive sector the requirement is to broaden the appeal of the offering in question in relation to those of the other players. Related to this is often the extension and expansion of the offering range (real or differentiated). There are diversification elements in this which will be discussed fully under that heading below.

6. Expansion into new locations, both indigenous and international.
7. Diversification, integration, acquisition, merger, joint ventures and alliances. All of these are discussed fully under their own headings below.

Expansions take place for their own configurations of the rational and irrational. Rationally, organisations expand because they have spare or under utilised resources, finance, staff, production and output technology.

Some organisations in some sectors may need to grow in order to remain viable players in a turbulent sector (as with national and global companies in the civil engineering sector). Organisations make acquisitions to seek more and alternative outlets for their products (for example, the purchase by Sony of Columbia).

Organisations expand production volumes by using their existing technology more effectively and thus bringing unit costs down (and generating the opportunity therefore to bring the price down also). The irrational must also be considered. Some organisations have overwhelming pioneering cultures which require constant prospecting and exploration. This, in turn, leads to a constant expansion and extension of the range of activities.

Organisations may choose to go down a particular line because it is a high-profile or fashionable area in which to be involved. Organisations may pursue a particular strategy on the whim of the Chief Executive, a bunker mentality, . or an overmighty subject or group. Organisations may choose to go into a sector because it is, or is perceived to be, highly profitable (rational enough) but without having any previous experience or expertise in it. In regard to all the above points, the rational does not of itself lead to success, and neither does the irrational lead to failure. The key to success in expansion is again rational, however.

The proposed direction has to be subjected to the same standards and level of scrutiny as any other strategy. Timescales, targets and intermediate markers are established. The extent of investment and resources required for the purpose is the same. The capabilities, capacities and expertise required to be a successful player in the sector are analysed and evaluated. Whatever the source of the proposed expansion, it will succeed only if these elements are applied.

This occurs in the following circumstances and conditions, and where new organisations are able to satisfy them. In passing, it should be noted that there are very few sectors that are not open to potential entry.

1. Where the overall market is growing, can be made to grow or has growth potential. In this case there is a capacity or potential that existing players may not be able to fill and they may not be willing to fill it either, preferring to concentrate on keeping their existing customer bases satisfied rather than diluting their efforts in this regard in the pursuit of larger volumes.

2. Where organisations leave the market, again, leaving spare capacity in it.
3. Where the potential entrant has a real, perceived or differentiated advantage to bring to the sector in question. In real terms this is likely to be a cost-price, value or quality advantage over the existing operator. These were the overwhelming advantages borough to the consumer, electronics and car sectors by Japanese companies coming into Western Europe and North America.

In perceived of differentiated terms new entrants bring associations, image and lifestyle connotations to the sectors in question. Again, these were the main qualities brought to the take-away food sector by McDonald's and Burger King. They are also the basis on which Coca Cola and Pepsi Cola is sold, and any potential entrants to the soft drinks sector must be able to compete on this, or else find something that supersedes it.

4. Where a niche operator builds up sufficient reputation, resources and capacity to engage in offensive strategies with a view to taking share from the main players involved.
5. Where complacency exists on the part of the existing operations in the market where there has been a fall-off in the levels of quality or service; where profit-taking exists; where sectoral norms exist; and in all of these cases where there is an opportunity in relation to these. This would tend to indicate sectors where entry barriers where in reality relatively low. The capacity for complacency, fall-off in levels of quality and service, and profit-taking tends to be greatest in sectors where entry barriers are relatively high.

6. Where an organisation is able to bring its reputation from one sphere to another and to gain a foothold in a sector as the result of expanding in another. This may apply where the new sphere is related to previous experience or not. In either case a high levels of existing reputation is necessary.

This occurs where an organisation either finds itself in the position of being the major player in the market (for example, as a result of mergers or take overs, or withdrawal by competitors from it); or, conversely, the organisation sets out to become the dominant player. Dominance may occur in a variety of ways. It may come about because of sheer organisation size and the resources that are available to it.

The company may be the only multi-national or public company in the entire sector. It may have a particular national, regional, sectoral or local appeal. Dominance may be of a large sector (cosmetics, for example); one that is more clearly defined but still large, such as toothpaste; or more specialist still, such as non-silicon based toothpaste; or highly specialised, such as herbal toothpaste. It may mean command and production or process technology that give enormous cost advantages. It may mean control of the critical sources of supply, or critical retail and distribution outlets.

One organisation may be able offer premium salaries, thus enabling it to attract all the best expertise in the field. The nature of the market in question may have given rise to virtual monopolies, or oligopolies, which have in turn created entry and protection barriers making it very difficult for anyone to enter who does not have ready the capital, equipment, resources, technology, expertise and distribution outlets (oil, banking, energy supply, transport and telecommuni-cations are all examples of this). There are clear advantages to be gained from being in the position of dominant operators. There also particular responsibilities and obligations that are related to market management, stability and influence. It is possible to regulate price levels, delivery dates, production runs and the volume of the item in question that it available at any one time. However, these capabilities are not eternal. If the business relationship that is part of the strategic focus is lost, the capabilities may only last until the customer organisation either redesigns its product or finds another source of supply.

Brands and branding

The purpose of brand creation is the establishment of identity and uniqueness for a product or service. The following types of brands may be distinguished.

Company — Where the company itself is a brand (for example, Marks & Spencer, Sony, Ford, British Airways).

House — Where the product range of the company is branded. For example, the Ford house brands are Mondeo, Escort and fiesta; the Sony house brand is the Walkman; British Airways house brands include Poundstretcher, Club Class and Concorde.

Individual brands — This is where the owning company's name often does not appear in the branding process. Offerings are allowed to stand on their own: for example, Persil (owned by Lever); Daz, Radion (Reckitt & Coleman) detergents; Singapore Airlines is owned by the Swire Group; Butterley Brick is owned by the Hanson Group; Jaguar is owned by the Ford Company. The owning organisation has no prominence in relation to these brands.

Generic brands These exist as a form of umbrella for a range of products. To all UK consumers Bird's Eye, Ross and Findus are frozen food brands. The range of each is constantly being varied. It is easy for the companies in question to do this as they have the general strength of the brand on which to base the new product. These is no need therefore to engage in a separate marketing activity as each new offering is made. Further marketing activities conducted on behalf of one of the offerings under the generic brand also promote and reinforce its strength.

Distribution This is the branding of retail establishments such as Currys, the outlets John Lewis Partnership, Tesco and Sainsbury's; wholesaling such as Booker and Arcoll; transport such as Norbert Dentressangle, National Freight Corporation and TNT; mail order such as keys and Great Universal, and catalogue stores such as Argos.

Universal brands These include Coca Cola and McDonald's which have a global general identity and perception.

Specialist brands These have no meaning or identity outside their own sector but they are of critical value within it. The properties of distinctive branding therefore apply to the manufacture of components are parts for assembly, and to industrial business just as they do to consumer orientation and distribution. For example, the manufactures of aero engines have to use components of a particular distinctive brand strength.

The amins of branding

The purpose and function of branding is as follows. Commercial advantages are gained by supplying large generic markets. Organisations that make dolls' clothes, for example, are able to charge much more for then if they are to be sold on as part of the Sindy or Barbie range. Manufacturers of copper piping are able to charge much more for this if they are able to generate a positive identity and confidence in the construction sector.

Organisations normally register the name of the brand and also any distinctive slogan, description or slang that has been generated as part of the branding process. Thus, Gillette and 'the best a man can get' are both trademarks. Coca Cola, Coke, Diet Coke, Cherry Coke and Fanta are all registered as trademarks by the Coca Cola Organisation. This also extends to intellectual and creative property:

Terry Pratchett, the UK best-selling author, has registered the name Disc World and the characters in his novels so that a range of other products, including figurines, pictures, T-shirts, videos and tapes may be developed.

The brand mark is a part of the differentiation process. It offers distinctive benefits, both operational and behavioural, to customers and consumers. These are the realities of value and quality; and the intangibles of expectation, esteem and identity. For example, this is the element that enables Coca Cola to charge premium price over supermarkets and other non-distinctive Coca brands. The distinctive Nike, Hi-Tec and Reebok logos all add value (and therefore price premiums) to their trainers and leisure wear.

The purchase of an item brings with it levels of expectation, satisfaction and performance; and an actual or perceived statement of price quality and value. The repeat purchase of familiar brands should must be sate consumer activities.

The brand is the cornerstone of customer loyalty. Thus the person who always books her holiday through Thomas Cook, always flies Virgin Atlantic or British Airways, or always buys here groceries from Tesco or Marks & Spencer does so because her loyalty has been engaged.

The brand name effectively acts as a summary of everything that is known, understood and perceived about the given item and its value and benefits. Thus when Coca Cola is mentioned the consumer perceives not only a drink but also the sunny happy images that are associated with it, its even and universal quality, and its lifestyle associations. The person using Wolf tools not only perceives their usage and dexterity with them, but also the finished job or products, the feeling of satisfaction (and profit) that will go with it, and the positive response of the person for whom the job is being carried out or the product being made. Where the process of branding is successful the returns are considerable. Brands with a market share of 40 per cent generate three tines the return on investment of those with a share of only 10 per cent.

The top UK grocery brands generate six times the return on sales of the number two brand. Premium brands earn 20 per cent more than discount brands. Differentiated brands command premium prices rather than having to rely on cost advantage. The best feasible strategy to achieve high brand profitability, reputation and growth is therefore to differentiate.

This is where the characteristics of other brands which are seen to be successful are taken on. Thus all airlines have a club or business class, and this is now being extended to rail and sea travel and car hire. Business facilities, computer terminals, typing pools, fax and quiet work areas were first offered by Hilton hotels and have now been introduced by all the other global chains. Cadburys have brought out their own version of the Irish cream drink of whisky, brown sugar and dairy cream first designed and introduced under the Bailey's name in the 1970s.

This is where organisations use other brands for their won advantage. Car companies, for example, use particular brands of tyre, spark plugs, seating or in-car entertainment. Clothes manufacturers use proprietary prints, distinctive fastenings and ornaments, and may coordinate these with the offerings of other producers or of the retail outlets in which they are being sold. Retail and mail order outlets may also expect to gain from the offering of proprietary brands as part of the total portfolio. They may enter into promotion and brand development partnerships with the manufacturers of other offerings. They may also be able to introduce a range of other offerings on the back of one proprietary.

This is where one company uses another's brands to add value to its own offerings. A travel agent, for example, may offer the ability to stay in a Hilton Hotel as part of a package, or they may offer Thomas Cook travellers' cheques or Avis care hire at special rates, also as part of the total package.

Brand leadership

This is where the organisation sets out to have its product or one of the range of its products established as a brand leader in the sector. This is measured from a variety of standpoints. It may be to get the product established in the language of the world. On a truly global basis, examples of this are Coca Cola, Pepsi and McDonald's. Or, again, it may be designed to be the most profitable of a range of generic offerings, or that with the strongest image. A brand leader also helps to sell the rest of the product range.

Brand leadership is often confined to leadership of its own sector, the holding of a high reputation and status. It is also often confined by national boundaries. Nescafe Gold Blend is the leading brand of instant coffee in the UK, for example, but it is virtually unknown elsewhere. Indeed, it has different names in other countries, and therefore the branding is overtly national. In France the competition for brand leadership in the motor car sector is confined to Peugeot, Citroen and Renault; the multi-national and foreign marques have all has to take their places behind these. In all cases, the key to high brand strength and leadership is the ability to reflect customer and consumer requirements rather then (or at least as well as) technological excellence.

Consolidation occurs when an organisation seeks to preserve its position in its markets, niches or sectors, its range of activities and operations, and its customer bases. Consolidation also implies the reinforcement of an existing position. This may be sought through increased marketing and public relations activities, improvements in efficiency, productivity and the cost basis of the organisation, and improvements in quality or delivery targets.

It also depends upon the nature of the markets in which operations are being conducted. The major players in the oil sector undertake general marketing campaigns, television advertising, offers and price moves in response to moves by others in the sector, and in this way consolidation may be seen as form of defence. Johnson and Scholes also include the concept of consolidation in declining markets.

As the fact of the decline becomes apparent, organisations will seek to gain every last possible benefit through 'strategies of harvesting'. These include the sale of the brand themselves and also of licenses, franchises, technology, distribution rights and the leasing of premises and facilities, as well as the maximisation of product sales.

The purpose is to be left with as few unrealised assets as possible, having gained the maximum possible harvest from the sector before it finally ceased being a profitable area of activity.

Withdrawal, retrenchment and contraction

Withdrawal, retrenchment and contraction strategies take place as a result of decisions to move out of particular activities and/or to concentrate the resources of the organisation and its expertise on a reduced portfolio of offerings. There is nor necessarily a negative connotation to this. Withdrawal from particular spheres may take place as the result of reviews and activities, which arrive at the conclusion that loss-making or resource-consumptive offerings are being carried by the organisation's profitable and positive activities.

It may also be a response to economic conditions: for example, where charges and interest rates are sufficiently high to make it worth sub-contracting transport fleets and distribution outlets rather than owning them. This happened in the UK in the late 1980s and early 1990s when both insurance companies and building societies divested themselves of estate agency chains that they has originally acquired when they were seeking additional outlets for their financial offerings, and when general investment in property was considered worthwhile. Organisations wishing to divest themselves of loss-making activities must, however, first consider the effect on their remaining range and on their continuing image, prestige and confidence.

Concentration of resources on a more limited range of activities may lead in time to opportunities for expansion and intervention elsewhere. Within this context withdrawal strategies take one or more of the following forms.

1. Concentration on core business at the expense of niche operations. Much depends on the criteria used

to define 'core'. These may relate to volume, profit margins, income or resource consumption. They may also relate to reputation, confidence, image and identity.

2. The sale of assets, liabilities, subsidiaries, patents and brands. These activities raise an instant cash windfall in return for the loss of the opportunities that each is to create in the future. Balances clearly have to be struck between the need to divest on the one hand, and the need to gain a realistic, even credible price, for the asset in question on the other.

3. The end for the useful life of a hitherto profitable product. This normally arises for one or more of the following reasons. It may be that the result of these have been superseded by a superior, more modern or more fashionable alternative, as for example, in the cosmetics and car sectors. It may be the result of the loss of regard. It may be the result of changed expectations: for example, it may hitherto have been the norm for a sector to have a six-week delivery time for its offerings, but a new entrant can now deliver in six days. Rather than reinvest or re-engineer in order to be able to compete with this the player in question withdraws.

The most common circumstance for this is where the organisation is faced with massive investment, transformation, modernisation or rehabilitation bills on which it cannot see an adequate rate of return. It also occurs with trading relations and activities taking place in volatile areas and sectors. Organisations that operate in these areas know that in extreme circumstances they may lose their entire capital investment if it is nationalised or destroyed by the government of the country in question, or if there is a revolution or civil war. The other area where escape is an option is were there is a sudden loss of regard, confidence or demand for the offerings in question. In the pursuit of withdrawal strategies, full consideration will be given to the exit barriers concerned. Again, having taken the decision to divest or withdraw, the process must be conducted in an orderly and rational manner (whatever the spark that set off he withdrawal, whether rational or irrational).

Diversification

Diversification strategies occur where the organisation seeks to extend its current range of offerings or spheres of activity. This may be through means of integration, or it may be through new product development or new market development. It may arise as a result of the assessments of the current range of products and markets which are deemed to have arrived at maturity and which therefore require development and new introduction. Diversification may be classified as either related or unrelated.

This constitutes the development of the range of offerings and activities within the current ambit or experience of the organisation in question and according to its current expertise. It may be a direct relationship as, for example, where an industrial building company seeks to diversify in the house building sector. It may be a generic relationship as, for example, where an electrical goods company adapts its technology in order to produce electronic calculators and digital wrist watches. It may be related to the market sectors covered; for example, a confectionery company moving into the dog and cat biscuits sector may gain advantage because the product outlet is the same. it may be related to the capacities of the technology and technical expertise that the organisation has: for example, radar was originally invented for military purposes, but now has a variety of commercial uses.

It may constitute the development of a complimentary range of products as, for example, moves by dairy companies into the sale of bread (to complement butter), cakes and scones (to complement the cream), and biscuits (to complement the cheese and cream). It may be an extension of the use of the production technology owned by the organisation (for example, the output of components for one sector may easily translate by modification into components that are suitable for others).

This is where the organisation treads it won new ground. The best recent UK example of this is the Virgin Group transition from records and music retailing into the airlines business. It represented a complete change of direction on the part of the organisation; a move from the known to the unknown. It recognised the fact that effective performers in the sector made profits and that there was scope for a small, high-quality operation in a field dominated by global and national flag carriers and United States multi-national operators. Any diversification should have this as its driving force: a combination of capacities in both niches and organisation together with the need for change and progress in the existing activities of the organisation. The effect is compounded where there are slack capacities, underutilised production means and technology or surplus cash in the organisation in question.

In order to understand the strategic concept of integration we must look again at Porter's five-force model of competition.

Backwards integration is where organisations buy up or into their suppliers, usually to control the raw materials and components. It may also serve the purpose of limiting the volume or quality of a component or material to competitors. This is especially true where the particular material or component is of critical importance or value.

It also occur when the organisation purchases the makers of its own production or information technology and the means of transport of the raw materials and supplies. In some cases also organisations buy up scientific research, market research and information and other consulting firms in their sectors to ensure an early supply of new products, ideas and proposals. Finally, organisations may establish their own financial services groups for the purpose of underwriting customer credit, extended payment schemes, loans and charge cards.

Forwards integration is where the organisation in question buys up its customers. This can be extended onwards: to their customers, the means of distribution, transport fleets, retail outlets, the retail chains that service these, and any agencies that provide after-sales or repair activities. This may also be apparent where component companies require the means of setting up assembly plants; and where assembly plants set up the means of finishing and packaging.

Northern integration occurs where organisations buy up those seeking to enter the market sector in question in order to prevent this from occurring or as an effective move to use the additional capacity that would become available, as part of a drive towards some form of market domination (for example, in terms of size, output, volume, technological capacity or other economies of scale).

Southern integration is where organisations buy up the means of production of critical substitute products. This, again, will be carried out for the purpose of sectoral domination or increased influence, or to preserve and maintain the position of the original offering at the expense of the substitute. It also gives the organisation in question the opportunity to hedge its bets; it has the ability to offer both the original product and substitute at its disposal and will do this according to the whims and demands of the market.

Integration with sectoral rivals occurs in a variety of forms. It may take the form of a straight merger between tow or more organisations in the sector in order to create a dominant or more influential organisation; or for reasons of synergy in regard to the technology, customer base, location, distribution and outlets available at each of the organisations contemplating the merger. It may take the form of joint ventures. It may enable collaboration in specific sectoral projects to take place. It may enable sufficient resources to be put together for the organisations in question to be able to finance and control specific projects and developments. It may also take the form of take-overs.

Take-overs and acquisitions

These take place for one or more of the reasons indicated under the integration and diversification headings. The major general benefits of pursuing this line (rather than developing an organisation's capacities in the area) are the relative time and speed of operation advantages, economies of scale, and market advantages.

Take-overs and acquisitions may also be contemplated for the purpose of: gaining access to and control of customer bases and portfolios; specialised technology and expertise; high-profile brand names; high-value companies; prime sites; footholds in new markets, sectors, locations and countries; prestige, image, profile and promotional objective; and to maintain control over capacity, output, price and value in the sector.

Take-overs may be either friendly or hostile, the organisation being taken over can go into the new relationship willingly or unwillingly. The latter occurs when the acquiring organisation either buys enough of the other company's equity to control it, of else dominates the existing business relationship to such an extent that take over is the only option for the dominated organisation. The former occurs where the organisation being taken over agrees to sell a controlling interest to the dominant company because of the advantages that are to be gained from this arrangement, whether perceived or real.

Mergers tend to be for the same purposes as take-overs. The difference is the way in which the relationship is entered into. A merger is normally much more collaborative, voluntary and mutually entered into than an acquisition, which (however friendly) is normally dominated by the organisation doing the taking over.

Mergers take place for all the reasons indicated under integration and diversification. They also take place for the more general and offensive and defensive reasons of generating a size and strength sufficient to take advantage of opportunities in the sector in question, or to generate sufficient strength to resist and respond to offensive moves by other players in their sector.

Collaborative strategies and alliances

Joint ventures and consortia are lesser versions of the merger approach. They occur where two or more organisations pool their resources for a project, piece of research, offensive strategy or initiative. The overriding principle behind the joint venture conception is again synergy; that the different organisations concerned pool their resources, expertise and technology in order to carry out the work in hand to the highest standards of each of the joint venture organisations. Joint ventures and consortia are to be found above all in construction, building and civil engineering projects.

They also occur in the computer information, medical research and drug sectors, car manufacture, military equipment manufacture, and leisure sectors. It is normal, but by no means universal, for the joint venture to be given its own distinctive identity. In some cases this leads to the formation of a company for the duration of the matter in hand. The advantages of size and resource concentration referred to elsewhere also apply. Some engineering and construction projects are too large and complex for the expertise to be held in one company. The same applies also to computer and information technology and expertise.

It also enables the elements of risk to the shared out between the member companies. Again, this problem is compounded if one organisation not only has to carry the weight and complexity of the project in hand but also the risks of failure.

It is also a way of organisations gaining 'toe in the water' experience of areas in which they may have only a general capacity or expertise.

Hook-ups, associations and networks

This is a variation on the same theme as joint ventures and mergers. It occurs in situations where for example one organisation agrees to give prominence to or provide an exclusive outlet for the products of another in its activities. The overriding concern is the mutual commercial benefit that accrues: by providing the exclusivity and taking a percentage, both organisations benefit.

The distributor has a constant and confident source of products that will always be provided by the manufacturer because of the certainty that the outlet will continue to sell it. Other more general *ad hoc* associations and collaborations may take place where some future mutual advantage or benefit is perceived, again driven by the synergy principle. Collaborations on research tend to occur in the expectation that they will yield mutual benefits more quickly than if each company works on its own. Licensing and franchising are variations on this theme. In the former case, licenses are sold by the holders of patents or blueprints for the right to manufacture, distribute or sell a product under licence in return for a fee or share of the profits. In the case of franchising, the division of activity is more clearly delineated.

Again, in return for a fee payable to the main company, the franchisee operates the business in question as if it were his own, to the extent that he has the responsibility for any manufacture, distribution and sales. The franchiser undertakes national advertising and promotion maintaining the brand name. The franchisee carries operational responsibility for quality and service. He may normally sell only the franchiser's products or a range of products agreed with them. If he falls down on any of this, or on related matters of quality, expertise or service, the franchise may be withdrawn.

Sub-contracting is akin to the normal general relationship between an organisation and its customers. For a fee (the price) the sub-contractor agrees to provide products and services to the agreed volume, quality, value and deadlines. Any dispute over this is resolved in the same way as any dispute over any purchase at all. The idea is attractive to organisations as they pursue the identification of core and peripheral activities (the latter are open to sub-contracting). Many organisations sub-contract cleaning, security and canteen services to those companies that specialise in these fields. Other forms of this relationship exist in the use of recruitment, selection and staff agencies, and technology, business and management consulting services. Every sector also has its expert sub-contractors.

These ply their expertise across its entirety, working at some stage for all organisations with it. For example, in building construction and civil engineering, specialist companies are brought in for specialised jobs, such as draining and earthworks in construction, and the fitting-out of buildings, ships and aircraft in the civil and other engineering activities.

These forms of activity are likely to be fully successful only if the characteristics and expertise of the organisations concerned are effectively blended and harmonised.

For any collaboration that is to take place over any considerable period of time it is usual to have a distinctive identity for the following reasons. It is necessary to give those working on it in turn a sense of identity and belonging in regard to the venture itself as distinct from that with their parent organisation. Continued reference back to the parent organisation is likely to emphasise differences among those who are actually supposed to be cooperating. It creates a specific point of reference for all concerned. It becomes 'the project' of 'the venture'—indeed 'the job'. In the case of computer, civil engineering or construction projects, there is also the need to have this point of reference in regard to the client or project commissioner. More generally, it is part of the process of energising the activities surrounding the project or initiative. It is also part of the process of resource-gathering and allocation that the matter has its own identity.

Some form of steerage or directorate has to be established. This is to ensure that the basic mutuality of interest and harmony is preserved to establish a review process, and as part of the general aim of giving focus and identity. It is also a problem-solving forum. Again, in the case of commissioned projects, it is likely to include client representative as well as the partners in the collaboration.

The collaboration must be capable of being supported throughout its useful life by the partners. In these cases, it is normal for staff, resources, expertise and technology to the committed to the collaboration and, as a result, away from the partner company. Collaborators must be able to sustain this.

Joint ventures and networks must be acceptable to everyone directly affected. The matter may arise for a variety of reasons. For example, one of the potential collaborators may be (or may have been) involved in unethical or unacceptable activities elsewhere; it may have a history of bad or controversial employee relations; one company's levels of pay and benefits may be substantially higher than those of the others.

It may also be necessary to take into account the views of existing customers and clients.

This is currently held in high regard by experts in management as a vehicle for pooling and maximising expertise and resources, and for developing expert managers. Many major projects are now beyond the scope of one organisation's resources. In order to manage a project or initiative successfully, and especially in a joint venture or collaborative situation, the manager must have a range and complexity of skills, qualities and attributes, and must be able to bring these to bear in a great variety of ways. Such managers must be capable of developing and improving this level and range of expertise. The testing ground or microcosm for this is in projects and ventures of this type. The managers concerned will either exhibit this expertise here and therefore indicates there potential for greater things, or else they will not, may therefore be channelled elsewhere.

It is normal for any form of collaboration or alliance to be subject to some formalised measure of agreement or understanding. For joint ventures and consortia project work, sub-contracting and franchising formal contracts always exist.

Each party involved therefore understands the nature, extent and duration of the commitment undertaken. Specifically, matters related to resource input, financial state, the benefits of success and liabilities of failure are addressed.

All organisations and their activities interweave with their business environment, customers' environment and the communities within which they operate. They are also subject to general, legal, economic, social, ethical and political pressures and influences. Any strategy to be formulated must therefore have regard to these limitations. It is no use producing something that cannot be delivered for one of these fundamental reasons, for no strategy is any use if the environment in which it is envisaged taking place cannot or will not permit it or allow it. Related to this is the more general question of the acceptability of the organisation and its products.

Part of the strategy of any organisation must therefore consist of the means of addressing this. The basic level of acceptance and mutuality of interest between organisation and environment must first exist if there is to be any chance of success. Mention should also be made of the extent to which an organisation may influence its environment. In many cases this capacity is very limited. Organisations must therefore work within the constraints imposed.

They must also be prepared for any new limitations or hazards that may arise under the legal, economic, social, ethical or political headings to which they would have to respond (again from a position of limited influence). Once in existence, the capacities of organisations for changing their spheres of operation are limited by the capital and financial liabilities that they have incurred to get to their present position, their real or relative expertise in the current field, and the behavioural or expectational impressions that they have built up, together with their reputation in it.

The point therefore is that organisations tend to be limited to their own area and spheres of operations. They will thus tend to formulate strategies within this context. In sectors where this is heavily dominated by process technology-for example, oil, chemicals and telecommunications-business strategy is likely to be concerned with guaranteeing raw materials, attention to costs and charges, technological improvements, the optimisation of processes, and the search for potential new outlets.

The extent of capital investment in such technology ensures that the organisation in question continues to operate in this field. This is quite apart from the extensive effort that would be required to change the wider perceptions of the organisation if it were to move into a new field entirely. It is also necessary to convince the new sector where such a change is made that the organisation has expertise in it, however good it was at business in the previous sphere. Some organisations do clearly make such transitions, however.

The move of the Virgin Group into the airline business is a case in point, although the charges incurred by the organisation in this move consisted of the creation of the airline itself, creating a distinctive image for it, gaining an operator's licence, and obtaining landing spaces at the desired airports.

3

Decisions-making

Several articles in the management science literature have pointed to the following trend in decision making: Organizational decisions are much more technically and politically complex and require frequent group decision-making meetings. Decisions must be reached quickly usually with greater participation of low-level or staff personnel than in the past. Many of these articles also focus on the development of computer-based systems that support the formulation and solution of unstructured decision problems by a group (i.e., a group decision support system of GDSS).

One of the a decision aiding tools that can be used as part of a GDSS to help promote effective group interaction and participation is the Analytic Hierarchy Process. Our goal in this paper is to report on experiences over the last ten years of so in using the AHP in a group setting. In particular, we provide guidance on how a management science practitioner might structure a group decision-making effort in which in the AHP is the central analysis tool. The discussion on three key areas:

1. assembling the group,
2. running the decision-making session, and
3. implementing the results.

The inherent complexity and uncertainty surrounding an organisation's major problems usually necessitates the participation of many individuals in the decision-making process. In some cases, the composition of the group is fixed (such as the National Security Council advising the President), while in others, it is necessary to select a mix of "actors" to form the decision-making group (such as choosing a panel to investigate the Challenger disaster).

The latter selection process requires specifying the number of experts, non-exports, staff personnel, and upper-level managers to participate, as well as choosing the appropriate individuals. This process can be difficult and time-consuming for many reasons. Decision makers who are considered "powerful" members of the organization might refuse to participate in the process. These members are aware that their level of control and influence might be diminished in a group setting. They fear that the social and interactive nature of the group process might dilute their power and ability to direct policy within the organization.

However, if powerful individuals actively participate, they are likely to strongly influence the process with respect to their preferences. In contrast, results generated by a group that consists solely of "low level" managers with little power may not be useful. The danger is that the powerful managers into account the valuable opinions and observations of others in the organization. We point out the participants who are considered "exports" can be especially troublesome. They may have strong ideas on the appropriate course of action and may note be easily swayed in their assessments. One way of dealing with the "power differential" problem is to assemble a group of participants that have equal responsibility and stature within the organization. Collectively, these individuals can be treated as a decision-making "subgroup" that could help formulate and solve a part of the problem with which they are most knowledgeable.

They could also contribute to discussions that involve higher or lower levels of management. This can be viewed as a sort of "shared " decision making responsibility in, which high-level management cooperates with subordinates. It has bee our experience that high level management often depends on low level employees to gather the appropriate information on which to base their decisions. In this regard, the use of the AHP can serve to facilitate this data gathering. The AHP helps expose various levels of management to a broad range of information views and arguments.

After the groups has been chosen, the members should begin preparing for the decision-making session by formalizing their agenda, structuring the allowable interactions between participants, and clearly defining the purpose of the session in advance. They can seek answer to several questions (such as the ones listed below) that are designed to establish the ground rules for the session.

— Is the purpose of the session simply to improve the group's understanding of the important problem?

— Or is the purpose to reach a final solution to the problem?

— Are the participants committed to generating and implementing a final solution?

— What is the best way to combine the judgments of the participants on various issues in order to produce a single group judgment?

Since the AHP is the specified decision-aiding tool, the group must first construct an appropriate decision hierarchy that reflects the problem under study. Most groups are willing to accept the basic hierarchical structure of the AHP as a rational way of modeling their problem. It allows a group with widely varying perspectives to decompose a complex problem into its most basic and important components. Debate and discussion among the participants can be used to generate a hierarchy that adequately represents the problem.

Each member presents his own definitions arguments, and viewpoints about factors at each level of the hierarchy. Of course, reaching agreement about the overall hierarchical structure of the decision problem may prove to be quite difficult. The hierarchy may be unacceptable to some participants who have already "made up their minds" about the final outcome. Still others may be unwilling to have one of their key decision factors relegated to a lower level in the hierarchy. For example, consider a group that is trying to decide one the best course of action to combat illegal drugs in a city.

The police department's representative might argue that crime is one of the key decision factors and favours placing it near the top of the hierarchy. Another member might take a broader view and talk about the political social and economic factors. Crime then appears as one of the sub-criteria of the social factor. Of course, the police now feel that the importance of crime has been substantially diminished in this structure.

We point out that in our experience when the group has agreed to use the AHP in advance of the first meeting, the initial group interaction exhibits form and direction. When the judgment process begins in the next step, the hierarchical structure helps the group focus on only one aspect of the decision problem at a time.

Once the group has agreed on the hierarchy, it must then generate entries for the pairwise comparison matrices at each level. There are two ways to generate these entries:

1. consensus vote and
2. individual judgments,

The first method requires that the group reach a consensus agreement on each entry in a matrix. At the first level, the group must pairwise compare the three decision factors and reach an agreement on each a entry in the matrix. Of course, a considerable amount of discussion (and initial disagreement) among the participants might be required to produce this number. Additionally, if the hierarchy is large, this step could require a significant number of comparisons that are usually tedious and time-consuming. Recent papers by Harker develop the incomplete pairwise comparison method that can be used to reduce the number of comparisons in a large hierarchy.

Now suppose that there is substantial disagreement amongst the participants concerning an entry in the matrix. The AHP allows each decision maker to specify a value and then combine individual judgments as follows: Use the geometric mean of the individual judgments to obtain the group judgment for each pairwise comparison. As shown by Aczel and Saaty, the geometric means is the uniquely appropriate rule for combining judgment in the AHP because it preserves the reciprocal property in the combined pairwise comparison matrix. An interesting question now arises: How well does an individual's set of judgments correspond with the group's set of judgments (as determined by the geometric mean)? We can give an answer to this question by examining the consistency measure of the AHP.

Factors such as personal charisma, perceived intelligence and expertise and size and strength of an outside constituency can make some participants in a group decision-making effort "more powerful" than others. A key question is: Are such individuals members have "equal" voices and are they willing to a abide by the outcome of the group effort? To help coal with the inequalities of power, the group at the outset of the process can develop weights for the importance of each participant.

These weights can be used to emphasize judgmental contributions or to increase voting power. If the AHP is used in an organization where the formal ranks of participants are known and relative power can be assessed then developing the weights is easy and natural. Developing these weights is difficult in groups where the power of each participant is nearly equal. Furthermore, in newly formed groups or ad hoc groups. It may not be possible or practical to gather enough information about the participants to make informed judgments about relative power. In such situations the AHP can be a valuable interactive learning tool before powerful subgroups or individuals have been able to assert themselves.

An alternative to developing weights for each participant is simply to encourage the expectation that the process interaction, combined with the participants knowledge of each other, will enable individuals to influence others, even though the votes are equally weighed. More powerful members of the group can persuade others to vote as they do. We recognize that there are two kinds of power present in a group setting: the ability to vote which is equal among members and the ability to influence votes which is unequal among members.

Participants in a group decision process are not always willing to reveal their true preference. In fact, they may wish to conceal the most important item on their agenda because explicitly stating it might lead to its defeat, e.g., if it becomes a focus for the opposition. Therefore, decision makers may support other proposals or present reasons that obscure their true thinking.

They may even lend support to an extreme position in the hope that it will be defeated and a very different solution will be adopted. If participants a re unwilling to state their true preferences, then the definition of issues will be incomplete and the analysis and priority settings in the AHP will be flawed. One way of dealing with hidden agendas is to assemble a diverse decision-making group that includes a broad range of participants. In such a group, some participants may be able to uncover the hidden agendas of their "opponents."

Another strategy is to design the rules of the decision-making sessions so that the final outcome or set of weights can only emerge from the set stated issues. Participants can also conceal preferences by intentionally distorting a position or opinion on an issues. Because the AHP uses comparisons to determine weights, participants can cast "extreme" votes in order to raise or lower the score produced by the geometric mean. Such votes would not reflect the actual assessment of the pairwise comparison but would represent an effort to distort the final score. This may happen when an individual perceives that he is the minority position or that there are diametrically opposed opinions in the group. When a group is evenly split between opposite positions, the group will easily anticipate the compromise value that results and will understand that an exaggeration of votes from one side can be countered by an exaggeration of votes on the opposite side.

A group's reaction to a single extreme position is less predictable. If a group is convinced by an individual's argument that the position is sincere, then the outlying vote will be seen as legitimate. However, if the individual is perceived to be a manipulator or trouble maker, then the vote could lead to retaliatory seifts in the majority consensus position. Often disruptive judgments can be identified by their inconsistency with the remaining comparisons and the individual may be challenged to justify such extreme thinking. A decision-making group may decide to police itself by appointing references who can judge the motivation of extreme voters and rule on allowable values. It is important about the rules during the decision-making sessions can be avoided. (Arguments of this type trend to jeopardize the willingness of the group to engage in the actual process) for example, consensus can be used for those judgments on which there is substantial agreement, while more controversial judgments may be synthesized from individual responses.

The effects of intentional distortion on the outcomes of the process can also be diminished if, after the initial structuring of the problem, the entire group of decision makers is divided into several small groups. The smaller groups can make the pairwise comparisons simultaneously and separately and the final results can be obtained by averaging over the groups. Finally any group process is susceptible to breakdown when several participants refuse to continue. As mentioned before, setting ground rules and choosing referees would serve to give a group the ability to reprimand and remove disrupters.

4

Communication in Corporate Management

Communications is a current catchword, both as a problem and as solution. It is worried over by manages and trade union leaders as much as by priests and politicians-and with reason. Failure of communication can be identified as part of the cause of many industrial, commercial, and social troubles. But only as part of the cause. 'Public relations as an applied social and behavioral science is that function which: i) measures, evaluates, and interprets the attitudes of various relevant publics; ii) assists management in defining objectives for increasing public understanding and acceptance of the organization's products, plans, policies, and personnel; iii) equates these objective with the interests, needs, and goals of the various relevant publics; and iv) develops, executes, and evaluates a programme to earn public understanding and acceptance.'

The word *public* is used throughout this volume to refer to any group of people who share a common interest. The employees of a company are an example of a public good pay, the company' stability and future, and the opportunity for advancement are a few of the common interests of members of a company. Some publics, such as employees, are part of an organization; these are called internal publics. In contrast, customers are an example of an external public. Other examples of external publics of a typical manufacturing company are suppliers, the community and retail dealers.

The internal and external publics will differ from one kind of organization to another.' The basic problem is quickly seen in these three examples. They all cross the barrier between what is public relations and how it is done. Most definitions are a description of the practice of public relations, or its function, rather than descriptions of its objectives. Thus Sam Black, in Practical Public Relations, said; 'The fundamental purpose of public relations practice is to establish a two-way flow of mutual understanding based on truth, knowledge and full information.' He was nearer the mark than the cynic who summed up the function as'....the truth, nothing but the truth, but never the whole truth.' In *The Marketing of Professional Services*, Aubrey Wilson noted that the difference between PR meaning either public relations or press relations was not just semantic.

Public relations was the methodical attempt to promote all company activities and interests in every way possible. In his comprehensive book *The Nature of Public Relations*, John E. Marston, Assistant Dean in the College of Communication Arts, Michigan State University, listed a series of definitions to illustrate the steps along the path from the general to the specific. Having said, rightly, that 'public relations is as hard to define as religion or education,' he started with: 'Public relations is planned, persuasive communication designed to influence significant publics.' He ended with a definition taken from Public Relations News, to which he added a brief but worthwhile contribution. It then read: 'Public relations is the management function which evaluates public attitudes, identifies the policies and procedures of an organization with the public interest, and executes a programme of action to earn public understanding and acceptance. Once again, it will be seen that these are all definitions of the practice of public relations: what it does more than what it is setting out to do. They are accurate, although they tend to be long. Trying to arrive at a concise definition engaged the close attention of many pioneer members of The Institute of Public Relations.

The result of this study was for many years the standard formula: Public relations practice is defined.... as the deliberate, planned, and sustained effort to establish and maintain mutual understanding between an organization and its public. However recently, the Institute has felt it better to try to make the worked more clear, and has adopted the following: Public relations practice is the planned effort to establish and improve the degree of mutual understanding between an organization or individual, and any groups of person or organizations, with the primary object of assisting that organization or individual to deserve, acquire and retain a good reputation.

The search has always been for a reasonably small number of words which will contain the agreed elements of public relations work in action and which will be readily understood by anyone. To describe fully how a public relations practitioner exercises his calling takes a book. It is impossible to crystallize it in two or three lines. Acceptable definitions at least achieve the results of clarifying it and simplifying the practitioner's task expanding and explaining it. In the process of clarification, the vital words are 'planned effort', 'mutual understanding', organization or individual', and deserve, acquire and retain a good reputation'. *Planned effort*-because a public relations man must always remain in control. The job is important, and he must thus work always to a plan and on a planned basis. The through is sufficiently vital for it to demand the double emphasis of 'planned' and 'effort; since it really does need a great deal of hard work. Success depends on seeing that nothing happens by accident.

Mutual understanding - because of the difficulty of bridging the awful gap in any process of communication between what the sender means and what the receiver thinks he means. They are not necessarily the same thing. Mutual understanding is necessary to remove any trace of doubt in the minds of either sender or receiver.

Organization-because no man can work in a vacuum. Every body works for somebody. A public relations man works for an organization, whether it is a government, a charity, a commercial company, or a pop star. To put it at its most simple, it is job to see that the organization is understood and appreciated. The principles remain true for individuals and should not be forgotten.

Deserve, acquire and retain a good reputation-because unless an organization is worthy of its reputation it will not keep it. It is an much the task of the public relations man to hammer home that thought as it is for him to devise and undertake whatever work is necessary to enable the organization to acquire and then keep its good name. It has been correctly said that it takes moments to wipe away a reputation it has taken years to build up- but the right to have it must have been there in the first place.

'Public' was deleted from the end of the previous definition in recognition of the fact that there is no such thing as the general public. Here it may help to imagine an organization as the hub of a wheel. The rim is made up of special groups who are attached willy-nilly to the hub by the spokes. They can include customers, shareholders, suppliers, wholesalers, retailers, national or local government departments, the communities in which the organization has factories or branch offices, the press, employees, opinion formers of all kinds, children , and so on. The spokes are the lines of communication between the hub and the rim. Possibly the most important of all the words in the new definition is, as it was in the original, *understanding'*. Without it the public relations man can achieve nothing. At the same time, it is a mistake to try to learn them parrot fashion. It is best to try to find alternative words to explain them, to make the meaning clear to the person reading or hearing the definition. Words mean different things to different people.

The twelve words from the IPR definition are a good example. To an antagonist of public relations it is easy to regard the words as baleful and sinister. A protagonist will regard them as sharp and packed with meaning. Attempts to achieve public relations purposes have been going on since the dawn of time. The channeling of these attempts into an organized craft is more modern, dating from the last quarter of the nineteenth century.

A great deal of twentieth century though has been focused on techniques-the 'how' of life-and public relations is no exception. Since it is, and always will be, an imprecise science it is bound to thrash around rather more than the exact sciences. It is only important to understand that there is no evil intent in the verbal acrobatics. It is not difficult to describe public relations as opposed to the practice of public relations, although it is equally difficult to sum it up in a few words.

To this end, the Institute has also adopted the *wording: Public relations is the state of mutual understanding between an organization or individual and any groups of person or organizations, and the extent and quality of the reputation that exists.* The reasoning is clear, but there is now the key recognition that relationships exist in any situation. They may be active. They may be passive. They may be good or they may be bad. They are nonetheless there-to be accepted, ignored or altered as desired. As already pointed out, the key to all this is seeing clearly that there is no such thing as one public. Here is one attempt at an explanation.

The world is divided into three sets of people. There are those who know you and like you; those who know you and do not like you; and those who neither know you nor care. The third are usually the large majority. The aim is to reach a position where those who know you and like you stay that way; where those who know you and do not like you change their opinion; and where those who neither know you nor care wish they could meet you and do business with you. Then you are enjoying good public relations. Much is made in print of public relations practitioners as 'Image merchants'. It is important to realize that identity comes before image. In a crowded society, it is the differences between one individual or organization and other that give each its own identity.

A great deal of management time goes into trying out produce these differences. It is the identity that is then projected. The image is the view held by outsiders. There is no reason why an organization should not wish to do something to ensure that good and mutually beneficial relationships with others are well maintained. That is the reason why public relations practice continues to grow throughout the world.

When Ralph Waldo Emerson produced his aphorism about the world beating a path to your door if your made a better mousetrap, he was demonstrably correct in terms of a society where deliberate communication was virtually limited to religion, politics, education, and current affairs for most people the media of communication where newspapers, pamphlets and books speeches and lectures, and most powerful of all-individual word-of-mouth report and comment. The fame of a better mousetrap might lead to newspaper reports, read by a far smaller public than today's marker's reputation would be built and sustained by those who talked favourably about him.

Small businesses operating in small communities where there was little demand upon people's mental time and receptive powers did not need to use the skills of the professional communicator for their messages to be acceptable and understandable. Now there is rapid transport over any distance and instant communication around the world.

The small business have taken their place as parts of large industries and the small communities are seen as part of one vast industrialized society. Television commercials assault the eye and ear in Bangkok as much as in Birmingham. Coloured magazine advertisements tempt readers in Helsinki and Hawaii, offering the same brands through the same selling techniques. The latest news from the remotest area is seen and read everywhere within hours and may be watched as it happens via telecommunications satellite. The demands of every form of communication upon the time and receptive capacities of men and women in the advanced nations has increased enormously over the past twenty years, and is increasing still. At the same time, the media of communication have grown in number and complexity. Communication itself has become a twentieth century skill, or rather a group of skills with the attendant need for professionalism and the resolution of ethical problems. This does not mean, however, that public relations is a new phenomenon.

The first man who had a product to barter, the first leader with an idea to convey had an involvement in public relations: they needed to find their audiences and get their messages across effectively. The tavern keeper who started the tradition of hanging a bush outside his door to indicate that he sold drink was engaged in advertising . The later tavern keeper who devise the phrase 'good wine needs no bush' was alert to public relations, because he realized that, in his business, reputation was more important than merely making an announcement. The demagogues of the past, form Tamburlaine to Hitler, crudely practice some of the techniques of public relations.

They knew their audiences and what they card about, whether it was loot or nationalism, and they fired their imaginations by conveying to them dramatic concepts couched in colorful words. Their effectiveness derived much, of course, from the ruthlessness of their approach, careless of the effect on others, and the single-minded approach, careless of the effect on others and the single-minded directness of their propaganda. They were not troubled over the morality of their actions; for them the end justified the means. Today, society having learned something from the past, the terms of reference of communication have largely changed. The audience is better educated and more people are equipped and willing to make objective judgments on the messages they receive. At the same time, the forelock-touching meekness of previous centuries has long been left behind by the average western man and there is everywhere an impassioned belief in the right to be told what is going on and why. The objectives of those who communicate are constantly and rightly questioned; there is much healthy scepticism and the mealy-mounted can expect no mercy.

The checks and balances of what is known as civilized society have brought about a situation in which it is rash to contemplate a course of action without at the same time weighing its effects on others and its acceptability to them as groups or as individuals.

Public relations is by no means a universal specific for every situation, by it is at least a concept of analysis, action and communication which can do a great deal to help.

Public relations as it is known in Britain today first began to be generally recognized in the nineteen-thirties, although he phrase and been used long before in the United States and a few pioneers were operating many years earlier on both sides of the Atlantic. Not surprisingly, the though that relations with the public mattered tended to mature first in those organizations where a major sector of the general public could be identified as of commercial importance. Service corporations like London Transport and national promotional bodies like the Empire Marketing Board were, understandably, among the first to adopt public relations thinking and practices in Britain.

The functions of what would today be known as propaganda and psychological warfare were, of course, in use during the 1914-18 war and there developed the planned presentation of information, much of it ruthlessly doctored to meet the government's needs. After that war, the first information posts in ministries and government departments appeared.

The 1939-45 war suddenly enlarged the official need to inform more people in greater detail than ever, to relate the objective and progress of the nation's battle. For plain information and as we now know-for far-from-plain propaganda, the government developed machinery for issuing news, background information, and ideas through the press and radios posters and pamphlets, films and lecture tours, such as had never previously been known or needed. The informative and motive powers of radio were fully exploited for the first time during the war and the British-American public's devotion to spot-news coverage has continued more strongly still with television.

After the war, both in central and in local government, the information concept remained. Many of today's successful public relations men learned their craft in government departments or the larger local authorities, most of them having previously been newspapermen. From this point the realization of the potential values of public relations began to spread slowly into industry and commerce.

At first staff appointments were less common than the use of the services of a consultancy of advertising agency department, of which only a pioneering few had existed before the war. Now these developed at a mushroom rate, many of them with an inadequate appreciation of the nature and techniques of public relations of the nature and techniques of public relations and sometimes with little motive other than to provide a fashionable service to clients. The poor reputation of public relations people among journalists and businessmen that persists in some quarters today can be traced back to this period of uncontrolled and unthinking growth. A few charlatans and more than a few old-time publicists contributed during the late' forties and the 'fifties to the confused reputation of public relations from which skilled and honest operations suffered and, to some extent, suffer still.

Changing social attitudes have since forced a new responsiveness and sense of responsibility in official and commercial like. The average mans's belief that he is entitled to be told is gradually becoming matched by a sense of accountability that was largely missing from life and affairs as little as thirty years ago.

Governments are felt to be more directly accountable to the electorate, and MPs to their constituents. Boards of directors can no longer dispose the ordinary shareholders money without adequate explanation. Local authorities are unlocking the doors of their committees to press and public. Industrial concerns can expect a bitter reaction if they offend in some way against the communities around them. Each part of society is felt to be accountable to the rest for its policies and actions.

It is in this social climate that an appreciation of public relations as a management and advisory function has slowly been won, not by words but by the deeds of the professional communicators who have proved the value of their work in all walks of life. They have managed to make it plain that planned communication, ethically conducted from the base of a soundly consider policy, is a worthy and valuable activity.

Almost forgotten now are the extravagant claims of those who spoke of public relations in the terminology of a new way of life, a philosophy, almost a religion. The merits of ensuring that mutual understanding is achieved by the skilled analysis of attitudes, the planning of programmes of action, and the carrying through of deliberate communication by a great variety of techniques, have won recognition in their won right. Almost.

The growth of awareness of public relations and the increase in the number of practitioners has been phenomenal over the past twenty years. The recognition of the need for organized public relations activity has been equally remarkable. No era of rapid growth is without its problems. Public relations practice has been no exception. It has been one of the major difficulties of practitioners to carve out their place in business life and society. Their own difficulty has been matched by that of the users of public relations services in trying to work out where the PR people fit in the structure of management. In the process there have been many misunderstandings and misconceptions on both sides.

Some of them still linger. In the early twenties of this century, when the first public relations consultancy was formed, it concentrated on publicity. Over the years the allied functions of promotion publicity, and organized public relations practice grew at uneven rates. If the growth were illustrated on a graph it would show a fairly recongnizable pattern. The different jobs met and parted steadily. They diverged wildly, overlapped frequently. Slowly they came closer and close together and began to run along parallel lines. Most public relations men are now agreed on where each part fits, even though they may disagree on matters of emphasis or method.

If another graph were prepared to show the recognition of public relations practice by users, it would demonstrate the same jerky steps. Laid under the first graph it would show a few points in time when both sides were thinking the same way. Since all public relations is concerned with human beings it is not surprising that the development of its practice have been over shadowed by human beings. Clever men, stupid men, sharp men, honest men, dishonest men, an-women-have all appeared on the public relations scene.

Some have been larger than life. Some have crashed in a spectacular fashion. With the development of expose and in-depth journalism, the spotlight has been turned more than once on pressure groups. Inevitably this has sometimes included public relations men. It is in the nature of public relations that it is difficult to explain exactly where it fits. This has left the door wide open for the fast talkers. At the same time, the techniques of communication and the need for it are constantly changing.

Nobody who was in public relations practice twenty years ago doing the job the same way now as he did it then. The first operators have had the twin tasks of learning the job while they did it and trying to create the conditions in which they could do it properly. They have had to work out for themselves what relationship they should have had to work out for themselves what relationship they should have or need to have with other in management on whose work they impinge. They have also had to present heir needs in such a way that they could not be accused of merely seeking status. They have often not succeeded. Equally, when they have succeeded it has not always been for the right reasons. A man may have been able to walk his proper path along the corridors of power because he had luck, or because he married his employer's daughter, or because he choose his staff well. His ability to exercise judgment, to achieve the right public relations results for his employer by his sheer efficiency or professionalism, may never have entered in to it. Basically speaking any organization-commercial or industrial undertaking, government, voluntary body, and so on-should consider the public relations consequences of any action it proposes to take. It does not matter whether those consequences are immediately beneficial or harmful, short-term or long-term, major or minor.

It should always remember that there will be an effect of some sort on some part of its state of public relations. Any organization must retain the right to decide to ignore the consequences, provided it is clearly understood that ignoring then does not make them go away. If that premise is acceptable-and it must be-than it is also the duty of the organization to have available the best public relations advice it can afford. It goes without saying that, having go it, should use it. There are two aspects of public relations advice in this context.

One concerns the principles involved, the other the methods. It is in this dichotomy that public relations people have found one of their biggest problems. Public relations men do not have the sole prerogative of ideas or ability to gauge human reactions. Many of them have believed that they do indeed have this prerogative and have become hidebound.

They have also become presumptuous. For example, in the floating of a new issue of shares, a stock broker is just as capable of knowing likely reactions as a PRO; in most instances he will probably know much better. The public relations man can skills entitle him to a place at the decision-making table, but once there he is no marathon a man among his peers. It is because too many people in the past have tried to insist that theirs should be the sole deciding counsel that public relations has been exposed to many of the attacks upon it.

Once a decision has been taken the public relations man comes into his own. It becomes his job-often, but not always, alone to communicate the decision, to interpret it, to maximize or minimize its impact. This is what he must be trained to do. It is from this second part that the attitude of many public relations people has arisen. They are fond of explaining carefully that they are advocates. They add that it is their duty to communicate facts, opinions and decisions whether they agree with them or not. In this they are right. ,

Of course, it is always open to them to resign of they disagree fundamentally with a decision. Once the need to communicate has arisen, the public relations practitioner can begin to work with other people. And in so doing he must understand the ways they work and the rules by which they work. This is an area of human relationship which he must study carefully if he is to succeed. There are many simple examples of this. They have to do with the method chosen for communication. If advertising is the method then he needs to understand how advertising works and how advertising men work.

He may feel that the advertising schedule would include a magazine he known is read by the chairman's wife because this will please her. He must listen when the advertising man carefully explains that by doing this the public relations man firstly will not reach the people he wishes to influence and secondly will have to miss out a publication which is vital. The advertising man knows what he is talking about. The PRO may at the end of it all decide for a variety of reasons that the magazine must be included, but at least his decision will have been reached after hearing the facts.

If the communications to shareholders, the public relations man must listen to the company secretary, who will explain the rules of the Stock Exchange. However wrong either may think those rules, they must be observed. The closing of a factory is a further example of the two-headed problem that is at the root of many of the difficulties both side users and practitioners-experience in setting the right place for public relations in management structure.

The decision to close a factory is hard to make. It is dictated by many factors and can only be taken by the directors of a company after long, serious thought. Some of its effects will be obvious; some will not be seen until later. The directors most closely concerned in the reaching of the final decision will probably be the managing director, the financial director, and the production director. The views of the sales director or marketing director will be sought. At some point, the views of the public relations expert-be he director or not should also be sought. It is not an essential prerequisite that he should be a member of the board. It is only essential that he should be brought in as early as possible.

There are many reasons why public relations people are not called in as early as they would like. Their professionalism could have been higher in the past. The readiness of directors to hear public relations advice could have come more quickly. If the senior representative of public relations in a company is not a director, then he must work to one. If it is true that public relations is a management function then he must report to the chief executive, whether that is the chairman, the managing director, or another senior doctor. In practice, he will also almost certainly woke with other directors.

There are many facets of a company's operations which involve public relations techniques and need public relations advice but which do not involve board decisions. It is a matter of debate what position the public relations man needs if he is to exercise his function properly and not become a slave to be pushed around by anybody. If is impossible to generalize on this question since it can only be related to the particular structure of the company in which he works. A further consideration is that just as the function of public relations is to pass information both inwards and outwards, so the public relations man himself must be a bridge between the different islands that comprise a company. He must be equally acceptable -and for good reasons-to the directors and to the personnel on the factory floor or at the sales point. He must be impartial. He must never grind the axe of one side against another.

It has become acceptable in many companies that the public relations officer has the same standing as the advertising manager and that both work to the marketing or sales director. There are dangers in this, and there are countless variations on the theme.

To say that advertising is a tool of public relations is correct. To say that therefore the advertising manager should be sub-servient to the public relations manager is not correct. The same applies when the public relations officer or manager is on the same level as the marketing manager. They are all servants of the company in the same way as the directors are the servants of the owners. The argument is not affected even if the owners are also the working directions.

It is a common practise for one man to combine the jobs of public relations and advertising, with staff below him to carry out the day-to-day functions. Clearly there is nothing wrong in this, provided that the man in the job is properly qualified. To understand all this it is necessary to consider briefly the structure of a normal commercial organization, whether it actually manufactures goods or provides a service.

The running of the company is in the hands of management, usually a board of directors. Not all board members necessarily work full-time in the company, but some will. The chairman may be chairman of many companies, but in each he will fulfil the same function of over all direction and of ultimate responsibility to the shareholders. The broad day-to-day control of the company will be in the hands of a managing director. Around him will be specialist full-time directors covering finance, production, marketing, sales, export, research and development, personnel, and so on. They will draw the information which allows them to do their jobs form what is often called 'middle management'- departmental heads who should be the directors of the future. These will include the public relations man, the advertising man, and a host of others.

This is not the place to argue whether the marketing director is more important in the scheme of things than the finance director, or the sales director, or the production director. It is important to record that the public relations officer faces one special difficulty. He becomes involved with all the directors, since every activity the company under takes produces a public relations reaction. Thus the more senior he is the easier it is for him to put his point of view with some hope success. What he has to do is to earn whatever standing he gains. Once again, it is almost impossible to make sensible generalizations. In a company making motor-cars and having a bad record of labour relations the most vital function of the public relations man for some years may be to concentrate on that aspect of the business. If that is so he will work extremely closely with the personnel director, but much less with the marketing director. In another company making, say, plastic toys the important job may be to earn the goodwill of children. This will bring the public relations man into close contact with the marketing or sales director. It is merely a question of setting the right priorities and then adhering to them. The public relations consultancy, large or small, is a slightly different situation. There is no genuine clash of interests between the consultant and the staff man; indeed, many staff men deliberately use consultants.

The reasons for this are not hard to find, but are summed up neatly in Public Relations and the Chief Executive published by the Public Relations Consultants' Association: the breadth of experience of judgment to a wide range of communications opportunities and problems. The consultancy's resources in terms of people also give it flexibility in carrying out the work. Many companies use consultancies.... to obtain an independent outside view and a wider range of experience, skill and talent than would normally be available economically within a single organization.'

The PRCA grew out of the Institute of Public Relations and maintains close working links with it. Whereas Institute member ships open only to individuals, PRCA membership is for firms. They must have been in business for a prescribed time and either provide comprehensive themselves or be in a position to recommend services from other firms.

The Association publishes a code of practice, similar to that of the Institute, and a list of members with their clients. Not all consultancies belong to the PRCA. As with outside organizations of many kinds, consultancies are given to pointing out that they are as good as a client will let them be. To quote again from the PRCA: 'Once appointed, the consultancy team will need to have complete confidence and to be kept fully informed. Bring consultants in early and do not present them with a *fait accompli* or use them as a barrier between organization and those interest which may properly seek information about it.' Up to now, the comments have been dealing with what can properly be termed the 'creative' public relations practitioners.

This means those who conceive programmes of activity, even if they may sometimes also implement them. However, there are many people in the whole filed of public relations who hold down what may be termed 'passive' jobs. This will include press officers, information officers, house magazine editors, assistant executives in public relations consultancies or agencies, and others.

The distinction between 'creative' and 'passive' is not intended to cast a slur on the latter. A press officer is called upon to exercise his initiative and ingenuity in the implementation of a programme. He is expected to contribute as much as he can to the creation of that programme. In certain circumstances more his time may go into answering press queries than in trying to generate press interest in a subject. He is not given the responsibility for the total programme, but only for part of it. He is therefore working to general direction. The organization and structure of a public relations department must be settled at the beginning. Its size is dictated by the scope of the job it is trying to undertake.

The public relations needs and duties of a small company making cricket bats are clearly not comparable to those of a major civil engineering contractor. The cricket-bat manufacturer would probably need only one man, or part of an executive in a consultancy. The contractor may need a number of specialists- mostly on the staff, but possibly also outside consultants- and someone to co-ordinate their work. This can lead to the growth of a large department. Basically, there are three jobs to be done. One is the creation of a programme of activity, which carries with it the responsibility of ensuring that the programme is undertaken properly.

This is followed by the job of disseminating information, as for the press or for internal use. The third job is the handling of print and other techniques. As the practice of public relations becomes more professional, and the definition of its tasks more exact, it becomes less and less possible for a one-man department to do a proper job. An organization of any size should employ specialists and may well expect to have at least three people in its public relations department, who in turn will need a minimum of two secretaries. Form that base the department will grow to whatever size is needed. In the process, one of the main tasks of the manager will be to see that the growth does out of hand.

Costing

It is vital that a public relations man should understand the principles contents, and elements of costing a programme of public relations activity. Although his involvement in the setting and final control of the budget may be minimal, he can make a vital contribution to its success by remembering the need for financial commonsense.

A public relations campaign devise with no heed to the money available is bound to fail. This is a principle which must not be forgotten at any stage. For example, a company which has consistently returned profits of £50,000 a year cannot consider a full public relations programme which would cost £75,000 a year. Equally, in an organization which has regularly made profits of £5,000,000 a year, it would be unwise to conduct a public relations programme which cost only £2,000 a year. In both instances the budgeting would be unrealistic for either the likely results or the likely needs.

The difference between the apparent cost of any item in a public relations programme and its true cost must be remembered. For instance, a press release sent to 100 newspapers will apparently cost £15.50- that is, the cost of first-class stamps. The true figure will be much higher. It must take account of the cost and upkeep of the typewriter on which the press release was cut as a stencil; the cost of the desk on which the typewriter was placed; the cost of the chair on which the typist sat; a proportion of the cost of cleaning, lighting, and heating the office where the typist sat the cost of the stencil; the costs involved in buying and maintaining the duplicator on which the stencil was produced; the cost of the paper and envelopes and a proportion of the costs of the stationery store; and the incidental equipment which all offices must carry, such as erasers, pencils, ball-pens, and a host of other things. Above all, the true cost of the release will include the time of the executive who wrote it and checked it; the time of the girl who typed it; the time of the girl who ran it off; the time of the office girl who stamped or franked the letters; the time of the messenger who took it to the post; and the time of the management and supervisory staffs who exists in all officers.

Any money spent, however little, is only well spent if it makes a direct contribution to the achievement of the public relations objectives. Success does not necessarily come only to the big spenders. The really important point is that however much is spent none of it must be wasted. It is the PR man's duty to himself and his employer, whether a company or a public relations agency, to make sure that he does not waste money. There are many ways in which this rule can be proved.

The public relations man should be ready to look for ways in which he can do a job for less money. He is, after all, spending somebody else's cash. He would like to feel that they would not waste his money, so he must not waste theirs. If it has been a practice to send out 12 x 10 in. Photographs to publications, he should find out whether 10 x 8in. would not be equally acceptable. If he telephones somebody and finds they are not there he should not wait. He should call back; it costs money to hang on.

This is not a doctrine of penny-pinching. It is advice based on the fact that it is the easiest thing in the world to spend money and one of the most difficult to spend it wisely.

The general rules by which a budget is crated, whether in a commercial company, a non-profit making organization, or a public relations agency are the same. There are only two basic elements: time and operating costs. A company employing a public relations officer or department costs time in one way, and will often not cost it completely. As an approximate rule the total cost of the department is double the actual salaries paid. Thus if a public relations officer is paid £12,000 a year, the actual cost to the company will be about £24,000 a year.

The difference between the salary and the total is made up by a proportion of normal overheads , pension and insurance costs, car or car allowance, equipment, and share of services. The items included in this breakdown vary slightly from company to company. Naturally, the overhead recovery necessary for a public relations officer working in a 20 ft by 20 ft modern office block at a basic rent of £18 a square foot is much higher than for a man working in a smaller office in a provincial factory at a rent of less than £8 a square foot. A public relations agency must make the same calculations in arriving at a fee for its professional services, with the all-important addition of a margin for profit. A fairly standard procedure is to treble the total of staff cost. This will usually produce a profit of 10 per cent before tax, or 4 to 5 per cent after tax.

Once again, the three-times rules is a dangerous generalization. An agency with offices in central London and considerable resources for the provision of extra facilities or services must charge more than a one-man organization operating from an office in the provinces.

The point is made only to show fees are calculated, and does not suggest that a staff public relations man is better than a consultancy, or that the mammoth London organization can necessarily do a better job than the solitary man in Birming-ham.

The operating costs of public relations programme will be much the same whether it is controlled from within a company or by an outside agency. The Institute of Public Relations has published a guidance paper on the subject entitled Fees and Methods of Charging. It makes the point, sometimes forgotten, that fees are the income of a consultant and expenditure is the cost of implementing an agreed programme. The latter is usually mainly a debit and credit transaction. It is normal practice, although there are no definite rules on this, to charge operating expenses monthly in arrears. They will tend to fall into major and minor categories.

The former can include research, market analyses, and similar surveys; advertising exhibitions, displays, and visual aids; the design, production, and distribution of printed materials, including house magazines; films and filmstrips; direct mail; the organization of speakers' programmes and special events. Minor cost can include travelling; entertainment, including press contact; toll and trunk calls and telegrams; press-cutting and monitoring services; photocopying or duplicating; and special stationery.

The detailed items of major expenses are usually charged according to the customs of the particular trade, while minor expenses are charged at cost. For instance, advertising budgets include agency commissions, and printed material often includes a commission element.

If anything extra is added to an invoice to a client, especially when it is added to an invoice to a client, especially when it is commission, the client should know and be able to see clearly how much has been put on. At the same time, it is the responsibility of the public relations man, whether on the staff or outside, to supervise all work done and check the expenditure and invoices. This remains true even if a client has agreed to pay major invoices direct, such as for advertising.

It is normal practice for the agreed budget for a programme to be placed into categories, so that all involved can see show money is being spent and can maintain a regular check on the rate of expenditure. A fairly common list for predominantly minor expenses, with explanatory clauses, could read like this:

1. *Travelling.* Travel within London is normally charged. Out-of-town travelling is charged, including subsistence and hotel accommodation.

2. *Press contact.* When an account-the consultancy's term for a client-calls for regular meetings with the press the bills are charged.

3. *Press releases.* When releases are regularly issued to a long list of papers in Britain, the postage, paper, envelopes, and handling are charged. The cost of special envelopes and postage for photographs is also charged.

4. *Photography.* The cost of photographs and photographic sessions is charged, including the purchase or hire of special equipment or props, model fees, and any fees paid to specialist consultants.

5. *Media Monitoring.* The costs of press-cutting services, radio and television transcripts, and subscriptions to papers and periodicals are charged.

6. *Special events.* When special functions are needed, the costs are charged.

7. *Special stationery.* If it is decided that special stationery is needed, this is charge and may be subject to commission arrangements.

8. *Temporary services.* It is sometimes necessary to call in temporary help-executive, secretarial or other-to deal with particular jobs. Costs incurred are charged.

9. *Demonstrations.* Some accounts call for

demonstrations and lectures. The costs accounts call for demonstrations and lectures. The costs incurred are charged.

10. *Specialist consultants.* Routine advice from outside specialists is not charge, but for extensive work a special fee is calculated and agreed in advance.
11. *Print.* Commission, normally 15 per cent, may be added, subject to discussion.
12. *Films and exhibitions.* Such work may be subject to a special additional fee.
13. *Direct mail.* A commission may be charged in certain circumstances, subject to prior agreement.
14. *Telephone calls, telex, telegrams, document transmission, and photostats.* Calls are normally metered and charged; messages are recorded and charged; photostats and charged at an agreed rate.
15. *Overseas assignments.* These may be subject to an additional fee, and out-of-pocket expense are charge in all instance.

Another simple example is press-cuttings. Whether papers are cut or a cuttings service is used, the public relations man may be required to circulate copies within his organization or to his client. The papers are relatively inexpensive in themselves, but added together over twelve months they can represent a sizeable chunk of the budget.

The point behind this-one which must always be kept in mind-is that he must always be kept in mind-is that he must always clearly be seen to be in contrail of the spending. In addition, it is vitally important that the public relations man should demonstrate clearly his integrity by never trying to hide costs or charge for something that was not a greed in advance. All it needs is care when making estimates to see that they are as accurate as is reasonably possible. Naturally, a budget cannot cover every eventuality. It is for that reason that it should contain a reserve.

However, this must be a reserve for unforeseen contingencies and not an excuse for floppy, uncontrolled forecasting. Once the budget has been set it dictates the broad scope of work for twelve months. It should not be allowed completely to control the PR man, otherwise he will lost the initiative that is a part of his stock-in-trade. Another task is to keep a running check on expenditure. It is easy to do this, either with a small notebook or a chart. The categories in which money is to be spent are listed and the accounts department provides up-to-date figures each month.

There are two essential items of information: what specific jobs are in hand and what suppliers' invoices or petty cash have been paid or are due to be paid. Naturally, it is never possible to tie up all the loose ends between the time a job is commissioned or handled and the time invoices either come in or are paid out. With a good system it should be possible to produce quickly adequate accurate figures at a moment's notice. There are two further points. Hieroglyphics that only one person can understand should never be used; somebody else may need to refer to the figures. Secondly, many companies work on general financial systems of running estimates, quarterly estimates, annual estimates, five-year projections, and the like.

The chart or book should show what is available in the budget and what has been spent up to any given point, plus expenditure that has been incurred even if not actually yet met. In this way the figures will be genuinely useful as a guide. Many young people are afraid of figure work. They think it may turn them from being in public relations to being in accountancy. This is not so. It is the job of the accounts department to monitor or collect the money passing through an agency or department. It is the executive's job to see that he can explain why money has been spent and to ensure that, when it is his responsibility, it is not spent wildly. This is not accountancy or book-keeping; it is merely commercial commonsense.

Ethics

Public relations, like most other forms of human activity, can be measured in moral terms. Indeed, it is highly desirable that it should be, since all communicators by the nature of their work are capable of influencing other and therefore having a responsibility to society to maintain decent ethical standards.

The ethical considerations of public relations are not easily decided. As the business is young in comparison with the established professions, there is as yet no universally acknowledged code of conduct and the case law that has accumulated is relatively slight. Similarly, since public relations is not a fully organized or controlled business, and it is still possible for anyone to endeavor to step in practice, there is no disciplinary control outside the provisions of the law, apart form that covering members of the Institute of Public Relations, Public Relations Consultant's Association, National Union of Journalists and Institute of Journalists.

Even the codes and disciplinary powers of these organizations are far removed form the strictly regulated and enforced standards of the legal, medical or architectural professions. In effect, of course, there are other indirect controls which have a bearing on public relations practice. The rules and regulations governing advertising, the case law being built up by the Press Council, the pressures of the consumer organizations, the watchfulness of hundreds of groups representing particular interests, and, of course, the opinion of his colleagues and contacts in the communication business, all have their effect on the public relations man's attitudes and actions. Endless ethical questions can be raised in an ordinary week's work in public relations, but most of them fall into four categories: social responsibility; relationship with the client or employer; relationship with the media of communication; and relationship with fellow public relations people. Social responsibility, in addition to basic commercial honesty and fair dealing, is very much a matter of not engaging in practices which are contrary to the general good, and of not supporting or condoning such practices on the part of a client or employer.

For instance, if a process is to be installed in a factory and it becomes apparent that the noise level will be harmful to employees and constitute a major nuisance to the community, it would clearly be contrary to the public interest to deny or discount the hazard. The public relations man would be failing in his duty if he did not draw the attentions of the management to the social and human problems involved, encourage preventive and remedial measures, and do his best to explain to employees and other the necessity for the process and the mitigating action taken.

Responsibility for the process and its hazards lies with the management; responsibility for honest assessment of the problems created and for frank communication with those concerned lies with the public relations man. A negative, but equally important, form of social responsibility is to avoid and prevent misrepresentation. This is far more complicated than not making exaggerated claims for products or services. The choice of what type of product to make or service to offer, what to charge, and how to sell is management responsibility, although the public relations man can contribute to the marketing thinking preceding the decision. It is a public relations responsibility, often a matter of personal conscience, to be sure that the presentation of the product or service is honest and that not direct or indirect deception of the audience takes place.

This does not mean that it is only possible to work for a Rolls Royce type of organization; there is nothing wrong in promoting a cheap ballpoint pen for what it is, although there would be in presenting it as a luxury product. Misrepresentation can also take the form of suggesting in-correct or only partially true reasons for an organization's policies or deeds. For example, it would be unethical to suggest that a price reduction had been brought about by increased efficiency in production if it had been forced upon the manufacturer by failure to compete in the market place. One of the most insidious forms of misrepresentation is the creation of 'front organisation'. For example, an organization might purport to be a research trust when in fact it promotes a medical product or appear to be study group when in reality its purpose is political propaganda. Even when this type of organization is set up with good intentions, its operation must involve deception and half-truths, if not worse. Anything less than complete honesty in public relations work is bound to harm all those involved.

In the communication business, falsehoods and deceptions seldom remain unrecognized for long and when they are discovered the trust which is essential among those who convey messages is damaged. This trust is just an important in the public relations man's dealings with his client or employer. Confidence based upon frankness and honesty is necessary if a relationship is to be built up within which the full benefits of inward and outward communication can be enjoyed. The public relations man must be happy that the clients or employer's affairs are decent, honest, and useful-or, at the very least, harmless and innocent.

On the other side, the public relations man must be trusted as a person of integrity. The client or employer must be sure that his affairs are regarded as matters of confidence and be secure in the knowledge that no detail of his business or item information is transmitted without explicit agreement. Another aspect of confidence is that of loyalty. It is clearly not ethical to accept payment form or engage in work on behalf of any competing or potentially competing organization without the consent of one's client or employer. Consultation among all parties when such an issue arises is the only fair way to determine any conflict of loyalties.

Although a few people in public relations do no agree, it is generally held to be unethical and unprofessional to work on the basis that reward shall be related to specific achievement: for example, a fee of £X for Y column-inches of editorial coverage, or a fixed percentage of a sum to be raised for charity. The public relations man's dealings with the various media of communication are usually critical, in more than they need his, and he there fore has to understand and play by their rules.

At the same time, his activities is are frequently regarded with scepticism and the man who offends against the unwritten laws is not readily forgiven. The cynicism of the press, radio, and television towards those who wish to give them information is a healthy safeguard which protects the public from deception and dishonesty; it should be welcomed rather than resented, even when it acts against the acceptance of entirely worthy approaches. Corruption of the media of communication by misinformation. By the with holding of relevant information which can reasonably be held to be in the public interest, or by attempting to influence editorial judgment on the use or rejection of information is one of the most distasteful and damaging forms of unethical behavior. Immediately, however, problems of ethical judgment are raise.

What is the dividing line between information that is in the public interest and facts which by normal commercial prudence, should be confidential? Is telling a journalist some additional background to a story over a friendly drink an attempt to influence his editorial judgment? Is a lunch for his news editor on a getting-to-know-you basis an endeavour to undermine his independence or merely an attempt to establish personal confidence. Is placing a series of advertisements in a trade paper to be interpreted as liable to affect the editor's view on the news value of store is about the advertiser?

The answers to questions like these mostly lie in the realm of commonsense. It is barely possible to lay down hard and fast rules, but the development of an objectives approach and a sensitivity to the attitudes of others can, with the growth of experience in communication and the help of mature advice, keep the public relations man on the straight and narrow path of unimpeachable behavior. In his relations with his colleagues, his competitors, and his employers, he is on surer ground.

It is accepted that it is unethical to injure the reputation or practice of a fellow public relations man, to endeavour to supplant him with his client or employer, or to encroach upon his business in any way. This includes the soliciting of work by unfair means, such as misrepresenting another's ability or reputation, or implying that his work could be performed better or cheaper. The common practice of agency and consultancy executives leaving their employer and taking with them certain accounts so that they may set up a business of their own may be ethical dubious, although when agreement has been reached among all parties this procedure is quite proper. On the other hand, for a client to engage on a staff basis a consultancy executive who has served him well is, far from being unethical, often a logical development even if it means a loss of business to the consultancy. The IPR and the PRCA have codes of conduct covering most of these points. The NUJ and the IOJ have codes which contain basic ethical principles applicable to public relations as well as to journalism. The advertising Standards Authority and other advertising and sales promotion organizations have also laid down standards of good practice, many of them concerned with the ill-defined area of good taste. There will always remain issues that cannot be decided by rule nor even by generally accepted practice.

These must be a matter for the social, moral, and professional conscience of the individual. The responsibility of the public relations man is to remain alert at all times to the ethical aspects of his work, to act honestly and decently, to guard his loyalties and to respect the integrity of other. When all else fails, and his attitudes, advice, and opinions are not respected, his ultimate action must be to resign from the job or the account.

Communication is easy; everyone does it all the time. Effective communication is difficult. It involves attracting attention, compelling interest, and conveying information with impact, accuracy, and lack of ambiguity. It also requires that the audience should be clearly defined and that means of reaching that audience should be identified and skilfully used, which involves understanding and operating a variety of techniques.

As if this were not problem enough, there are also the physiological and psychological barriers of the selective and subjective mechanisms of every individual member of the audience to be appreciated and overcome.

For example, it is usually accepted that colour is a subject of infinite difficulty to talk and write about without misunderstanding. Apart from those who are wholly or partially colour-blind, colours are seen differently by different people. Some shades of blue to one are green to another, and so on.

In other words, the physical apparatus of the eye and the nervous mechanism for transmitting its messages to the brain are unique to every individual and what one person sees is never seen as precisely the same by any other person. What is seen is also selected by a variety of factors: alertness, experience, frame of mind, prejudices, physical surroundings, and many more.

The choice of facing fractionally one way instead of another immediately makes what is seen unique to the individual. No other person can be looking with the same eyes and attitudes at the same subject from exactly the same place at the same time. A street scene containing all kinds of activity will be seen by different people in different ways. A nervous old lady will see a frightening rush of vehicles and people. A man who is late for an appointment will see the big clock outside an office.

A house wife will see a supermarket sign. A youth will see only a pretty girl walking by. The validity of these subjective factors has been amply demonstrated. Examine any two eye-witness accounts of a street accident; ask any two people to carry a verbal message and check on its delivery. The 1914-18 war joke about the message, 'Send reinforcements; we're going to advance' being passed from man to man along the trench until it arrived as, 'Send three-and-fourpence; we're going to a dance' has a sound basis in observable reality. The spoken word has its own hazards and its peculiar differences from the written word are often overlooked.

Any shorthand-writing reporter will confirm that he transcribes what the speaker meant to say, for if he wrote what he actually said the speaker meant to say, for if he wrote what he actually said it would often be gibberish. This is true of almost any unscripted speech, apart from that of the gifted few who are able to compose sentences to speak as others compose them to write. Read any transcript of a radio or television unscripted discussion just as it comes from the monitoring organization and it becomes apparent that what sounds plain enough at the time is often confused, broken, and jumbled when seen in written from. Facial expression, inflection and tone, the interplay between speaker and audience, the visual context of the occasion—all contributed to enhancing the meaning of the spoken word and none can be conveyed adequately in a written report.

Only in rare case, such as Sir Winston Churchill's speeches, is the mastery of language such that the words are equally acceptable and effective whether read or spoken. Yet, however precise the words, there remains the obstacle of subjective reaction and interpretation to overcome. At its most macabre, it is possible to postulate that each separate member of an audience thinks he hears what the communicator thinks he is saying, and the fear begins to develop that clear communication is not possible. It is possible, but it is not certain. As long as everyone whose work it is to convey messages remembers that uncertainty and guards against it, there is hope for effective communication. Most communication is by word, spoken or written, or by some form of pictorial or visual presentation. That words are liable to be ambiguous, however carefully used, is obvious, but visuals can be equally ambiguous if their effect on the chosen audience is not the intended one.

A non-representational work of art may convey a variety of emotional 'meanings' to those who view it; it may also convey to some a representational meaning far removed from what the artist had in mind. The question 'what does it mean?' can produce many answers, according to the subjective interpretations put upon it by those who look at it. The question 'what did you mean?', addressed to the artist, may produce only one answer. The differing interpretations put upon the words of a politician by professional commentators, who may or may not have been present to hear them, instantly illustrate both the potential ambiguity of even cunningly conceived speech and the selective acceptance of a message by those who filter it into their minds through fixed attitudes. Subjective thinking is often a matter of believing that some things are 'right' and others are 'wrong' without necessarily defining at any time what those moral terms may mean.

Even if it is not possible to establish what someone else means by his subjective reaction, it is vital in public relations to recognise that it exists, that it is, in fact, a part of the make-up of every human being. To take a simple example, the steel-engraved company letter-heading with a vignette of the bearded founder looks just as right to the elderly manufacturer as it looks wrong to the graphically alert young manager.

Either might in theory be collect in believing that his personal choice of what is right is also right for the company's audience. The only way to try to find out is to seek the advice of those who are trained in the visual disciplines involved and of those who are trained to the techniques of measuring attitudes. In other words, subjective public relations judgment is dangerous-for all the value of flair and hunch-and the scientific approach of using available, proven techniques is more likely to produce useful answers to problems. Allied to this, there is a permanent need for the public relations man to retain a cold objectivity about his work. This does not mean any lack of loyalty to client or employer, nor any lack of enthusiasm for a cause or a company. It does mean the ability to see and hear through the eyes and ears of the audience as well as those of the concern he serves. Loss of objectivity, lack of the scepticism which motivates the best in journalism, of criticism and social analysis, can be mortally damaging to a public relations man's effectiveness.

Role of Advertising

The vast majority of advertising men are denied this privilege. It is a pleasure reserved only for that small minority engaged in the preparation of advertisements which have some criterion of effectiveness built into them, such as mail-order ads. Nevertheless, the experiences of this privileged minority have made possible the statement of certain principles which can be applied to advertising in general. Unfortunately, most of the advertising in our national media is witness to the fact that these principles are not very widely practised. On the other hand, advanced consumer research leads to conclusions almost identical to those which have been arrived at by advertising people who have been permitted to see directly the results of their own work. What are some of the conclusions about effective advertising which have emerged from consumer studies and experiments?

One conclusion is that intellectual gimmicks, cleverness, wittiness, or ingenious and tricky word combinations do not add to, but rather subtract from, the effectiveness of advertising. Even slogans are of doubtful value. In fact many of these so-called attention-getting devices actually operate as distractions. Efficiency in advertising seems to depend on the use of simple language—simple direct presentation of sales arguments—and the avoidance of tricky attention-getting devices unrelated to the product itself. Here are a few examples. An advertisement for phonograph records uses an illustration of a woman breaking a phonograph record by stepping on it.

Presumably this illustration is intended to catch the consumer's attention and lead to the next revelation: that steel needles also ruin phonograph records. To be sure, the needles do not ruin them as thoroughly or as quickly as a woman stepping on them, but nevertheless they do serious harm. After this devious opening gambit, we are finally permitted to learn the moral of the story—the true sales point: diamond needles preserve records. The creator of this copy apparently had convinced himself that the consumer would not be interested in the simple fact that phonograph records are ruined by steel needles but can be preserved by using diamond needles.

Therefore, the copy writer felt compelled to try to catch the consumer's attention by the "more interesting" picture of a record being brutally broken by a woman's foot. In another advertisement, traveller's cheques were offered as the right way to carry money. But in the headline the word "right" was spelled "write". The copy writer seems to assume that the reader of the advertisement wants to be entertained, to be impressed by wittiness and by an unusual use of the English language. He assumes that the reader will be pleasantly surprised to see this game of words. This pleasant feeling, he hopes, will generalize to the traveller's cheques and will increase the reader's interest in using them instead of cash when he travels. These examples are so extremes as to be almost unrealistic. However, in almost any copy of a national magazine we can find milder forms of the same disease: tomato catsup described as "what eggs scramble for," television picture-tube purchasers exhorted not to be "Vidiots," or a telephone instrument described as a "conversation piece."

We can also find roses growing out of liquor bottles, dogs dressed policemen, and women apparently walking on clouds. Are the products to be sold so pitifully drab and uninteresting that the consumer must be entertained or shocked before he will attend to them? An even more innocent appearing example was brought to light several years ago. For many years the Socony Mobil Oil Company used the symbol of "the flying red horse" to identify its service station outlets. The argument in favour of using this symbol rather than the simple word "Mobil" was that the flying red horse gave pleasure to the motorists who viewed it, and suggested lightness, power, and speed, whereas the single word "Mobil" was drab and colourless. Considerable evidence had been accumulated that the horse was an inefficient communication.

As a final assault on this question, the following experiment was designed:

An automobile equipped with movie camera was driven along roads where Mobilgas and other gas stations were located. As the camera moved along, it photographed every gasoline outlet on the way. After the film was developed, the number of Mobil stations and other brands was equalized. To avoid bias, the selection was random.

Various audiences were invited to see the movie thus prepared, and afterwards every member in each audience was requested to tell what brands of station signs were on the road, and approximately how many of each he thought there were. The frequency of the flying red horse sign was underestimated down to about one-half of that of its most efficient competitor.

The outcome of this experiment revealed that the station sign of Socony Mobil Oil Company was losing substantial parts of its competitive sales opportunities by clinging to a symbol which has associations which were pleasant but irrelevant to the problem of identifying Mobil stations. These advertisements and signs communicate in a manner that deviates drastically from communication as it takes place in other phases of our daily life... in the editorials of newspapers and magazines, in teaching, in simple conversation, and in ordinary sales talk.

Directness and simplicity have been replaced by carefully contrived detours, which can be very costly indeed. A simple change in the wording of a headline may increase the efficiency of an advertisement by several hundred per cent. For example, in a split-run test the following two headlines were compared: "New Jobs Are Offered In Television Station" and "Television Courses for $11.60 per week." The first of these headlines returned six times as many orders as the second—six times the value for an identical investment in advertising space. If a change only in a headline can produce differences of this order of magnitude, imagine how these differences might be compounded by changes in the whole copy treatment.

It seems a modest hope that an increase in the knowledge of the principles of advertising will enable an advertiser to double, at least, the value he receives for each advertising dollar invested. The average "expert" in advertising must apply a substantial part of his ingenuity and inventiveness to tricks and gimmicks which *lower* the efficiency of advertising, rather than *raising* it. If it is true that a simple change in the wording of a headline can produce a six-fold change up or down in the efficiency of the ad, why do we not more often notice advertising campaigns leading to business disaster?

The reason is that at least two mechanisms operate in advertising. One of these, the "Persuasion Principle," has been widely discussed in writings on advertising. The second, which we may call the "Familiarity Principle," has been much neglected. The familiarity mechanism in advertising is often overlooked in analytical discussion of advertising. However, it is possible for this mechanism to operate effectively even in an advertisement in which persuasion operates at an almost negligible level. The Familiarity Principle is fairly easy to state and simple to understand: *Something that is known inspires more confidence than something that is unknown*. Thus, a consumer confronted with two products, and having no knowledge of the physical characteristics of either of them will almost certainly choose the one whose brand name is more familiar to him.

Consequently, a piece of advertising which does nothing else but mention the name of the product will contribute something to the sales of that product, simply by creating an awareness of the brand name that generates this minimum amount of confidence. Advertising can survive, and even give the appearance of some efficiency, by trading on this unavoidable, minimum effect of familiarity. Many advertisers, in fact, can afford to rest their whole case on it. Marketers of chewing gum, soft drinks, and cigarettes often have gained a powerful position through the deliberate use of advertising that concentrates on simply making the brand familiar by merely showing the brand name.

But advertising copy is intended to perform a function *beyond* the mere development of familiarity with the brand name. Copy is intended to shape motives and desires, to build believability, and to provide a reason for selecting a particular brand over all others. It is the most flexible part of the advertising message. In the development of advertising, it is the copy function which demands the greatest skill, creativeness, and intelligence. Every advertising man wants to create "good" copy. And yet what criteria can the advertising man apply in deciding that one piece of copy is good and another bad? What are the criteria of efficiency in copy?

The great problem is that we cannot relate a *specific* sales increase or decrease to a *specific* advertising act such as a copy treatment, a sound effect, a headline or a sales point. Indeed, it is almost naive to imagine that any relationships can be established between specific advertising actions and sales. The reasons are manifold. For one thing, even in the most favourable marketing situation which we can contrive, it is difficult to separate the *familiarity* effect from the *persuasive* copy effect of advertising. A piece of advertising with "depressing" copy can fall back upon the familiarity principle as long as a brand name is mentioned.

Many advertising successes which are attributed to copy are in reality simply the unavoidable minimum success solidly secured by the Familiarity Principle. Furthermore, when we attempt to relate specific advertising actions to specific sales effects, we must get rid of the cumulative effect of advertising over a period of years. For an old established product, the cumulative effect of previous advertising will greatly outweigh any specific contemporary advertising action. Therefore, old established products make the observation of causal relations between specific copy and specific sales impossible. Nor do we realize any advantage if we are dealing with an entirely new product. It is never possible to separate advertising's effect from the contributions of ingenuity in product design, packaging, or distribution.

Thus, the copy writer must always be denied the advantage of being able to observe the effect of a specific copy action in a specific sales success. In almost every other field of human endeavour, the development of proficiency and skill depends upon being able to observe the effects of our actions. Let us imagine that builders of pianos were forever forced to build their products in a vacuum where there is no sound and sell them to "clients" without ears.

After forty years or so of working under such conditions, we should expect that the piano designers would be turning out very attractive pieces of furniture, but we should have no right to expect that this furniture could product music. If we should happen to mention to the piano builder that his instruments do not sound good and that his activity is inefficient, he would probably not be surprised. Indeed, he would consider us unreasonable if we blamed him for his inefficiencies, so long as she is denied the privilege of hearing the results of his activity.

Today the copy writer creates his message in the vacuum of the modern distribution system without being able to see the effects of that message unfold. Then he sells his creations to a client who has no sensory organs to observe what a specific phrase does to a prospective consumer.

The creative advertising man is deprived of the natural rewards that any sincere individual wants. He wants to see the results of what he does; and yet our entire marketing system forces a blind-fold over his eyes. The primary rewards of seeing the results of his actions are replaced by the secondary rewards of praise from his colleagues, bosses, and clients. And the people who confer these rewards are in no better position to see the results of the man's action than is the copy writer himself. Let us imagine that the copy writer proposes an entirely efficient piece of copy for his client.

This copy consists of simple language and uncluttered, straight-forward sales presentations—without gimmicks, tricks, or intellectual surprises—copy equipped with the most ingenious and most invisible device of letting the product impress the listener or reader. The client reviews the copy and before approving it, happens to think. "This copy writer does not seem to be using his imagination. He talks only about the product itself, and does not add anything of his own." So, the copy writer efforts but it actually rebuked for failing to show "imagination." It is quite natural, then for the copy writer to resort to the use of tricks, gimmicks, and devices that will entertain, startle, or humour himself, his intellectual friends, and the client.

The emphasis is shifted from ends to means—from *what* advertising should say, to *how* it should say it. It is unfortunate, but not surprising, that the creative man now diverts his efforts from making the *product* interesting to making the *advertising* interesting . Ultimately he is no longer selling the product to the consumer, but selling the advertising to his client. The difficult and even unfair position in which the creative man finds himself may be illustrated by the following analogy. Imagine a room with a large window that looks out on a beautiful countryside. On the wall opposite the window are three mirrors. The first mirror is uneven, spotted, and dirty looking. The second mirror is clean and neat, and in addition is framed by a beautiful ornamental engraving.

The third mirror has no frames or ornament, and is nothing but a plain, but perfectly flawless mirror. Now, an observer is taken into the room and his guide points to the first mirror and says, "What do you see?" The observer says, "I see a bad mirror." His guide points to the second mirror and asks again, "What do you see?" The observer says," "I see a beautiful mirror." Finally his guide point to the third mirror and says, "What do you see?" The observer says, "I see a beautiful scene out of an open window." Obviously, the third mirror has done the most efficient job. It is the function of an efficient mirror to reveal with perfect clarity the object to be mirrored without interference—that is, without making the mirror itself visible.

It is likewise the function of perfect advertising to step behind its own means—its own tricks and gimmicks—and push the products so much into the foreground that the advertising itself, psychologically speaking, can be overlooked. It may be disappointing to the maker of mirrors to discover that his most efficient mirror is one which the prospective customer is unaware. The very perfection of the mirror conceals itself from the observer. The advertising man, unless he takes pleasure in perfection, will also be disappointed to discover that the more perfect he makes his advertising, the less it becomes noticeable as "Advertising."

How can advertising rise above this situation in which only its inefficiencies are capable of producing reward for its creator? We cannot normally expect the copy writer to take the initiative. He is human, and must respond to the rewards and punishments which are offered to him. His client, the advertiser, on the other hand, is in a much better position because he controls the rewards and punishments meted out to the copy writer.

Let the client relieve the copy writer of the burden of having to prove his " imaginative" and "creative" powers by forcing him to resort to tricks and gimmicks. Let him trust the copy writer's professional competence to use correct grammar and an attractive style. Let him then concentrate on *what* the copy writer says, rather than *how* he says it. This would surely have the effect of restoring the sales point to its rightful position of importance in advertising. The development of a sales point is one of the most challenging problems in advertising. Sometimes the best sales point is intimately related to the main function of the product.

For example, the function of antihistamines is to relieve cold symptoms, and this turns out to be their best sales point. On the other hand, the main purpose of face soap is to clean the face. But the cleaning power of face soap is not an interesting sales point for face soap. It is not always easy to decide for a particular product what will be an efficient sale point. For hair tonic, for example, is it better to say that it prevents quenches thirst or that it has a distinctive flavour? Advanced marketing research justifies its existence in terms of its ability to discover the most efficient sales points for a particular brand. This is the real core of advertising and its most challenging problem area. This is the center where creativeness can makes it most fruitful contribution. Only the advertiser has the opportunity to bring the sales points back into advertising... to make the advertising product-oriented rather than advertising-oriented. Superficial reasoning easily sinks to the level of platitude where the following pseudo-logical argument sounds convincing. First of all, advertising has to get the attention of viewers, readers, and listeners.

A given advertising message competes within an inexhaustible number of other advertising messages. Therefore, a given, piece of advertising, to meet this competition, must put something out of the ordinary before the eyes and ears of the potential consumers. Ideally, a given piece of advertising should look or sound different from any other piece of advertising. This kind of reasoning bypasses the product and, therefore, the advertising function. The ideal statement should be to formulate: "A given piece of advertising should make the product look different from all other products, without violating the truth."

That the easiest and least "creative " mental effort leads to the "Attention-getting advertising" escapes superficial reasoning.

A printed ad under the headline "Your Father in the Cesspool" would get good attention. Not much useful imagination goes into the headline. However it requires a surplus of intelligence, analytical power, and useful imagination to find an interesting headline which leads the reader to read the text in the anticipation of learning about a useful product.

In advertising discussions, the term "create" and its derivatives are partially misused and misunderstood. "Imagination" is confused with "creativeness." Imagination is a fundamental and elementary requirement. Creativeness denotes the *advanced* form of imagination where it is *purposively* used by abiding to rigid rules and by meeting practical conditions.

Children on a playground and many patients in mental hospitals display extraordinary imagination. But the imagination in these instances is usually without the discipline of organization, selection, and constructiveness. It is not, in other words, *creative*.

An advertising man who claims that the acceptance of rules and conditions interferes with his creativeness is probably unaware of the fact that he is seeking a licence which the real creative geniuses in arts and sciences would consider embarrassing. Creativeness is the opposite of pure freedom of imagination. To create something means to *build* something along rules of usefulness or purposiveness... to build an intellectual or mechanical organism. Leonardo da Vinci spent a lifetime seeking the rules within his visual imagination which could produce more powerful creations. To be creative in advertising means to have so much imagination that it does not "fizzle out" as soon as product orientation is imposed.

If the advertising man believes that the product itself has no virtues worth the attention of the consumer, be should suggest taking it off the market. If he believes that the product has a right to be on the market, and yet believes that it has no property worth the attention of the public, he is obviously overlooking the most serious and most creative obligation of advertising—*to find an approach which makes a good product look good and thereby interesting.* If, in the advertising man's opinion a product is justified in being on the market, then the advertising man's consider it justifiable that consumers pay money for the product.

Fluid Media: Radio and television are fluid media—multilevel fluid media. They exist only in film or tape *or mind.* The printed word, the script, the storyboard, the shot list, the fact sheet, and the strategy *are* not the commercial.

There is no perfect way of presenting broadcast commercials. But there surely is a wrong way: read them. Never! That's deadly sin number 4. Listen, Dream. Imagine, Talk them out. And don't be shaken by surprises. They happen, usually for the good. But watch the face and moisture on the palms of the man who carried the seed in his brain. If he's ecstatic and he's good, bet with the house, but don't drag out a limp, folded, spindled, and tattered story board and think that it's a commercial. It's blueprint of sorts and a communications tool. But it's a long way from perfect because it doesn't move. It's statue, not a beautiful girl. Nevertheless, before we go any further, let's spend a few paragraphs on the most familiar tools, no matter how inadequate they may be, that are used in dealing with commercial ideas before they actually become commercials.The script is common to both radio and television, even though the two scripts may look somewhat different. Classically, the radio script is a double-spaced paragraph in the neighbourhood of 120 words per minute with sound and music instructions tossed in as they fall in caps and parentheses.

The television script is usually divided into two vertical columns. The left is typed in caps giving picture or video instructions. In the adjacent portion of the right-hand column the script and audio instructions appear.

Nowadays not enough people bother to write out a *bona fide* television script, but go directly to rough storyboards. In the early days of Revlon's historic television era when *all* commercials, even some of the shade promotions for lipstick and nail enamel, were shot *live* just scripts, set designs, and costume sketches. No storyboards. Since the beginning of television, the storyboard has been the basic blueprint and communications tool for the production of the television commercial. There exists much controversy today as to whether the storyboard is a help or a hindrance.

The mere physical existence of a series of drawn frames with video instructions and audio copy typed under them can be of no value unless the *story* clearly emerges. The story is important, the *board* is not.

Purpose of the Storyboard: Bear in mind that storyboard is an inanimate object that does not move, lacks the plasticity of film, makes no sound, has no music, and is generally crudely drawn. It is not a commercial. It is a tool which is often inadequate, but perhaps the most inexpensive and rapid way of gaining understanding and agreement among the many persons who will be involved in the production of the television commercial.

In apocryphal story about the cavemen sums it up best. Od and Ug were having a heated discussion one day and were faced with a complete failure in communication. Finally, in desperation Od said to Ug, "Leave me to draw you a picture." That's how we got the famous cave drawings in the south of France.

Often the television writer will make a rough "miniboard" to help communicate to his art director what he has in mind. Just as often nowadays, the television art director may start the process with a rough graphic concept, calling in his writing counterpart for help. As the writer and art director work together, a more polished storyboard emerges where the design of the commercial becomes more apparent and the action implications are sharpened. At this stage, the storyboard helps the agency account group understand the intent of the commercial. Next, it helps the many echelons of the advertiser. The storyboard also provides a basis for communicating with production companies in obtaining bids. Their initial attention to the storyboard deals primarily with technical requirements that emerge, size of set or location, types of equipment required, talent costs, length of shooting, and so on.

After approval is obtained on a commercial, sometimes the first step in production is to create a shooting board in which finer attention is given to camera moves, opticals, and editing techniques while in the stages of pre-production with the film company. This can be a waste of time or a great advantage, depending on the complexity of the commercial. If the desired technique is intricate, involves extreme cutting, montages, colour communication, or great imagery, it can be a help, but only to the people who are sufficiently technically oriented to understand it.

Hindrance of the Storyboard: Once again let us emphasize that this is a blueprint and communications tool—not the commercial. Whenever an advertiser or an agency directs his production house to "shoot the board," he is depriving himself of the immense potential creative contribution of the "hot" director and cameraman he has haggled so hard to get for the job. The other extreme can be equally disastrous. Certainly, this is no time to start from scratch on a basic idea. Under any circumstances, the finished commercial must reflect the strategy and intent implied by the storyboard. A middle ground must be reached through the strength of the agency people who have the trust and confidence of the advertiser. When this ideal relationship is established, beautiful nuances can be built into a commercial by intent or even by "happy accidents".

Some years ago, one of the major soap companies experimented with storyboard which had three typewritten sections under each drawn frame: (1) video instructions, (2) audio, (3) objectives. A hue and cry went up among the creative people in their stable of agencies that this was mechanistic, busy-work, and unnecessary.

Upon reflection, however, the idea has great logic. Often by stating what it is you are trying to accomplish by a given sequence of film, you not only refine your picture content and audio at the conceptual stage, but also communicate more clearly to your production house what you are trying to say and do and why. The longer you work with this system, however, the more you realize that such a statement of objectives is more easily accomplished and with stronger results, if instead of attempting to write objectives for each frame, you prepare an overall statement of objectives.

Different Types of Storyboards: Historically the storyboard has consisted of from twelve to eighteen pictures, each of which is accompanied with a written video section explaining what is in the picture, camera moves, optical effects, etc., and the audio section explaining music, sound, and script. Some agencies prefer to lay them out one frame per page and present the commercial in flip-chart form. Others lay them out horizontally with approximately twelve frames per page. Still other lay them out virtually with four to six frames per page. In many cases, it is matter of personal taste. Yet there are advantages for each of these techniques One frame per page helps everyone discussing the storyboard concentrate his attention on what is being discussed at that precise moment without wandering forward or backward to other frames. While the horizontal technique of twelve frames per page has the danger of permissive wandering, on the other hand it often provides a better overall grasp of the graphic concept.

The Six-Frame Board. This type is very much in vogue today, and works best where there is a good working relationship between a top agency TV team and a knowledgeable client. It reduces the concept to a simple clear-cut representation of the real key graphics. It leaves out the editing-room pyrotechnics, because the team instinctively knows how they're going out put it together. They're after agreement on the solid skeleton.

The One-Frame Board. This method is best applied when the commercial is truly built around one powerful graphic idea. You use one drawing or scrap photograph to indicate the central idea, then talk your way through the commercial with a script. It works well where a commercial depends heavily on a central-character study or an interesting location or set. Another variation is an actual sketch of the set—and you walk your fingers through it to communicate your idea. Some agencies I've known use this with paper dolls of the lead characters, moving them around.

Then There's the No-Board Board. The cycle now completes itself and you're back to a script and a key prop and a great presenter. Sometimes, the theatre of the mind can more clearly understand a commercial concept this way than with all the rough or comprehensive drawings in the world.

The almost-finished-commercial board: There's great temptation to shoot a series of stills or test film or tape to show commercials that are almost air quality. It frequently backfires. You're almost finished—but not quite. You've come so close but are missing the final polish of professional production nuances. I've seen it work like crazy—or fall on its face. Now that we've glanced over the mechanical tools, let's take up the far more important creative and psychological tools, rules, theories, and practices in broadcast execution. You can construct the most perfect marketing plan, product profile, competitive analysis, and creative strategy—and still blow the whole bundle. The only thing the consumer sees and hears is the execution. Think about that for a minute: The thing the marketers know least about and the creative man knows most about is often dominated by the introspective view of a marketer. And all the ground-work can be meaningless if the intimate, convincing moment of communication is self-serving to the advertiser instead of the consumer. To make things worse we live in an age of parity products. By the time you've innovated your product, your competitors' lab has stuck it under a spectroscope and is hot on your heels with virtually the same thing.

And now, let's consider that we have spent all the post-war years with the marketing maw chewing up every unique strategic or positioning idea that an entire industry can offer. There may be no totally new idea—or at least not enough to go around. All that is left to separate your product or service from the industry cliche is the uniqueness and excellence of your execution. So if it requires consideration of something unfamiliar or expensive—consider it. It may be the only fuse that can detonate the swamp. One can build a strong case for either side: (1) Write the best commercial you can. If it comes out as 30 seconds, run a 30-second commercial. If it takes 60 seconds, run minutes. Or (2) figure out the best possible media buy. If 30-second commercials are more efficient, write 30-second commercials, etc.

Neither is totally realistic. One ignores the money realities. The other ignores the communications problem. Somewhere in between with professionalism and mutual respect, the answer must be found in each case. The most efficient media plan can't work with weak 30-second commercial. Neither can the world's best minute commercial deliver enough customers if not enough people see it. And the real dilemma is that this is one of those decisions that research can't solve because you're adding applies and oranges.

Nevertheless, "target" length should be discussed before your first attempts at execution of your strategy. It makes a difference in the "mind clock" which every good broadcast copy writer had developed. You simply think differently in trying to solve a problem in 30 seconds as opposed to 60 seconds. And this pre-applied discipline can help you from becoming embroiled and in love with an idea that simple can't live in 30 seconds.

Don't, however, dismiss the other side of the coin. If great minute commercial emerges and your best pro's simply can't bring off a strong 30—it's time to go back for a heart-to-heart talk with your media director. Every creative director has his favourite form of organizing strategic information. But most strategies include at least six critical decisions:

1. Who's your friend? Or whom are you talking to and trying to convince?
2. Who's your enemy? Is it a competitor or some other obstacle—even apathy?
3. What's good? Or what real consumer benefit exists in people terms?
4. Why should I believe? Or what's in or around the product or service that substantiates the benefit above?
5. Who's talking? Or what personality are we projecting for the advertiser, tone of voice, etc.?
6. Anything else? Are the "musts" and lists really necessary or merely cluttering up the air?

Strategies are seldom brief and often longer. Sometimes they ever start defining execution ideas. All times these can be needlessly limiting, Nevertheless, it brings up an interesting disclaimer. No one can accurately and clearly define where strategy stops and execution begins. Nor can he define where execution ends and production begins. Like any good commercial they flow into each other smoothly and the seams never show. But that's production talk. This chapter is limted to a minimum of technical production, dwelling mainly on the creative philosophies of execution or strategy. Without needlessly rehashing how one arrives-at strategic decisions, let's take a moment to understand the critical importance of these building blocks as we enter the stage of broadcast execution. First, remember, you're dealing with a highly personal form of communication that is part of a person's life. His nightly bout with television can soothe away a hectic day, transport him to a stadium or bring the horror of war crashing into his den—while her daytime hours can be lightened by a soap opera or enlightened by history in the making. And radio, the constant companion, lessens the loneliness in the kitchen or the car. Because broadcast offers so vast a choice, it becomes an extension of the personality of the viewer or listener as she or she expresses that choice with the dial. so you see, it's terribly personal.

Arthur Godfrey's greatest contribution to radio was the impression that he was not addressing the masses but talking instead to one woman at a time. He may very well have been the first to articulate this philosophy. Many grasp it today as a matter of course. Yet may still fail to understand it. This is another deadly sin. But these observations may help build a foundation for the importance of truly understanding the prime target—not just demographically, but psychologically as well. Once having understood him, you must talk to him in his frame of reference and his idiom, not yours. So if you absolutely hate the music of the day, and feel that fashion is becoming downright indecent, you'll never reach today's young market unless you check your personal bias and let someone who's with it turn the young set on for you.This is perhaps the best advice for the creative adman. This advice is based on protection of your paycheck and pension plan.

The simple truth is that almost everybody's strategy *starts* with some sort of profile description of a market target or prime prospect or user or consumer. If he is changing with the times, either evolutionary or revolutionary, yesterday's awareness of his psychographic profile can make him a stranger today. Or worse, it can make you a stranger in his eyes! So don't talk. Not until you've digested today's breed of cat—or may be even tomorrow's.

Let us make it clear that this is not a plea for the cold-blooded murder of the English language. It is not a plea that we all master and use the language of either the jet set or the beat generation, the patois of the recording artist or the idiom of any ethnic group. Rather, it is a caution the people may very well think differently, feel differently, respond differently today.

Life is changing. Values are changing. Miles are disappearing. Drudgery is diminishing. Mammoths are being miniaturized. Moments are being minimized.

Can the human race survive this environmental about-face without reflecting some symptomatic changes in personality and philosophy?

An intimate understanding of your key market target is the most vital contribution creative people bring to broadcast execution. That's because it influences the way you handle all the other building blocks of the strategy.

From the culture into the product: Once upon a time all claims seemed to radiate from the product and into the culture. Nowadays the most telling claims seem to radiate from the culture and into the product. And if it may be abbreviated the dictionary. "culture" means the accumulated knowledge, whereas "society" means the accumulated restrictions. To understand the culture, you must understand the people *as* they are accumulating. And this braintwister has given rise to advertising which is much more people-oriented and emotional than advertising which is product-oriented and factual.

This requires the realization that he who would pursue creative execution must have a split personality. On the one hand he is part philosopher, psychologist, sociologist. But because it's a real world he must also be alert to the practical side, realizing that much of what his people are accumulating comes from the total effect of all the advertising to which they are constantly subjected.

While it is earnestly believe that imitation is the downfall of an advertiser. It is equally convincing that intensive exposure to other advertising is critical for the creative man. One cannot tolerate the lost arty souls who make a living in the advertising business while defaming it in toto, parroting the dissenter's favorite battle cry: "I never watch television." One has never known a really top creative man who didn't average a couple of hours a night with the TV tube and a couple of hours a day with the radio. He must—just to know what's going on.

In the first place, it gives an instinctive picture of what constitutes par for the course. You get a feeling of the total fabric of the medium. You get a rather clear picture of what the major advertisers of each industry are saying. You're better prepared to search out preemptive campaign strategies and executions. You avoid the embarrassment of coming up with a marvelous campaign idea only to discover later that someone else is already doing it.

On this latter score, don't ignore the distinct possibility of ESP or the fact that other professionals faced with the same problem may come up with the same answer. An Adman recalls following experience. Many years ago he was on a train from Baltimore to New York.

Just before leaving he checked the first run on some 24-sheet posters they were doing for Betholine-Sinclair. The subject was faster winter starts. The poster showed a woman's foot in a white fur-trimmed snow boot pressing down on the starter. The copy said, "Just touch and go... " It had a blue background and an oranges station sign. The train was drawing into 30th Street Station in Philadelphia. He looked out the window and got the surprise of his life. There atop a building was a giant spectacular in the process of being painted. Workmen on a scaffold were putting on the finishing touches. It had a man's foot pressing the starter.

In addition to the everyday awareness of these media, it's equally important to expose yourself to the cream of the crop, the best of what's going on. This sharpens your perspective, elevates your bench-marks, and helps you spot trends in the growth of the art of communicating and convincing. There are several opportunities open to you. Some for free, some for fee. First, the sample reels of film and sound production companies contain what they believe to be their best contemporary work. Usually, their judgment is rather sound. They're anxious to play them for you as a means to get some of your business. There are several excellent reels put together annually or more often by the industry's most informed historians, observers, and awards directors. Once you have armed yourself with insight into the typical family at the other end of the airwaves, *and* become current with what's going on, what do you do with it? One like to think of it this way.

Every good creative man has one head and four hats. He has a miner's cap with its lamp a green eyeshade with accompanying paper cuffs, the winged helmet of Viking, the powdered wig of jurisprudence.

First, he dons the miner's cap. And he digs out every scrap of ore in the vein. He is not selective. He simply exhausts the vein he is digging and tosses every possible nugget into his cart.

Second, he replaces the miner's cap with the clerk's green eyeshade and paper cuffs. He examines the load from the miner's cart, sorts it, and enters the valid pieces in his ledger, totals his columns, balances his books, and prepares his statement.

Third, he casts off his bondage from the accounting office and places the Viking's winged helmet on his head. He is free. The open sea beckons. He will fly under sail, sometimes running free with incredible winds, sometimes, be calmed, but everlastigly exploring uncharted seas.

And fourth, when his voyage is over, he removes his helmet and takes on the wig of jurisprudence, coldly to evaluate the discoveries of his previous self.

But remember, he has but one head. He would look absurd if he wore more than one hat at a time. If he were to wear the green eyeshade of the clerk with the miner's cap, he might be trying to evaluate while exhausting the vein. He could outsmart himself and miss the mother lode. If he were to wear the wig of jurisprudence along with the Viking's winged helmet, Judgment might restrain him from the risks of the greatest adventure.

This grim little fairly tale is merely a graphic way of saying that the creative mind must accept, develop, and defend a four-way split personality that many a skilled marketer may find alarming. You can help him while he wears the first two hats. You can help him with the fourth after he has had a chance to evaluate and judge his own work and even prepare a defense. But when he reaches the point of winged flight with the third hat, leave him along. That's when the creative mind is at work. That's what execution is all about.

Many attempts have been made to define creativity beyond the concept of talent or gift. Unfortunately, most of these attempts have been made by psychologists and researchers who do not possess the same brand of creativity or work at it every day of their lives. This is not to say that their work is not creative, rather that it is a different form of creativity.

So we are faced with a dichotomy. The scientists can be much more precise in their explorations of the process. The creative man may not be so technically articulate. But he has experienced it. And the part of him that experiences it most intensely is his *subconscious mind*. That's the reason one expouses the motto: "Prepare the mind—then free the mind" and its accompanying "four hat" theory. In essence it uses the *subconscious mind* as the real working tool.

In other words, if you absorb all the pertinent information and then formulate the objectives and strategy, your best bet at this point is to walk away from it and let it cook. Staring at blank paper is demoralizing. And an overt attack at execution at this point often turns out a commercial that is nothing more than the strategy statement set to pictures and music. On the other hand, if you suffer with the pieces your subconscious mind while doing something else to break the monotony, ideas begin to spill out.

No matter what degree of creativity you may have started with, no matter how you have refined it. Disciplines are important in every other stage, but this phenomenon can have no disciplines except those a good broadcast writer has accumulated from experience. His mind works on a plane different from that of the print writer. He is not so concerned with a stopper headline and illustration. He is concerned with the passage of time—a story that will move from something interesting and relevant to a, favourable conclusion. There are more tools at his disposal and more arts to be mastered. Sometimes a commercial may come out full-blow. Other times pieces begin to emerge. And every writer is different. One of the best ad-women, had the nickname "58-second mind"—because every commercial ideas she ever turned out was timed instinctively to fit. She used to start doodling until the doodles became delightful primitive drawings which became a sequence which became a commercial. Another successful writer did all his actual creative thinking on weekends while riding a tractor on his farm. He used the normal work week for digging, sorting, and evaluating. This may explain why writers often state out of windows, seem near to napping with their feet on their desks, do all manner of seemingly unproductive things which exasperate their managements. But if they are at the third-hat stage, forcing them to conform can force your commercials to conform to mediocrity.

Perhaps one has used the term "writers" indiscriminately. It really implies "commercial builders" regardless of their primary speciality. The break-through idea may be a picture sequence, a piece of music, a casting or location idea, a word, a slogan, anything that opens up a new path. More of these nuggets seem to pour out of the subconscious because it is free of inhibition and the need to evaluate. So we're now at the point where ideas are beginning to emerge. Is there any way to help them along?

Too often the urge to imitate overshadows the urge to innovate. In our opinion this comes from fear, laziness, and the urge to be "in". When it happens on the client side it's usually caused by overreaction to the advertising of competitors. When it happens on the agency side it's usually the result of who won what awards in the last competition. In either case it creates a massive cliche.

This is the costly phenomenon where virtually all the advertisers of a given industry turn out advertising that is so similar the poor consumer has difficulty in telling one from the other. Generally it starts with pressure from the sales department when they're falling behind the quarterly prediction, and you hear a question like, "Why can't we have stuff like the XYZ Company is running? That's really working out in the field." Before you know it, the pressure mounts and you're dealing with a stated objective to duplicate their campaign when what is really needed is a campaign that separates you from them.

Perhaps the most classic industry cliche was in the tyre industry in the early 1950s. The name of the game was colour spreads in the late-lamented *Saturday Evening Post* showing the largest possible head on retouched exaggeration of one's tread. Suddenly one advertiser had the wisdom to switch his campaign from strategy to execution to media. Goodyear blasted the swamp with the now-classic multi-awarded "Go Go Goodyear" campaign from Young & Rubicam. There was excitement and urgency and realism—and most of all an implicit consumer benefit in their television commercials. They also established an important musical theme which was to become a valuable continuing property for the future and a vehicle for radio "magnification."

In light of today's fresh airline advertising, it's difficult to remember the dreary "destination schedule" commercials that ran in the early 1960s. Today the list is almost endless, but as one set of cliches is broken another begins to emerge.

This cuts across industry lines and ranges from parody to plagiarism. Nevertheless, this is what happens when one advertiser has a breakthrough commercial and other advertisers in other industries adopt part or all of it for their own use. It can be as innocently simple as the rush to use *the* hot announcer or *the* hot director or *the* in sound or hand-held camera throughout or machine-gun film cutting or multi-image montage or whatever is new and different at the moment.

Slightly more serious is the case where one advertiser grabs something timely such as a movie plot or cast and suddenly six others are reshooting the same script with a different product shot. Parody of other commercials also seems to be very much in vogue. While it's often entertaining, it does split the sponsor identification.

It's also been charged that some agencies have "a look"—that all their ads for all their clients look alike. In some cases, this is true, but not of the agencies at whom the charge is usually levelled.

The moral of the twin cliches discussion is simply this: If you wish your advertising to stand out, then by simple logic it has to be new and different from the rest. So while it's a lot easier to imitate, the name of the game is innovate. And since production costs in broadcast are usually a lot higher than in print media, you're twice as obligated to make the grade.

Preemption applies to strategy as well as execution. In its simplest form, preemption merely means talking about something that competitors could talk about—but ignore.

In today's climate of parity products this becomes critical. It requires insight and guts. But let's assume that some basic, factor is common to your product and the products of all of your competitors. Because you, and your counterparts as competitors, are extremely close to the technology involved, you assume it is a standard operation or feature of that product category. *If* you can back off far enough and become totally philosophical, you may realize that here, at last, is an uncovered base. Your management may scoff. After all, all the competitors *could* say the same thing the day after you chose to break your campaign. But you are blessed with lead time. Under normal circumstances it will take them weeks to come to the realization, weeks to come to the decision, and more weeks to approve advertising to counter you, and still more weeks to produce and air what they have approved. By now you have developed a consumer awareness and the idea is yours. Every nickel competition spends in saying "me to" may only serve to reinforce your identity with the concept or execution.

Sometimes preemption pays off with a totally new idea. Often it works with an old idea the industry has discarded ten or twenty years ago—and it's time for re-run. Take, for example, the case of Macleans. Twenty years ago the toothpaste people discarded whiteness for more competitive and narrow positions. Macleans actually retreated to a generic toothpaste strategy, but did it with fresh, compelling television executions and shocked the industry virtually overnight. In its simplest form they said: Strong taste equals strong cleaning power; strong cleaning power equals strong appeal; whiteness wins.

5

Publicity Evaluation

There is a variety of ways to do publicity work. These can be broken down into three categories: i) Fully staffed in-house publicity group that does the entire job; ii) Small in-house group (often one individual) that uses the talents and resources available elsewhere in the organization; iii)In-house publicity director supported by outside services. Several things influence the method used in doing the publicity job. Foremost among them are company factors such as size, type of management, type of employees and their attitudes, type of products, internal costs, and budgeting methods.

Other factors are the size and type of marketplace in which the company does its business, and the media that serve the marketplace. There is little agreement on the question of whether it is better to buy outside services or to staff up to handle publicity internally. However, there are some considerations that apply in many cases. One is general acceptance of the rule of thumb that says companies with sales in the $ 5 to $ 10 million per year range probably do not have the resources to do the job internally; and companies with sales over $ 25 million per year should be able to do a reasonably effective job themselves. But even in the case in which a company can justify an internal publicity operation, outside services will probably be needed somewhere along the line because of work load peaks and special problems. It is probably safe to say that a combination of the internal and external approaches is best in most cases.

In comparing the cost of external *versus* internal service, one thing that is sometimes overlooked is the effect of indirect costs on the internal operation. In addition to the direct costs of salary and operating expenses, costs such as fringe benefits, vacations and sick leaves. telephone service, and working space must also be considered. Indirect costs can amount to as much as direct costs. Large companies or organizations usually use this approach. They generally have a group of publicity managers and experts in the corporate staff organization that serves the divisions or departments.

Sometimes the lower echelons have publicity people, or people who perform the publicity function, in addition to the staff group. These publicity groups use outside help usually only when they have an overload or when it is clearly less expensive. For example, if an east coast company wants to obtain a case history story on the west coast, it may be less expensive to hire a west coast writer or agency to do job than to send a staff man out. Smaller companies generally do not have the resources to have an in-house publicity group. Also, they might not have enough publicity to be done to justify a group. Small-and medium-sized companies or organizations often take the approach of giving a small group responsibility for a publicity program. In most cases these groups or individuals do not have the budget to spend much on outside services. In these cases, they use manpower and resources elsewhere in the organization to do the job. This means that the publicity director must persuade the managers of other functions such as marketing and engineering that it is necessary for them to support the publicity effort with manpower, money, or both. And with all the demands for resources made upon these managers, they are difficult to convince. Often this approach is not the most effective use of everyone's time, and it is probably used more often than it should be. Also, it often bogs down completely, as illustrated by the following example. The case involved a materials department headed by a highly competent materials engineer with an international reputation.

In addition to technical competence, however, he had a very good grasp of business and management ideas and practices. He agreed fully on the importance of a strong publicity program. However, he and the several engineers and technicians working for him were putting in long hours in lab work and were spending a great deal of their own time working on reports on the lab work and on proposals for contracts, both essential to the profitability of the department. Progress reports were overdue, a few key projects were behind schedule, and a technical paper the manager had committed himself to write was late. He agreed in principle, but felt unable to do anything to support the publicity effort. Such instances are not rarities. And in some organizations, they are the single largest block to an effective publicity program. What often happens in such instances is that the engineering group, or whatever kind of group it happens to be, promises to support a publicity program, with no real ability to follow through. They just want the publicity director out of their hair. Besides inefficiencies such as lip-service support, the use of "contributed" resources within the organization has another disadvantage. It diffuses both responsibility and authority. And "What is everybody's business is nobody's business". Despite the disadvantages of this approach, in many cases the resources are simply not available to do the job any other way. There are some things that can be done to alleviate the problem. They are:

- Use a "direct mail" approach.
- Enlist suppliers, customers, and distributors in a cooperative publicity program.

The so-called direct mail approach can make use of questionnaires, motivational material, and incentives. One company used a combination of a questionnaire and an incentive. It gave a cash award of $ 25 for every case history questionnaire its field salesmen filled out and sent in. The case history information was used in some cases for advertising and in others for publicity. Enlisting the aid of a supplier or other outside "volunteer" organization should be done by the individual who is its primary contact. In the case of a supplier, this would be a purchasing agent; for a customer, a salesman: for a distributor, a marketing director or manager.

These individuals know the companies or groups they deal with and are able to judge whether or not they will be receptive to a cooperative program. Another possible source of help is a technical writing group. Many companies, even small ones, especially those that do government work, have such groups. They work on all kinds of manuals, handbooks, and other material often referred to by the general term "documentation". The material is usually instructive in nature. Its most common form is military equipment documentation— operation, maintenance, and repair manuals. There are, however, countless other forms. Some technical writers know, or can learn, enough about publicity to produce useful press releases and articles. The caveat here is that most technical writers do not write anything original. They simply make more understandable and readable information they have been given. And this level of "writing" ability may in fact be all that is required in certain cases.

However, if any interpretation or generalizing is required in the writing, most technical writers will be at a loss. They usually cannot shift their specialized attitude enough to do an adequate job. In addition to their writing potential, technical writers can also be useful in illustrating material. They are responsible for illustrations in the manuals and other documentation they produce, and work very closely with illustrators and photographers. But here again, their specialized viewpoint may be more of a hindrance than a help. The types of external support available are individual producers, consultants, and agencies. Individual producers can include writers, photographers, or a combination of the two known as photojournalists.

Individual producers are used to write material and illustrate news releases and articles that support some objective of a publicity plan. Their role has nothing to do with planning or counselling. Consultants on the other hand usually do nothing but counsel. (High-calibre public relations consultants are known as PR counsels.) In some cases, their advice is in the area of organizing to do a publicity job; in other cases, it involves publicity planning as well. Some individuals who call themselves consultants go beyond the giving of advice and also do the work of carrying out a plan. In this capacity, they function as a one-man agency. Agencies are hired either on a retainer basis or as needed to carry out a specific program or solve a specific problem. The type of external support the company needs depends largely on its in-house capability and the state of its business. Companies needing external publicity support can be categorized as:

- Small company beginning or expanding its publicity effort.
- Small or large company needing external support for a limited time.
- Large company that likes to keep staff activities lean and prefers to buy service outside rather than enlarging its publicity unit.
- Large company that needs external support to help keep its publicity people objective and outward-looking instead of becoming primarily concerned with internal affairs.

When a small company just getting into publicity, or expanding its publicity effort, has a full-time publicity director with considerable experience, it will probably use individual producers and agencies. If a small company has a part-time director for this activity, or one who has little experience in the publicity field, the company may want to use both a consultant and an agency. In the latter case, the consultant either can be used initially to organize the publicity activity and then step out of the picture, or can stay on to supervise the agency's activities. Agencies and individual producers are used by small and large companies that need external support or a limited time to carry out a special project or to help solve a particular short-range problem. They are also used by large companies that need external support on a continuing basis. Consultants and agencies are used in the fourth case, where a large company feels it needs outside eyes the look at its activities to keep its attitudes relevant to the needs and opportunities among its publics. Consultants and individual producers usually work on the basis of a letter or memorandum of understanding rather than formal written contract.

Many agencies do also, but contracts are not uncommon. There are far more agencies than consultants and individual producers. Small agencies, and consultants and individual producers, are usually highly specialized. This is one of their strengths. The way to locate outside support is to ask professionals in other companies, talk to editors, and talk to as many potential contributors as possible. Some of the key questions in determining the type of external support needed are:

- Is the support required to be of a counselling nature, or will actual publicity work be needed? If it is counselling, a consultant is probably called for. If work is to be performed, an agency or an individual producer is in order.
- What are the short-and long-term objectives? Short-term objectives usually imply a one-shot or limited publicity project. In such a situation an agency or an individual producer is usually used. In the case of long-term objectives, a consultant may be needed to map out the strategy, and an agency or individual contributor to carry out the plans.
- What is the size of the job to be done? In the case of a very extensive program, a large agency is often used because it has the necessary resources.

- What is the extent of the funds available? If a very small amount of money is available. Many agencies consider an account of less than $ 10,000 a year unprofitable and will not accept it. Consultants are usually more expensive than individual producers, but the quality of the publicity program is much higher.
- How much in-house expertise is available? As indicated above, if the publicity director run a one-man shop and has little experience in the field, may need the advice of a consultant to start him down the right path.

Important to the effectiveness of any type of external support is the matter of accountability *versus* authority. If agencies or individuals are to be held accountable to a high degree, they should also have a lot of authority delegate to them by the client. They should be free to make commitments and decisions they feel are necessary to carry out their responsibilities and meet the expectations of the client. The least used, but not necessarily the least valuable, type of external support is the consultant.

The qualifications of a publicity consultant are much the same as for other types of consultants. He should have broad experience, proven performance, and an in-depth understanding of the way organizations work. He must be a problem solver, and he must always put the client first. Before bringing in a consultant, it is necessary to make sure that the key people in the company will cooperate and be receptive. It is also necessary to define carefully the purpose or the problem to which the consultant will apply his expertise.

The next step is to locate a consultant and work out with him the scope of his task. In conjunction with this, the fee should be negotiated. This may run from $ 100 to $ 250 per day.

Once the consultant is brought in, he should be given all the facts. It is essential to be completely candid, even to the extent of admitting the fears and prejudices of key individuals. Individual producers are individuals in the sense that they usually work alone. They are sometimes members of a group of associated writers or photographers, they may be employed by concerns that provide such services, and in some cases they are free lancers. The majority of individual producers are Journalists in terms of knowledge and experience. They know quite a bit about a lot of different kinds of things. Usually, they are ex-Journalists or ex-photojournalists. Other individual producers have specialized knowledge and experience.

Many are technically trained, and some are former editors of trade and technical publications. Some photographers come form specialized areas such as industrial photography. Individual producers may charge for their services on a flat fee or a time basis. On a time basis, writers usually charge by the hour for time spent in researching and writing. Photographers usually charge by the day. Whether they are on a time or flat fee basis, writers and photographers always bill expenses connected with the job to their clients at cost. Many companies prefer writers to work for a fixed price, so they know exactly how much a job will cost.

This is often more expensive than the time basis, because writers usually paid a fixed-fee quotation. It is not because they are dishonest, but simply because they are not willing to risk losing money. Every writer knows from experience that some jobs take more time than expected.

So he inflates the price to make up for the unprofitable jobs. Writers and photographers calculate their fees by adding together a salary, overhead costs, and reasonable profit, and then dividing that figure by the number of working hours in whatever time frame they have selected. It is probably safe to say that more individual producers, both Journalists and specialists, work on case histories than on any other type of story. Individual producers are in most cases be most "cost-effective" method of having case history material prepared. Those that have become known as effective producers at reasonable cost have developed clienteles.

A pattern that has evolved is that such producers make swings to various parts of the country to carry out specific assignments. By informing their clientele that they are making a particular trip, they often obtain additional assignments. By combining such assignments, they can spread the expenses around among several clients. Some have done this so successfully that they have developed a flat rate for job just about anywhere in the country. The other more-or-less common way outside writers are used in for ghost writing, mostly speeches and signed articles. Busy executives do not always have the time to write things themselves, so they or someone on their staff turns these chores over to someone else.

The writer is told in general terms what the executive wants to say. He then talks to staff members and experts, and may even visit a plant or other location to get a feeling for the atmosphere. The mark of a good ghost is the amount of work he puts into research before even outlining what is to be written. This of course takes a lot of time, and there may be expenses involved. Sometimes, those who are responsible for buying the writing services are surprised at the cost, especially if they have never done anything similar before. Outside the individual producers of course can be used to produce all the other forms of industrial publicity in addition to case histories and ghost-written material.

These forms of industrial publicity include various types of press releases, unsigned exclusive material, signed exclusive articles, speeches, papers, and material for company publications. Agencies come in all sizes and have all kinds of different characteristics and expertise. The first major problem is shopping for an agency is matching an agency's capabilities with the needs and characteristics of the organization. For example, it is possible that an agency performs brilliantly in creative work, but that the account executive or manager cannot communicate with his counterpart in the company. Another agency might have less creative power, but has an account executive who works well with the client. Most agencies are either advertising or public relations agencies.

Some large ones do both. With the exception of financial public relations, what is called public relations by agencies that operate in the public sector is usually industrial publicity. Evaluating agencies is a highly subjective matter. Some of the things that can be used in an agency evaluation are:

- *Accomplishments.* These reveal a lot about the agency's creative abilities and the kinds of things they are good at. The other side of that coin is that failures can also show a lot about the agency.
- *People.* An investigation of the abilities, attitudes, and experience of management, account men, and creative individual is also revealing.

- It helps provide a picture of an agency's total talent, its stability and reliability, and its integrity, and gives an indication of the compatibility of the agency and the company.
- *Cost.* Agencies usually charge on a time basics for publicity services. Everyone in an agency in required to keep daily records of how much time is spent working for each account. These accounts are then billed monthly for the total amount of time spent on them. If an agency is on a retainer, it provides service on an agreed-upon basis or on demand up to the value of the retainer. If additional service is required, a fee is then negotiated over and above the retainer.
- *Physical factors.* The location of the agency is a consideration. It should be easy for agency people to reach the company, and *vice versa.* Another consideration is the location of other offices of the agency, if any, which can be called upon if necessary. If, for example, there is a possibility of needing services overseas, it might be a good idea to try to find an agency with overseas offices. The size of the agency is another element—which can be either positive or negative.

It is important to recognize that there can be a difference between real and apparent competence in evaluating support of any kind. For example, for cost agencies, a fact of life is making presentations to clients or prospective clients. They put a lot of effort into these presentations, and justifying so because they are the primary means of communicating their abilities. Individual producers usually engage in a certain amount of salesmanship is sometimes confused with product quality.

The vast majority of agencies are of course ethical, and they do not try to sell their clients worthless services. But it is useful to remember that agencies, just like companies, must make a profit to stay in business. That does not mean that they are unscrupulous, but they practise entrépreneurship in looking for opportunities to increase their billings.

A final caveat: Free or non-profit publicity services provided by advertising agencies are often inferior. This approach should generally be avoided. The forms of publicity information are described in some detail, and the means of implementation are to large extent covered in the descriptions. However, some factors not covered there affect implementation. These factors are related to the nature of the organization and to the publicity plans. The type of organization is a major influence.

At one extreme is the small, limited-product-line unit which has high-volume production of relatively simple and competitive products. Such a unit may be a company, or it may be the smallest unit with profit responsibility in a corporate structure. Publicity for such a unit may be handled independently of the rest of the organization, even if it is part of a corporate structure. The publicity program for such a small unit is usually very specific and highly focused. It is most often completely marketing oriented, as opposed to supporting public relations objectives. It is aimed at very specific audiences—generally well-defined customer audiences and uses specialized media. The other extreme of organization type is the corporate unit in which publicity is handled by a corporate staff. This permits a lot of specialized ability to be applied to programs, but very often the corporate staff is not completely attuned to the needs and problems of the lesser units. It is probably safe to say that in most large corporations the main responsibility of the corporate staff is public relations publicity as opposed to marketing support publicity.

In cases in which the lesser units have responsibility for their own publicity activities to some degree or another, the corporate staff has the added responsibility for coordinating the publicity activities of the units so they do not work at cross purposes and get in each other's way. Corporate programs are usually much more general in nature and aimed at larger and less specialized audiences. They are oriented toward the large circulation media, the general interest magazines, newspapers, and the electronic media. Most organization units fall somewhere between the small, strictly limited unit and the corporate unit, so there is usually an element of both marketing and public relations support in a real-world programs. Whatever the type of program, it must at some point be translated into action. This is where the tools and techniques covered in the next chapters come in. Briefly, the forms of information used fall in two broad categories: syndicated and exclusive information.

Syndicated material is sent to many publications at the same time. Exclusive information is given to a single publication. Syndicated material is most commonly in the form of a press release. Exclusive material is usually in the form of an article which is substantially longer than a press release and may or may not be signed by someone. That is, someone's name appears under the title as a by-line. Also, there are two broad categories of methods of putting information into the hands of editors and writers. These are indirect and direct means. When indirect means are used, information is passed along to recipients by mail, teletype, or telephone. In direct transfer of information, the recipient is given the information personally. This can take place on either an individual or collective basis. The individual basis may be through a visit to or from an editor; the collective through a briefing or a press conference. A major problem in industrial publicity is what *Fortune* magazine once referred to as "a kind of overcapacity' problem. Its capabilities for spreading the message are immense.

The trouble is that it's hard to find message worth spreading; to a large and dispiriting extent, the p.r. output that lands on most businessmen's and editor's desks belongs in their wastebasket—and gets there within second of the landing."

Fortune's statement may not be completely accurate, but the point is valid. This is borne out by a comment made by Richard Koff, formerly managing editor of *Product Engineering* magazine. He said that the magazine receives about 15,000 press releases per year, but uses information from only 2000, about 13 per cent of the total.

The reasons so few releases are used can be viewed in terms of an editor's interest. If the release is not of interest to an editor, he simply does not use it. The editor's interest is of course an extension of his readers' views. If a release does not interest an editor, it is either poorly done or misdirected.It is usually possible to find an interesting angle in almost any subject area, but occasionally it is not. If the latter is the case, the project should be dropped from the plan as soon as it becomes apparent that it will be a waste of time. Another consideration under the heading of problems and limitations is that of proprietary information. This falls into one of two categories, competitive information and information about patentable inventions. Competitive information is of the company and trade secret type. It includes such things as market and financial data, and information about processes and product know-how. Information about patentable inventions can be extremely valuable to a company.

Patents give the company the right to the exclusive use of information on processes or devices. It can sell its patents, or license other companies to produce patented inventions. However a company handles its patents, they are usually worth a lot of money. Very often, a company goes to a lot of expenses to develop an invention, and if it cannot be patented, competitors may get the benefit. The patent problem in the United States is different from that in most other countries.

In the United States, if information about a patentable invention is published, the company has a year to file for a patent. In most other countries, the company cannot obtain a patent after the date the information is published anywhere in the world. So if a company does business overseas, it is in their best interests to file for a patent before they disclose information by publication. Even if a company is not doing overseas business and has no licensees overseas, it is a good idea not to disclose information on something that is patentable.

The reason is that it may stimulate a competitor to file for a patent on the same thing. The first to file is in a better legal position in any patent dispute. The burden of proof is on the company that files second. Being on the defensive is always a disadvantage, especially in patent disputes. A way to avoid the patent problem is of course to avoid premature disclosure of information on something that is patentable. The one that is in the best position to make a judgment as to what constitutes premature disclosure is the company's or unit's, patent attorney. He should therefore have a chance to see information about new products or procedures in advance of disclosure.

And since industrial publicity is concerned with new information, it should be one of the types of information the patent attorney is shown. Yet another item in the catalogue of problems and limitations is a rather nebulous subject that might be called sensitivity. One form it takes is knowing what *not* to say well as what *to* say. Saying the wrong thing can sometimes be worse than saying nothing. Sometimes, publicity done for its own sake can amount to saying the wrong thing.

Those responsible for putting out publicity often feel compelled, or are expected, to use numerous pieces of press information or clippings as a measure of their effectiveness. In many such instances, realistic planning and relevant objectives are given lip service, and the aim becomes the production of material whether it does any good or not.

Given such a situation, the odds are that at some point a press release will go out or an article will be placed or some other action will be taken that results in bad press. An example of a situation in which the wrong thing is said is the following hypothetical case: The ABC company makes an electronic tube that produces a television picture in almost total darkness. The main use of the tube is in a television camera that is part of a night bombing system on a military airplane. But there are other uses, such as watching streets, parking lots, parks, and so on, at night, possibly for crime prevention. Now suppose that the publicity director has a press release on the remarkable performance of the television camera tube in the bombing system and, wonder of wonders, obtains approval from the military customer to distribute it. In making up a mailing list, he decides that the press release should be sent to municipal and law enforcement publications because the tube can be useful in night surveillance for crime prevention. But one of the national municipal publications he sends the release to has an editor who is violently antimilitary.

The bombing system mentioned in the release so incenses the editor that in a fit of anger he dashes off an editorial about companies that build instruments of war and, to make matters even worse, try to exploit people in trouble using their ill-gotten technology. Although such an extreme case of bad press is unlikely to happen, it illustrates the problem of wrong information or information in the wrong place. Ineffective or misdirected information is not the mark of a professional. Another form of sensitivity is to be alert to the possibility of something unfavourable or even disastrous happening in the publicity process.

The second case is of course an extreme example which hopefully will never be duplicated. Nevertheless, both cases illustrate the idea that it is necessary to assess the risk of something unexpected happening and what the probable consequences might be. If lives are at stake, project such as the filming of an aircraft formation should not be undertaken. This also holds true if there is a possibility of expensive equipment being damaged or destroyed. Projects of lesser risk must be individually assessed.

Security requirements are another type of limitation. These can relate to company security, proprietary information, or government restrictions on information. For example, a part of every contract from the Department of Defence is a document designated form DD-254. This has a block in which a statement is entered indicating how information related to the work covered by the contact is to be handled. Usually it says something like: "All information relating to work done under this contract must be cleared by the contracting officer for open publication." Most other types of government contracts and commercial contracts have some provision in them for approval of information related to the contract. So it is necessary to be sure what the contractual obligations are before even beginning a publicity project.

Even though a contract may not require formal approval of information by the customer, it is frequently a good idea to inform him about a publicity project on work covered by this contract. It may even be advantageous to let him see information as a matter of courtesy and to maintain good customer relations. Yet another problems and limitations areas is that of working with people in the company. The two main categories are executives, and experts and specialists.

Top executives are by definition more or less good at company politics. They are of course usually very capable people to begin with, but as a general statement they are also very adept at company politics. The publicity director usually is, or should be, in a privileged position with top management. Consequently, it is often difficult for him to not become entangled in company politics. He should, however, make a strong attempt to stay aloof from such political activity unless he is in line for a top management slot himself. The reason is that he rarely win at that game. So he should try to stick to business.

Top-management men often have a reasonably good understanding of what publicity is and what it can do, because they see the operation of a company from an overall viewpoint. Since middle managers have a narrower view, they can create problems for the publicity director. A common way in which this is done is to exert pressure through budgetary controls and to withhold cooperation. He may have to resort to persuasion or, in some cases, arm twisting—which often amounts to playing company politics—to obtain the cooperation of lower-echelon managers on plans and procedures.

There also are special problems in working with experts and specialists. The majority of these individuals in practice turn out to be engineers. The main reason for the problems is that the experts often do not understand involved in publicity. And that goes for advertising people too. Another reason for the problems is that experts can be difficult to work with. Some are naturally uncommunicative and uncooperative, some cannot get their, minds off their work, and some are just prima donnas.

Difficulties in working with experts sometimes come from their not being involved in publicity planning. It may be argued that evaluation is not a sub-category under implementation, but as subject in itself. Even if this is the case, evaluation is very closely related to implementation and provides the feedback necessary to see if results are being obtained and if the plans continue to be meaningful. In industry, evaluation is usually thought of in terms of measuring something.

The effectiveness of publicity to measure. This problem is very much like the difficult of measuring the effectiveness of advertising. The most common gauge of publicity results is the volume of clippings generated by a press release, or the length of a feature article. But this does not indicate that anyone read the material or, if they did, whether the information had the desired effect. It is especially hard to measure the effectiveness of image-building or capability publicity. Here, the only worthwhile way to tell if anything has been accomplished is to survey the attitudes of a specific public before and after a publicity campaign. Because of the cost and the time involved, this is practical only where there is a massive and continuing problem.

An example might be the kind of ingrown awe of nuclear power that most people have. This is definitely a problem for electric utilities and their suppliers all over the world. On the one hand, nuclear power is considered in many instances the best, most economic way of dealing with the need for more power. On the other hand, there is a lot of opposition, some very powerful, to this energy source. For relatively minor problems, more "routine" objectives, and small companies, surveys are often not practical.

A workable alternative is to evaluate not the results but the performance of the program. The idea behind this is that a program carried out the way it should be generally achieved the desired results. The job must be done professionally by knowledgeable and thorough people. They will formulate meaningful objectives, at the audience, and use the appropriate media. Their strategy is coherent and their tactics are workable. The material they generate is well done and appropriate. Information being published is as effective, or more so, than what competitors are doing. Spot checks with the media can be used to obtain further insight into performance.

So results at the image-building and capability publicity end of the spectrum are very difficult to measure. At the other end of the spectrum is product publicity, and its results lend themselves more readily to measurement. And since more product publicity is generated than any other type, it may be useful to explore its evaluation in some depth. Some product publicity specialists evaluate results by determining the amount of editorial space obtained by publicity on a particular product and comparing that amount of space to other stories or to what competitors have done.

This method does not give an indication of whether or not the information was read, much less whether or not it was acted upon. It is more useful as a performance measurement device rather than an evaluation method. As a performance yardstick, it provides one indicator of how well the publicity group is doing its job. The use of amount of space garnered as an evaluation method is carried one step farther by some.

6

Corporate Behaviour

One of the biggest behavioural barrier in corporate environment is to break the aspect of negativity. Any negative connotation of an organisation or offering reduces its effectiveness, marketability, saleability and therefore profitability. Any product or service over which there has been trouble or complaint, or any history of unreliability, must have confidence in it restored by the sector or niche. It is nor enough that the producers of the product know that the corner has been turned, and that it does now actually work well all of the time the market itself has to be convinced of this. In extreme cases it is necessary to repackage, re-present or even redesign and rename the item in question. In other cases extensive marketing and promotional activity may be required. Where there are teething troubles for a new product or service, or where an organisation is going into a new sector for the first time, it is often necessary to support this with public relations resources and activities.

1. *Product confidence and reputation*: the combination of performance, utility appearance and perception that gives particular their standing.

2. Organisation confidence and reputation: the combination of performance activity and interaction with the environment that gives particular organisations their standing.
3. Products and organisation image: the combination of promotional, marketing and public relations activities with performance elements.
4. Internal reputation and colloquy: staff groups shareholders
5. Value chain reputation: Suppliers, distributors, competitors and substitute sectors.
6. External reputation and colloquy: community, environment lobbies and pressure groups.
7. The effects and influence of overmighty departments, divisions groups and individuals.

These have to be considered from both negative and positive standpoints. Serious problems are extremely costly and organisations go to great deal of trouble to avoid them. However, when they ado occur, there is a derived public relations advantage in getting the matter sorted out as quickly as possible. As a consequence of this, positive forms have to be found for negative features and characteristics. People do not wish to be associated with 'cheapness' because there are connotations of low quality, and also reminders that the consumers in question have not got much disposable income.

Alternative connotations have therefore to be found. The most universal positive and enduring phrase is that of good value. Others that are included in this alternative positive approach include seasonal, faddish and fashionable: that is, something with a limited useful life.

Neither is the concept of cheapness or cheapening confined to the bottom of the price scale. Those who purchase expensive or exclusive goods may be seriously dissatisfied if the producer brings the price down and thus cheapens them, reducing their exclusivity, and opening them up to those with whom the original clientele did not wish to be associated. People also do not wish to be associated with tackiness of advertising lack of or loss of ambience in the retail outlet or other means of distribution, and neither do they wish to purchase goods that are poorly packaged or presented.

Organisations operating in niches where advertising and promotion are basic, or from wholesales, warehouse or other good value outlets, must create alternative features, so that the benefits of going to the establishment on the part of the customer clearly outweigh the negatives. Successful approaches to this have included emphasis on access and the ability to park the car, and also forms of exclusivity.

Some sectors have negative associated with them over which they have no control. Trains are late, seas are rough, the air is turbulent roads have roadworks cars break down. Those operating in each of these sectors find benefits to emphasise as a means of counteracting thee negative. British Rail has had great success in the past with its Let the train take the strain campaigns and more recently with the sale of tickets to London that are integrated with London regional transport. Shipping and air transport design is now sufficiently far advanced to cope with all but the worst weather; and the companies have a great variety of benefits on which to concentrate. Carts are sold on power, range appeal and comfort as we have seen elsewhere.

There are always general sectoral negatives that must be either accommodated or countered. If an organisation is the slowest deliverer in its sector it must find other virtues on which to draw. If an organisation is the fastest deliverer in the sector, it will invariably use this as a major source of competitive advantage.

It is therefore essential to recognise where the negative lie, and to take effective steps to overcome them. There are general matters relating to all business activities the must be addressed. These are both generic and customer-or consumer-generic. There are specific issues that require addressing from time also. These are as follows.

1. Loss of confidence : in the organisation its products/ services, its staff (especially its Chief Executive and senior staff), its stability its future its quality and reliability.
2. Loss of reputation : of the products and services in question, of the staff (again especially the Chief Executive and the senior staff). Of the organisation ownership.
3. Loss of performance : both overall and by individual division department and offering. This includes performance aspects of quality, volume and reliability and the ability also to meet deadlines. Loss of performance in this regard also includes financial aspects.
4. Obsolescence of offerings marketing presentation and public relations, both in performance and behavioural terms.
5. Bad and negative news media stories, whether warranted or not.

6. Long-term gradual decline often based on long-term negative workplace relations lack of investment or lack of strategic stability. Again, the decline may relate to a whole organisation and offering range, or individual departments divisions and functions.

These have to be considered in reverse if one organisation is taking over another which exhibits any or all of the negatives indicated. The critical part of the strategy for revamping the organisation being taken over must therefore address these if any measure of success is to be achieved.

The converse of the negative is clearly the positive. It has the function of countering the negative of representing both elements of an offering and the circumstances surrounding it which have negative connotations and influences. It is useful only to the extent illustrated. Beyond this is essential to go on and create positive feelings, images and impressions about the offering for its own sake. It must become positively attractive. Again, there are pitfalls that must be understood. Whatever is presented must be attainable and achievable in the eyes of the buyer, customer, client or consumer. It must represent a view of their world, not some Utopia or Shangri La which is plainly beyond their range or scope.

Images of glamour, luxury, status, style, sex, appeal and sophistication must also therefore be presented in relation to the real world of the consumer group in question. If this is not present, or if the levels presented a re too high or unattainable for some other reason, the offering in question is rejected. As we have seen, the car company uses its glamorous brand to attract people into the showroom to buy the workaday variety. They do not buy the glamorous brand itself, and if this was the only offering they would pass it by. Holiday promotions include pictures of 'normal' families; people used in the pictures look happy and they re 'everyday persons'. Indeed the use of film stars, television, music and show business personalities has to be very carefully considered. For the same reasons—of unattainability and unachievability in the wrong places—the usage of these personages has negative effects on the products and services in question. For success and effectiveness, they must be introduced into the world of the consumer.

The use of laughter and smiling happy faces pervades the creation of all positive images and associations. The use is universal, to be found in life assurance and health-care promotions as well as those for consumer goods and services. The only variation on this is where pantomime-type baddies has to be very carefully assessed as even such an obvious and overt caricature may nevertheless give off negative impressions.

The other universal image is sunshine and the associated brightness and warmth that goes with it. Again, the only exception is for a contrasting effect. American Express ran one commercial set in the rain where the card user, a man, was portrayed as a rugged, tough and caring individual helping a woman change her car wheel in the bad weather. Otherwise, bad weather is used only to emphasise contrasting messages, such as warmth and comfort. It is also worth pointing out that ski holiday brochures, while making sure that they have plenty of snow in the picture always ensure there is sunshine.

The language that is used must also be entirely positive. This extends to the avoidance, as far as possible, of words such as 'but', 'not', 'no' (and their compounds of 'do not', 'cannot' 'will not', 'must not', and so on). This extends throughout all contexts. Whether the message being put across is negative or not, the use of negative words ensures that part of it is perceived as negative and the receiver therefore has a high tendency to reject it. One of the caveats attached to negative or critical advertising -which is where part of the message is the unfavourable comparison of competitors with those of the organisation in question - is the reading of the negative words in the advertisements themselves. Again, unless handled, the negative message rebounds on to the advertiser and not on to the products of the competitors.

Both the concept and use of size is important in this context. Images used will be as expansive as possible in the context. As well as being fast, cars travel long distances. Supermarkets have shelves stretching away into the distance, and they are all fully packed. Restaurants have plenty of room and plenty of tables and thus which emphasise perceptions of success, also an important positive image.

This is where shelves tables airlines and even town centres are full (in the case of people not too full: the desired image is one of bustle, prosperity and success, not overcrowding). In the particular context this reinforces the desired associations with success, prosperity, fulfilment and also choice and happiness both of the which are very strong and positive images themselves).

The motivation of buyers, customers and clients is clearly fundamental to the purchasing behaviour. It follows from this that any understanding of the motives of those in their sector or segment that can be achieved by organisations is going to contribute to competitive advantage. In general, motivation arises from needs and wants on the part of the consumer that occur and a re important at different times of the hour, day, week, months, season, period year or lifetime, and general understanding of where the offering in question lies in regard to this is fundamental to business success. Consumers prioritise their demands, into 'needs' and 'wants' food drink and shelter are essential, a car is desirable, a holiday would be nice. They also prioritise even the essential needs: food is essential biscuits are cheap; steak is expensive; caviare is extremely expensive and not very filling.

Strategic should also understand the importance of considering motivation in terms of expectation fulfilment and reward. People make purchases with certain expectations in mind. They expect particular benefits to accrue from the acquisition ownership, use and consumption of the product or service in question. Levels of expectation are set by a variety of needs.

There is the price paid and, in general the higher this is the greater the expectation. There are also always value and quality considerations. Additionally, there are impressions associations and images created by the marketing activities that surround the product or service in question. Packed cites 1950s perfume adverts which had an overt message to women users; Wear this perfume and get the man your dreams.' When the man of their dreams failed to materialise, the women rejected the perfume itself.

More recently top UK football clubs have brought out ranges of leisure wear to complement their sports goods offerings. Many supporters of the clubs would not buy the sports goods because they had no actual use for them (that is they did not play football but only watched it). They also might, by putting the football shirt on, be faced with or remained of their lack of powers at the sport itself, or their own physical or behavioural shortcomings that contributed to this (their weight or the fact that they smoke or drank, for example).

However, distinctive leisure wear both fulfilled the expectation and association and in ways neither threatening nor otherwise confrontational. If something is offered on the basis of status, prestige or esteem, then these elements must be conveyed by ownership, use consumption of the product in question. The top of the range car, executive home, or exclusive holiday must be exactly this, is the expectations be to be fulfilled. If these are not delivered dissatisfaction will ensue. The holiday may have been truly wonderful, but it was not exclusive. The car may be fast, reliable and economical but again it is not exclusive. Each organisation will therefore task steps to understand the motivations needs, wants and expectations of the client groups that it serves and wishes to serve as part of the strategy process.

Attitudes and behaviour

The fact people have positive or favourable attitudes companies and their offerings does not mean that they will form them or use them. Attitudes (the positive and favourable) and behaviour (the act of buying) are therefore different and distinctive. For approaches to the question of attitude to have any value, it is the attitude to the purchase ownership and usage of the them that requires consideration, not the attitude to the item itself. Otherwise the strategist must address the behaviour of the consumers or consumer group, their propensity to consume, the level of priority accorded the offering in question and other leaders and triggers that cause them to choose between them and to choose between brands. It is also true that where people have a negative attitude towards companies (for example because of the organisation's involvement in an accident or disaster, or because of the nationality of the parent company), this does not mean that they will not buy its products.

Many consumers buy Japanese goods in spite of prejudices against Japan, because the products are of excellent quality. French and German car sales are dominated by the indigenous brands in spite of the varying and uneven regard in which the organisations themselves are held in these countries. Consumers carry out the bulk of their shopping at out of town supermarkets, superstores attitudes towards the smaller town centre shops where service is personalised.

The larger stores have therefore addressed the behavioural rather than attitudinal issues. It is convenient to carry out a high proportion of purchases in one single visit, and in addition car parking is likely to be easier. This is compounded by the comfort that arises in an organisation when its products receive favourable responses in attitude terms: the question 'Would you buy/consume/use our products?' is always more comfortable than the question 'Will you buy/consume/use our products, and if so how often, when where, why (etc.)?' However, a general attitude to the product or service in question is of little value other than a passing comfort. It is the attitudes generalization by commercial success that reflect reliability quality and value that are important.

These are present in all patterns of consumption and have implications for esteem, regard, respect status and acceptance in different situations. People belong to a variety of groups which can be permanent, temporary, *ad hoc,* and transient. The family is perceived to be a special and relatively permanent group. This has additionally a variety of complexities such as the extended family and the in laws for example, and it also changes its maturity and to old age. Clearly an understanding of this is essential in the successful and effective devising of consumer goods orientated strategies.

For example, the consumer or user of a toy is the child. However, its appeal has to be sufficiently positive in general to persuade the adult to buy it for the child. Similarly sellers of male and female clothing must consider the opposite gender. Men are likely to be put off if the women in their life do not like their clothing for any reason, and versa; and the reason and vice, versa; and the reason for dislike may be ethical associational or related to a bad past experience, as well as concerned with price appearance quality and value. Other groups to which people also influence their patterns of consumption. Social, sports leisure and work groups to which people aspire-higher status groups, lifestyle groups peer groups exclusive groups and hero identification—which influence patterns of consumption and behaviour. Related to this are notions of fashion and opinion leadership. This is deemed important to this the point of view of influencing the groups, the onus is placed on supplying organisations who identify and influence the most important members of the group, in the knowledge that other members would tend to follow.

It is also important from the point of view of fashion leadership': the ability to persuade film, sports and music stars to use or wear a particular item or brand eat in particular restaurants or travel in particular cars or with particular companies. It is essential to recognise and be able to influence positively patterns of group think conformity and other influences that are always present.

In more general terms, a similar approach is required when establishing the needs, warns characteristics and aspirations of sectors segments and niches.

Perception

The basis for the study of perception is that all the senses of each individual are constantly assailed with far too much information to interpret all of them accurately all of the time. People therefore recognize and receive certain cues and signals and interpret the gaps between them. This extends to what is seen, felt, tasted, touched, smelt; and also to what is thought believed and valued; and a also as the trigger for actions and behaviour. The keys to a good understanding of this are as follows.

This is the ascribing of a range of characteristics to people items, places and services on the basis of a known single or small group of characteristics. For example, professors are absent minded? Japanese electrical goods are reliable. Spain is hot and full of British and German holiday makers National Health Service hospitals are places where the sick and injured have to wait a long time for bad service. None of these statements is necessarily true yet each has the feeling or perception of truth because of the stereotyping process which is upon anecdotal evidence that has received a wide coverage.

This is where the product person place or service exhibits one extreme characteristic and everything else is perceived it. It happens all the time in interpersonal relations a firm handshake must mean that the person is strong a strident voice must mean that the person knows what he is doing; and so on. It also happens with places service and products in the same way. For example as

Spain is full of British and German holiday -makers' those who believe this will notice these groups of people to the exclusion of all others. People notice and remember the bad ways in which they were treated at National Health Service hospitals to the exclusion of the good. People remember the good Japanese products and put any bad ones down to abberation or exception.

Following on form stereotyping and halo effects, there is the great tendency for people, products places and situations to conform to pre-expectations and preconceptions. People who are thought to be clever, brave powerful or influential are treated as if they were so, and thus become so (and more so). The unreliable product becomes treated as such because of this preconception and reputation and any failure of performance on its part will reinforce this; eventually the users of it will (perceive themselves to) have had enough of it and change it for a substitute.

People use a restaurant because the service is good they consequently become known by the staff and so tend to get good service (if there are any lapses in this, it is put down to a break between courses they are busy, or new staff who do not know them). British Rail attract complaints about UK railway services to such an extent that examples of poor service are actively sought out. This has led to a collapse both of public confidence and staff morale. This is in spite of the many examples of good and high service with which the organisation is endowed. The self-fulfilling prophecy must be considered from the opposite point of view also. It is easier for people to live up or down to the expectations that others have of them (especially in work, political or social positions) than it is to change the expectations, especially in the short to medium term. Places that have built success and prosperity on a particular reputation will tend to ensure that the reality behind it is maintained if something is perceived to be reliable then it had better actually be reliable.

This is important in this context for a slightly different reason. Initially it requires a recognition that a person's view of the world and what is important in it is constantly and often suddenly, changing. For example the person who is cycling home from work early because of his daughter's birthday, and suddenly realises that he has not bought her a present has the overwhelming need for a toy shop or sweet shop. He makes his purchase and returns to his bicycle only to find that he now has a puncture. He therefore has a need for a new tyre or puncture repair kit. He also has a need for a telephone, to let his family know that he will be late (or possibly to try to get someone to come out and fetch him and the bicycle).

This in turn causes disappointment and anger because he will be late. He therefore returns to the shop to buy a box of chocolates for the others to try and make up for this. He finally gets home and needs a hot bath and a cup of tea.... and so on. The converse of this is when organisation have to be able to offer acceptable alternatives for products and services that they no longer maintain. The person who goes to the shop and asks for product x only to be told that it is no longer stocked always experiences an initial frustration and disappointment.

Dependent upon the nature of the rejection and the current importance of the product in question to the customer at the time, the shop may lose all of that person's business for all time. Behaviourally, therefore there is the necessity to be able to respond with a rider to the effect that there is now a good, ideally better, alternative available. This is a strong behavioural reason to explain why organisation maintain the extremities of their product range.

The behavioural needs of customers and consumers may be summarised as follows.

This can be related to bulk purchases of food in the freezer sector, safety features in cars, and domestic security systems. The comfort confidence and security needs of the customer in question are satisfied in turn because there is plenty in the house; we are safe in the house; and we are safe in the car. This is a clear response to the basic needs identified by Maslow of security survival and stability. It is also a particular response to the domestic crimes of burglary and the carnage on the roads of Western civilisation.

Purchases must make customers feel good. They have to satisfy themselves both in their own eyes, and in those of their circles of friends acquaintances and colleagues. Successful products and services therefore exude reinforcements of these. It is also essential that where the product is for menial or domestic use, it must be presented and self-worth.

Packard quotes research carried out in the 1950s by the soap powder and detergent sectors; this research found that unsuccessful marketing of the products was directly related to those campaigns where no self worth on the part of the user was evident. It is also essential in the purchase of major items. Domestic appliances and cars are required to have a long useful life. They are also required to have a long behavioural' value. Styling and presentation of these has to reflect this. Those bringing new products on to the market must ensure that this is done alongside maintaining a current and residual value for the existing products otherwise customers may respond unfavourably to the organisation. They have been left with a product that is operationally excellent but behaviourally obsolete, and there are clear implications for overall levels of customer satisfaction to be considered.

Anything that is sold successfully must include a measure of products/service/offerings/customer in harmony. Part of the initial resistance to television dinners, instant mixes, cook-in sauces and instant coffee was related to the fact to their convenience: the host, cook, wife mother husband father or friend who was producing them effectively had no input to them. They were created by the company and the person serving them up simply acted as the middle person.

Approaches based on lifestyle convenience luxury sex and opulence as well as involvement and satisfaction had to be generated for these in the same way as for other product and service ranges. Packard quotes two further examples. Earthmoving equipment which met resistance because the machine (rather than the drier) was perceived to do the work, had to be represented with the driver at the centre of the promotion. The other example was the success of vanity publishing which promised (and continues to promise) immortality rather than riches, and which remains a huge industry.

A variation of the ego need is creativity. For example cake mixes that required the addition of eggs were found to be more successful than those that simply required the addition of water. The perception was that there was a greater input on the part of the user or consumer while at the same time maintaining the benefits of convenience. The requirements to make a positive addition or contribution ensured a measure of involvement so that the very least that occurred was a perception of a partnership between the manufacturing and the consumer. It is also worth drawing at this stage to the opposite side of this coin; the extreme value and identify that people place on something that they have themselves created. It is very difficult to tell somebody that what they have produced is of no value (whether in a commercial or domestic situation).

Nevertheless in organization terms, if the item in question has no value then ways have to be found of letting the individual who produced it know this which both satisfy the organisation's requirements not to have unless or worthless products and at the same time measure the individual of her general worth and value to the organisation. There are thousands of ex-organisations that have followed the brainchild, creation or invention of their originator into oblivion.

This aspects may be summarised as cuddly toy dear little child or sweet/cute little animal. Andrex the major suppliers of toilet tissue to the UK retail sector, has used labrador puppies as the central feature of its commercials throughout the 1970s, 1980s and 1990s. The images are so strong that the company now the end of the all its presentations during the period of November, December and January of each year. Children are used extensively commercials in the pursuit of engendering this sense of love and warmth. This usage extends to washing powder washing-up liquid grocery shopping fast food cars, car parts petrol holidays central heating and double glazing. The image of the child in each case is extremely powerful and central to its success.

Power

The power of the product or offering is reflected in the user of it. This is manifest in a variety of ways. There is a power = strength = security aspect to be considered (as in the presentation of health care, for example). Nearly all automobile advertising and marketing is on the basis of power, performance and speed. Many newspaper and magazine advertisements and public relations material for cars contains the phrase 0 to 60 miles per hour in x seconds. Where the product range includes offerings at the least powerful end of the range, these are often not used in the marketing strategy at all; or where they are used, a small engine is described as lively or nippy. The power and strength elements are integral to the successful promotion of cigarettes.

The central images generated all reflect this: Formula one motor racing cars; power boats; personal strength and fortitude athletic power and strength. Power is also a progressive theme. One's first car (a three-or five-door small saloon, for example) has a certain amount. The second has more. The third is in the executive range. Power has been used in peripheral ways to reinforce messages in other spheres. British Gas ran commercials entitled Being in control, in these celebrities were placed in different situations to illustrate the virtues of suing gas as a domestic power source.

The punchline was always the same. Don't you just love being in control? The celebrity would then raise his or her thumb and the gas would appear to come out of the end of it. IT was a very effective presentation of control and influence.

This is use of a sense of the past to create positive and comfortable images. Food promotions use phrases such as just as good as mother used to make. Morgan cars retain their traditional design as the distinctive selling feature and mark of exclusivity. Also in the car sector Rolls Royce maintain the tradition of fittings and furnishings and reliability on which their original reputation was built. Other aspects of this also bear illustration in this context. Baileys Irish Cream, the after-dinner liqueur was invented and created on this basis in the 1970s. Its traditional image with a rustic-looking label and distinctive bottle is thc kcy to the commercial success.

Elsewhere politicians exploit perceptions and visions of golden ages with calls for returns to traditional values and back to basics', because there is a very strong association with historic success order stability and prosperity. Traditions and roots are also the key to nostalgia booms, period revivals and fashion recycling.

Reference has been made to this above in the Vanity publishing example under the ego gratification heading. It is also important to consider it from other points of view. Stability, order and control are all associated with longevity and are important in the presentation of long-term offerings such as bought housing life assurance, other insurances loans and other financial products.

Those that are successful are presented alongside images of steadiness increased prosperity and value and also alongside a stable, happy and successful domestic situation. Even in days of high levels of divorce and the consequent traumas of family break-up, these remain powerful and positive images. By association reassurance of worth and value and emotional stability are all so very positive. This constitutes an outline of the main elements of the behavioural and perceptual impacts on strategy. The mixture of these will vary between sectors. They will vary between organisations operating in the same sector, and there is no reason why a variety of approaches should not be applied with equal effectiveness within a sector.

A variety of cues, levels and triggers motivate and induce buying within the customer group, and it is likely to be beyond the means of one organisation to strike them all successfully. It is also likely that consumers will view the organisations and their products in a positive and comfortable way if they have strong images and attractions rather than a diversity. Organisations will therefore tend to follow those cues and levers that have been successful in the past, and that are successful at present. If they do propose to make radical changes, they must be aware of the risks of this: the Abbey National plc, a UK bank, lost impact confidence and, above all market when they attempted to change their marketing cornerstone from. The Abbey Habit to Abbey Endings.

The Abbey endings campaign was stopped and the organisation retrieved the situation with a revamp of the previous slogan as The Habit of a Lifetime'. Endings' is highly negative and certain to fail the immortality and ego gratification tests indicated above. As well as choice and understanding of the behavioural elements is the key to generating confidence in the organisation its products and services, the level continue to be of service into the future. The converse is extremely destructive and potentially fatal to the organisation if there is no confidence in the organisation or its products, it does not matter how good they actually are since they will not be bought or used. Engendering and maintaining confidence is therefore a combination of the behavioural processes indicated above to ensure that both organisation and offerings are presented in days and with benefits and usages that appeal to the sector or segment in question. The final element is this is to recognise that people do not act rationally. They may buy something and then rationalise why they bought it (especially if they are not sure they made the right choice or if their peers have chosen something else).

7

Sales Promotion and Public Relations

The exploitation of a sales promotion campaign or a sponsored event presents special challenges to the public relations man. To be successful, it calls for rigid adherence to high standards of presentation and meticulous attention to detail. Sales promotion has been defined as the art of pushing the product towards the consumer. Thus the national tour of fifty theatrically consumed salesmen in specially labelled cars shouting the merits of a new synthetic detergent is sales promotion. So is the employing of half a dozen girls wearing some national costume to visit grocers' shops and decorate them with point-of-sale material advertising an imported food product. Sales promotion campaigns, of course, do not necessarily mean people. They include leaflet distribution, the merchandising of retail outlets with display material, and many other exercises. News of sales promotion drives is usually acceptable to trade papers, since they can see it as part of their job of informing the trade they serve.

For lay newspapers, they seldom make news without an excessive degree of stunting. Sales promotion is often based on a proposal put up by an advertising agency, whose news values are different from those of journalists. Is an understandable enthusiasm on the part of an advertising executive that leads him to call in the public relations man and ask him to try for editorial coverage. If the public relations man sees that there is some genuine news value in a promotion, he will act in the same way as in the handling of any other story. If the wants to invite the press to see the departure of a team of bikini-clad girls on a national sales tour, he will work by exactly the same rules as if he were inviting the pressmen to a factory opening.

He will have to resist the pressure to make his invitation and press information too excitable, or to use too florid a style of writing. In this way he will have a better chance that his story will be seen as a piece of possible news. He will still be fortunate if the brand name is mentioned anywhere, even in photographs. It is, of course, perfectly within the right and duties of a public relations man to suggest that a sales promotion campaign should be used to solve a particular public relations problem.

However, if he does so, he will then exceed his rights if he does much more than make the proposal and afterwards hand it over to the experts, either in the sales department of an organization or its advertising agents. Sponsorship is an entirely different matter. With rising costs making life difficult for many sports, the arts and a vast variety of desirable social activities from youth clubs to conservation schemes, industry and commerce has come to recognize that sponsorship is a doubly valuable activity. It can provide a means of demonstrating participation in the wider community and at the same time offer useful promotional exposure.

Just how sponsorship can work for an organization must depend very much upon its own character and activities. To a certain extent, it should arise naturally from the character of the company itself. To take the simplest example, while it may be wholly acceptable for a chain of dance halls to sponsor a beauty contest and an insurance company to support an opera tour, it would be quite out of character for those roles to be reversed. Equally, petrol companies and type manufacturers turn naturally towards motor-racing, rallying and so on. It all depends on what the sponsor hopes to achieve. A consumer goods company may find the greatest value in sponsoring a mass appeal sport, and go on to feature it within a marketing programme by advertising, point-of-sale material, packaging and the full range of product promotion. The basic object is to increase sales. On the other hand, a national service organization may choose to put money into a conservation project or an education scheme of some kind with the principal objectives of achieving exposure of its name in a favorable context. Either way, results are difficult to monitor.

Sponsorship is often, although not necessarily, an expensive exercise and its evaluation is exclusive. Usually, of course, it has to be assessed as part of an overall campaign. Media publicity may be the objective, in which case a rough evaluation is possible. On the other hand, if the aim is a continuing favourable exposure to a given audience—teachers, gardeners, yachtsmen or whatever—only careful research is likely to be able to indicate value for money. Frequently, sponsorship over a period pays better dividends than the one-off occasion. To pay for one concert in an arts festival is not likely to within sponsor more than the most ephemeral kudos, but to sponsor an instrumental competition over some years and back the annual concert at which the winner performs is more likely to attract the approval of the music-loving public. If the music-loving public is not at least part of the target audience, do something different—even if the chairman's wife is an avoid concert-goes! The tendency has developed to treat sponsorship.

Particularly of the arts, as if it were a clear social duty on the part of commerce and industry, virtually a replacement of the rich patrons of the past. This is unrealistic. Of course, corporate bodies have social responsibilities, but in the realm of sponsorship they should not be expected to be entirely altruistic. A partnership from which each side derives reasonable, planned benefits should be the aim.

There are still sports promoters, artistic entrepreneurs and intrepid trans-Saharan unicyclists who seem to feel that any large company should be an easy touch to fund their activities and who invariably have inflated notions of the publicity benefits likely to accrue. Charity is one thing; sponsorship another; and wasteful extravagance yet another. As in almost all public relations activities, the essential first move is to determine what audience is to be reached and with what message. If a sponsorship proposition offers a means of conveying the determined message to the desired audience then it deserves examination. A sponsored event may have short-and long-term objectives. It may be costly. It should not be recommended lightly.

For example, an international architectural contest with a first prize of 5,000 will probably cost many times that sum to administer. If it is to be kept up over a number of years to begins to add up to a great deal of money. Thus it is simple sense to work out carefully the value of such an event, its true cost, and its place in a public relations programme before making a firm recommendation. To reach that point means taking a series of simple steps.

A good example is a golf tournament, since this has become one of the most popular types of sponsored event. There are, of course, two reasons for holding a folk tournament. One of them so because golf day for his firm's or client's customers or suppliers may be a useful piece of promotion. Golf may have nothing to do with either his professional interests or these of the people he is inviting; it is simply a social occasion. A decision to hold such an event will then be based on whether there are enough executives in his company who are interested, and whether there are enough guests who want to play.

The decision once having been taken, the public relations man is only involved in making sure that the organization is right. He will need a working committee, a budget and enough planning time to ensure that everything is done properly. It is worth recording that one of the greatest problems is in matching players so that all enjoy the day. Incidentally, the public relations man can make a useful contribution to a memorable day by providing prizes which are slightly unusual.

Certainly such a day can have a tremendous value in bringing together company executives and customers. However, this is an entirely different operation form a tournament sponsored by a manufacturer of golf equipment or clothing. The company golf day may cost £2,500; the tournament can cost £500,000. The first is only intended to clothe business talking in a pleasant atmosphere; the second is intended to focus sharp attention on the manufacturer's products. The first is a relaxed day off; the second is a tense competitive occasion.

The forest can survive even of there any mistake is sudden death. The first step is to survey the scene, to find out how many golf tournaments are already in existence, when and where they take place, what results they bring, and what sort of prizes they offer. This study will show whether there is a gap that could be filled with a new contest.

The public relations man will then consult experts-especially golf associations-to discover whether the gap has been noticed, and whether the initiative of fill it would be welcomed. If there is immediate resistance it is usually not worth trying to pursue the idea. If, on the other hand there is some interest, then the public relations man must go exhaustively into detailed planning. He must find out the form of tournament that would make the event attractive. He must find out whether overseas entry would be acceptable to desirable. He will then have some basis for costing. The first thing to remember, of course, is that planning for an event of this magnitude takes at least twelve months, and can quite easily take two years. It is unwise to try to cram the planning into less than a year and such an attempt can be disastrous. To arrive at a final costing needs the creation of a timetable and checklist.

The timetable will work back from the date of the event, and forward to the eventual settlement in the preparation of the checklist, and to make absolutely certain that everything is covered in it. What has to be covered includes; advertising; print accommodation, travelling and subsistence for competitors and staff, especially if overseas entries are being accepted; special amenities and facilities at the club where the tournament is staged; photography; press facilities; postage; prizes; souvenir wallets and the like; flags for each hole; caddies and stewards; transport, road signposting; extra policing; insurance; and so on. No item can be left out and the list is endless.

During all the work involved, the public relations man must also guard against the danger of becoming so immersed in the excitement of the event that he forgets the objective. The objective is to support the games and to draw attention to his organization and its products. He must ensure that it is attained. One obvious thought is to incorporate his organization's name in the title of the event.

For a sporting event such as a golf tournament it is the hope of most public relations men that it will learn television coverage While this should not be a governing factor in a decision to stage an event, it is sensible to open discussions with special departments of the BBC or commercial television programme companies who consider the coverage of these functions. For one thing, their needs may dictate part of the timing of the event and it is as well to know this from as early in the planning as possible.

Other arrangements, such as advance press information and the provision of proper press facilities during the event, are important, but they need no special knowledge. They are the same as the arrangements made for anything which the press is to report. The real key to staging an event is good organization.

Of course, that implies that everybody who is involved anywhere along the line must know what is happening, why it is happening, when it is happening, and what part they have to play. Proper written briefs for everybody, as well as regular meetings of an organization committee, are essential. A simple but wise course is the appointment of an organizing secretary, who may become involved full-time in the work. In the world of sport, where there are already many sponsors., it is fairly common practice for the sponsoring organization to share the limelight with the body which organizes the sport as a whole.

Consolation is essential in any sport and in all the major activities the national and international controlling bodies have strict regulations governing what is permitted. At the same time, professional bodies are helpful in making available to the sponsor case history material in other, similar events. The public relations man will find that studying this material will save him a good deal of time. He must also take heed of the advice and guidance the professional body gives him. After all, they know the framework, history, made traditions of the sport. He does not.

The work on the event does not finish at the end of the day on which it happens. Often the follow-up activity is what makes it a profitable and worthwhile investment for the sponsor. If it is an international tournament, there are advertising possibilities to consider. There are also endorsement possibilities: so-and-so used the maker's equipment when he won the tournament.

This may lead into pack redesign jobs, window display us, and, indeed, sales promotion campaigns. For a sufficiently important event, the future value of a film should be considered. Golf clubs, for instance, are often willing to arrange special showings for their members of a film of an international tournament. It is at this stage that the male value of good advance planning will be realized. The example of a golf tournament has been given at some length, since it contains most of the elements needed for the conduct of a successful event.

In essence, the real need is attention to detail, Whether the event is golf, table-tennis, pigeon racing or and other sport. Of course, sponsorship is by no means limited to sport and performing arts, although these dominate both financially and in terms of public attention. The visual arts, architecture, education, conservation, medical research, even journalism itself, have all attracted sponsors of awards, competitions and the like. In an increasingly competitive world, the standards of practice in any craft, trade or profession become more and more important.

Only those with the highest standards will succeed. It is in the interests of manufacturers to help customers to attain high standards, and equally to identify themselves and their products with these standards. In any group of people with common interests there is the opportunity for a sponsor to advance standards by providing an award, trophy, or other prize. If it is truly relevant or sufficiently large it will attract the best people to compete. It should also set a target for entrants to the business. Repetitive sponsored events such as an annual competition depend in good organization. This is true, too, of a valid one-off event.

A good example is an architectural competition to provide a design for the forecourt or entrance of the new head office of a company, or one to provide the landscape surroundings of a factor in knew estate. Once again, the advice of the professional body in this instance, the Royal Institute of British Architects should be sought. They can guide the public relations man into acceptable methods and prize structure. Even more, they may provide or recommend the judges.

The reasons for deciding to enter into something of this kind do not belong here they have to do with community relations, or employee relations, or half-a-dozen other subjects. The only issue which crises in this context is one of method. A one-off event cannot be skimped any more than a repetitive event. Proper budgeting is essential. A single event may well draw more press attention than a regular one, since to satisfies the condition that it is unusual: it has not happened before and may not happen again. Unlike a regular event, there is no reason why press comment in a single event should not be seen as a major part of the reason for running it.

It is worth restarting a principle: the reason for entering into a sponsored event must be genuine of to so to succeed. It does not really matter of the event is international to purely local in scope. The public relations man must study carefully his objectives and decide whether he can attain them by creating something which excites the interest of any group he wishes to influence. It is not possible to generalize becomes this point. The PR man needs to look at his own particular circumstances and forge his who particular method. A sponsored event may draw the attention of the general public, if that is what the public relations man wants. It may interest only a handful of highly erudite specialists. It may be used for great dramatic effect, or it may be used to additional knowledge to research programme. It all depends on what you seek to achieve.

Community relations

No man so an island. Today Donne's dictum so more than ever true for every type of organisation. Every group has a relationship with community around it, whether to thinks about it or not. A beneficial relationship can be sought and fostered, given the right attitude of mind and the application of much time, although not necessarily a great deal of money.

There are three basic motivations for operating a community relations policy: a sense of corporate social responsibility; an acknowledgment of the attitude that nowadays all organization are expected to participate in life beyond their own doors; and quite bluntly, because the understanding and appreciation of everyone around is of genuine practical value.

Community relations may involve many of the techniques of communication that are used in other areas of a company's public relations. It needs the same disciplines of selectivity and control, but it differs in that it is almost impossible to lay down general rules. The reason for this is simply that no two communities are the same and that no two relationships between an organization and the various communities in which it may find itself are the same either. Even more that in other sensitive areas of public relations, careful study is vital before taking the first diffident steps to implement a programme.

There is no institute for local advice to ensure that an apparently good idea does not in fact turn out to be a local laughing-stock, or to identify a problem that is not obvious to the outsider. The idea of community relations is not new; to might be said to be as old as organized society itself. The ancient city states like Athens existed on the strength of good relations with the citizens. In the middle ages, the powerful guilds set the pattern of charity and education in the towns, while something benevolent landowners did the same in the countryside. Even in the dark days of the industrial revolution he were an enlightened few, usually prompted by religious motives, who accepted that industry and society had mutual responsibilities.

Unhappily, the majority of employers neglected the community as much as they neglected the welfare of their employees, and some four social relationships which exist today can be traced backs of their disregard of others. On the one hand there are innumerable hospitals, schools almshouses, and charitable trust which are a welcome legacy of the past and have been integrated into the modern welfare state, and on the other hand there are rows of dwellings barely fit for animals, mountains of slag, and polluted rivers still besmirching the countryside.

Today there is power under the law to prevent irresponsible behavior, such as the poisoning of the air with fumes or the uncontrolled jumping of waste. Yet the feat of transgression is not enough. It is quite possible to be a bad neighbor, or at least an in different one, without ever breaking the law. An attitude of mind has to be encouraged, a clear understanding of responsibilities as to be developed. Few companies lack appreciation of their obligations to their customers and in the past twenty years or so progress in employee relations has been considerable. Yet the concept of a deliberate endeavour to build a good relationship with the community has lagged behind.

As with other facets of public relations, before action can be proposed, management must be satisfies that it is both necessary and viable. This means thinking out and putting across a clear case to show the value of a community relations programme. All too often, good intention are believed to be enough. Perhaps the simplest way to start is to formulate one or two questions relevant to the company's operations. Is it a good thing, for instance, for a wife to ask 'Who are they?' when her husband tells her that he is going after a job at a certain factory? Does the management link it would, be helpful for the borough surveyor to recall the firm's unco-operativeness with disapproval when the factory needs permission to enlarge an effluent outflow? Will it assist recruitment of school leavers for the headmaster of the local technical college to remember that the company never accepts visits by students to see the process? Is it desirable to let the plant next door gain all the kudos for helping out organizations when the factory's own sports ground is hardly used? Within the context of a particular organization and its surroundings, needless appropriate questions could be put. Even if the general turnover of response to them is understanding and helpful both at top management level and on the part of the senior executive at a given location, the difficulties of building and applying a consistent community relations policy are only starting.

The possibilities for action are probably many; the money and time particularly at local level to carry them out are probably limited. The individual situation has to be assessed meticulously and the character of the community gauged to determine what can most effectively be done. This means taking time to investigate the social structure and to listen to local people. Attitudes vary enormously from one part of the country to another. The approach which works in the Welsh valley will not necessarily go down well in he Lowlands of Scotland, and what goes in lowlands will in very likely not work in the Highlands.

One common factor in all regions is suspicion of interference from the centre, whether that means London or Edinburgh, a head office in Britain or a parent company in the United States. Local affairs need to be handled locally, preferable by someone who knows his community and is perhaps known in it. The public relations man may establish the need persuade the management relations man may establish the need, persuade the management to act, create a programme, and provide the means to carry it out, but its effectiveness is bound to be hindered if it all appears in the community to be something artificially applied from outside.

A large organization building a huge project in a remote place may be able to afford a full time community relations man. A company with a PR department or using a consultancy may be able to put an executive on to a community project for a good part of his working time. Mostly the handling of community affairs, however, falls upon the management on the spot.

Usually, the public relations man must go beyond his programme to advise and assist those who will directly carry it out. He will have the techniques and the resources; they will have the awareness of local attitudes. The public relations man must learn to understand those attitudes, to put himself in other people's shoes. Basic principles are easy to state: reputation depends not only on what is done but on how much is known about what is done and why. This means that communication is at the heart of community relations. But what needs to be communicated? Is it a precise message or a general impression of the nature of the organization. The answer depends entirely upon the circumstances.

The problems facing a mail order house moving from London to a market town are not the same as those of a contractor building a power station in a rural area. The needs of an established company which has long dominated a small town and is now liable to be swamped by a bigger new comer are lastly different from those of an average engineering firm competing for labour in a flourishing new town.

All have in common the need to be understood. The local press, and this includes the provincial dailies and evenings and the regional radio and television services, are generally sympathetic to local stories. The independent endorsement of the editorial judgment of local media means that their stories are likely to be more acceptable among inhabitants than if the company blows its own trumpet.

This is not to say that direct published communication is not valuable. It may range from a selective outside distribution of the internal magazine to the issuing of an occasional open letter about progress on a large development; from making a back-ground leaflet available through libraries, council offices, and so on, to buying advertisement space in the weekly papers to make an important announcement.

The possibilities for graphic communication are considerable, too. It may be expensive to set up a touring exhibition, but it costs little to recognize a photographic display in a shop window. Permanent exhibits in local museums and libraries can keep the company's name, process, and product in the public eye.

Films can have a long and valuable life and are often in them-selves an attraction for local groups, so that illustrated talks can be offered and human reactions and questions met face-to-face. It is not essential to have films of one's own; many film libraries have production of sufficient relevance to be suitable for a company talk and most trade associations and technical institutions have film lists for the PR man to draw upon. The provision of educational materials and guidance for schools is a subject in itself and may be of major importance in a community relations programme.

This may mean lending a technician to lecture or demonstrate, or allowing craft classes to examine and use machinery. It may be a matter of giving information leaflets or donating scrap material on which pupils may try their skill. In the raw materials industries many large companies and trade associations deploy considerable resources to provide teaching aids: booklets, lecture notes, slides and filmstrips, wall charts, boxes of labelled specimens, sections of finished goods, and so on. The very fact that these are basic, rather than branded, products overcomes the sensitivity to any form of commercial pressure against which most educations feel they must guard their charges.

Nevertheless, plenty of forward-looking commercial concerns ensure that their future customers are made aware of their goods by the legitimate means of offering to schools free, or almost free, publications and all forms of advice and assistance for teachers. These can range from a complex business game to be attempt by sixth form economic students to simple project kits for junior schools. The criterion is genuine educational value.

Direct communication to the community can take many forms. The conducted tour of the plant may be for housewives to see for themselves how a food product is hygienically prepared, or for engineering students to view a process from start to finish; it may be for members of the river board to see how the company controls the release of effluents, or for careers masters to learn enough to be able to advise school-leavers about potential jobs.

An open day may be seen as mainly for the benefit of employees and their families, but each one of them is a member of the community and is in some form or another a communicator to others. If a new plant is to be built in an area with little experience of industry, an open meeting, organized with the help of the local authority, offers an opportunity to meet the people, present a case, and attempt to answer questions and allay fears.

Whatever aspect of the organization's activities needs to be understood, the communications techniques of public relations can be brought to bear—provided, of course, that the attitudes of the audience and the suitability of the method of communication are taken into account.

The second common denominator, regardless of the type of organization and the nature of its social surroundings, is the desirability of direct participation in the life of the community. Again, this may take any number of forms, but it is essential for participation to be active rather than passive. Mere donations to charitable causes do not constitute playing an active role in local life. Indeed, to try to buy one's way into a community by easy generosity is usually an expensive failure: it leads to the company being regarded as a 'soft touch', an outsider with more money than sense rather than an insider willing to help. Charitable generosity must be selective. It should be controlled: in a big way by a small committee to decide on the disbursement of an agreed sum have year, or in a small way by disbursement of an agreed sum each year, or in a small way by establishing a short list of worthy causes and stricking to it, with a modest contingency fund for special occasions.

Cash donations do not necessarily help very much to establish the company as a good corporate citizen. A name in the small print list of sponsors at the local sports, for example, is less likely to gain a good impression than the free provision of the public address equipment and the electricians to operate it. To help is fine, but to be known to want to help is better when reputation is at stake.

The forms of participation are endless, dependent upon the nature of the community and its institutions, and of the talents and time of those who are willing to help. In some ways it is as well to allow the contribution to local affairs to grow naturally, to let those with the enthusiasm or desire to do so lead the youth groups, take over the secretaryship of the film society, become Red Cross instructors or whatever it may be. Still, it is reasonable to encourage this genuine desire to help and make it part of the company's approach to the community.

Men and women who wish to take part in local affairs, and local government in particular, can be given time off for their duties. If a foreman takes over a scout troop, the firm's sports pavilion might be put at his disposal. A local debating society may find a programme organizes among the office staff, but could they use the office duplicator occasionally?

The plant manager will probably find it useful to belong to Rotary or the Chamber of Commerce, and senior executives to branches of their professional institutions, but beyond this is can be made known that the company is prepared to encourage participation by other employees in productivity associations, voluntary fire services, the special constabulary, having groups, and so on. It helps to know what is going on in the community, particularly for newcomers. Established local information points, like the librarian, the newspaper editor or someone in the town hall, can help build a list of organizations and activities.

Equally, it helps to know what skills and interests exist within the company: who might want to start a bee-keeping club or a children's theatre, who runs a pop group in his spare time or gives up his weekends to entertaining the sick. Needs and talents, opportunities and inclinations can often be matched. This is a matter for subtle human judgement and the thoughtful assessment of whether an idea is workable as well as superficially attractive.

A blatant attempt to foist company people or facilities on to local organizations would be as disastrous outside as a bald suggestion that all employees should take part in community affairs would be within. The impression that a company is trying to muscle in could easily result from an over-eager attempt to take part in too many activities too soon, however well intentioned. Just as a new resident in a village is not immediately accepted but has to earn his place, so a firm news to a community must take its time getting to know and be known. Even an existing organization that has previously kept to itself cannot expect to change its reputation overnight by starting a bold community relations programme. A contribution or a form of local participation that arises naturally from the company's own affairs is automatically more acceptable than a contrived endeavour to join in.

A printer can do charitable work for nothing. A fruit packer can give to hospitals and old people at Christmas. A builder can repair a church, and a timber yard can give materials. A coach hire firm can provide transport for an orphans' outing. A waste merchant can help school children dispose of scrap materials collected for some good cause. The company's experts can give their services, and maybe the company can contribute facilities to help them. Plumbers, painters, and carpenters can refurbish a failing youth club, but it may also need an accountant to straighten out its finances. It the company's activities and skills do not lend themselves directly to the adding of local activities, direct cash contribution is not the only alternative.

Sponsorship may well have a role to play in the support of the arts, education, sport or the environment on a local or regional scale. A scholarship in a technical subject for a local college may appeal to one firm as much as becoming the patron of a local choral society may to another, Cultural leadership is not necessarily expensive; the gift of stereophonic equipment to a music group may well be more welcome than the endowing of an art gallery. It depends entirely on the local situation.

The position in large cities is difficult as, generally speaking, only the largest concerns can make a noticeable contribution to community life there. Education and the arts again offer openings for named awards, anything form a scholarship in metal-working to an annual piano contest for teen-agers. Some activity crystallizing local or regional outlook, a bi-annual arts festival or sponsoring the revival of some ancient ceremony or sporting event, might be appropriate. In many large towns the majority of companies can remain quietly anonymous unless they actively wish to participate in community affairs, but for a major organization with many branches and a reputation for civic responsibility, the problem for the management in an urban area is delicate. It all comes back to deciding how a firm wishes to be thought of in its surrounding community. To be a good employer and to make a sound product will earn in time a reputation of one king, in many ways the best king. But to be known as a good corporate citizen, a thoughtful neighbour, and a discriminating supporter of good causes with money, facilities, and human effort may be of incalculable value, too.

The choice of what to do, how and when can only be made with a full understanding of local circumstances and attitudes. It is not beyond the bounds of possibility that a friendly letter of explanation and apology to nearby residents for noisy night working on a new plant extension could do more for a company's reputation than the gift of by covenant to a national charity. Size and expense are not the criteria of value in community relations.

Human relationships are always complex and for the public relations man there are few times when this is more clear than in the dealings between a seller and a buyer. At one end of any commercial transaction is a buyer, or customer. He may buy directly across a counter, or through the mail, or indirectly via a third party. In direct buying an immediate relationship is created between the seller, who may be a manufacturer or a distributor or a service company, and the buyer. In indirect buying, the buyer will have two relationship: One with the manufacturer whose good he buys, and the other with the agent who actually sells them to him. In extreme circumstances, he may dislike the agent but want the goods so much that he suppresses the dislike. In the pattern of commerce, wholesalers and retailers are, of course, also customers. Mostly, the customer is taken to mean the person who buys over the counter or by mail order and personally uses the product or enjoys the service.

In the most easily recognized form, that person is the housewife purchasing the week's groceries, the football fan, the couple buying furniture in a department store or the man ordering garden tools form a mail order catalogue. However, there kinds of customer whose attitudes must engage the study of a public relations man. The motor manufacturer who buys accessories and equipment form other manufacturers is just as much a customer as the woman buying groceries. The industrial organization building a new factory is a customer for materials, air-conditioning installations, machine tools, and a host of other items.

The differences between individuals and organizations are really one a matter of size. The seller makes a series of promises through his promotional and selling activities: his products are good and will thus give satisfaction; his handing of queries is impeccable and friendly.

For as long as the promises are fulfilled, the relationship with the customer will be good. At any point at which they are broken, the relationship will end. But always the state of the relationship will be helped along by a degree of understanding of each other's problems. This is the area where an efficient public relations man can make a solid contribution. There are two kinds of complainant: the genuine one and the 'professional'. However, action, whether by the complainant or the company, has to be judged against the legal background.

The 'rights' of the consumer are covered by the Trade Description Acts the Supply of goods act the Consumer Credit act the Restrictive Practices act and the Competition Act doubtless others will be a passed. It is important to be aware of their provisions, as well as those of the regulations covering the labelling of food. Lastly, it is vital to watch the directives issued by the European Commission in Brussels. Above all, the guide to the public relations man should be to observe the spirit of the law and not just the letter. However, when a customer feels a complaint coming on, it is not unusual for appeal to be made to the highest possible authority. This can be the managing director, or the sales director, or even a public personality who is known to be associated with the company.

The appeal is made to them partly to flatter the ego if the complainant, partly in the belief that the higher the complaint goes, the quicker will be the action. The receiver of the complaint feels in honour bound to take action or to look as if he has taken action personally. Since he has almost certainly not been involved in the transaction beforehand, he must institute a chain of enquiries, which takes a certain amount of time.

There is, therefore, one rule which must be observed strictly. All complaints, genuine or not, must be acknowledged promptly, preferably on the day they are received. The acknowledgment should, if possible, indicate how long it will be before the matter can be resolved finally. Inevitably there are points along the lines of investigation when people will be trying to justify themselves or their actions. It is sometimes extremely difficult for the truth to be extracted. Meanwhile, the customer is sitting and fuming, and if he is a professional he will be gossiping to his acquaintances and telling them how badly he is being treated. It almost goes without saying that prompt acknowledgment must go hand in hand with prompt attention. It must not be seen as an excuse for procrastination. In all circumstances, the customer must have the feeling that the complaint is being handled with the priority he feels it deserves.

Selling, in this context, is a business in which reputation is a paramount consideration. Reputation is created and maintained as a result of many seen and unseen influences. It can be earned over years and lost in minutes. It may be justified or unjustified. For the public relations man, it is entirely vital the he lays his groundwork properly. He must advise his management or client on their policy towards complaints, service, replacement, and the dozen-and-one other aspects of customer relations. When he has obtained management's agreement to the policy, he must see that it is made clear to all levels of staff.

He should try to define it in a few straightforward phrases which will apply to all personnel, including directors, however infrequently any of them may come into contact with customers. He should add extra explanations on steps to be taken by specific departments, for example, counter staffs, service engineers, outside representatives, and so on. He must aim at simplicity, so that both the policy and its implementation are equally easy to understand and follow.

Many people bemoan the passing of the 'shop on the corner' where many minor things-cigarettes, papers, candles, groceries, and the like-could be bought at almost any day of the week. What they liked about it was partly the convenience, but more importantly the friendliness of the shopkeeper. In many ways this was an archetypal public relations situation. The shopkeeper depended enormously for his business on the relationship he built up with his customers. In contemporary society the 'little, an' has largely disappeared because the economics of production and distribution are forcing him out.

Vestiges of his assets remain in the voluntary group chains which try to achieve the economies of scale while continuing to focus the customer's attention on one easily identifiable shopkeeper. The stores, supermarkets, and chains that are taking the place of the small man are most anxious to create and then preserve this same relationship with their customers, the ways in which they do it are necessarily different.

He dealt with a few people, know most of them by name, and often ran his shop in a hap hazard fashion. They deal with hundreds of customers, most of whom remain anonymous, and they are extremely cost and profit conscious. The size of the operation and the anonymity of the customers should, in theory, increase the importance of the products, since it is the products themselves and their quality which create the loyalty of the customer. But this fact cannot allow a diminution in the effort to be friendly and helpful on the part of managers or counter staffs. However, since much of the buying in, for example, grocers' shops is done on impulse a great deal of sales promotion the art of pushing the customer towards the product is needed. Special offers, window displays, leaflet promotion, local advertising, all these are common features of the store business. Their prime purpose is to increase store traffic, that is, the number of people who enter and walk through. Behind the purpose is the certain knowledge that once inside they will buy something, and often something more than they has intended to buy. One of the most important aspects of the customer relations job is staff education. It is one in which the public relations man may well overlap with other executives: staff or personnel officers, floor or departmental managers, welfare officers and so on.

The best displays, the most enticing products, and attractive prices can all be nullified by surely or ill-informed assistants. It is not easy, of course, for a shop assistant to maintain a cheerful appearance or manner especially in stores or departments which require the staff to be on their feet most of the day. It is also true that turnover in staff is usually high, whatever the pay and conditions are like. Enthusiasm is difficult to create and must be consciously fostered. On engagement, any shop assistant should receive a booklet telling him or her something about the store.

The information it contains should cover the products sold, the arrangement of departments and layout of the building, working conditions, holidays, time off, late night working, benefits, social amenities, and the like. It must tell newcomers something about the company that owns the store and whether there are other branches. If the store does any advertising, examples, should be shown. The booklet should be produced by the public relations man, working closely with the personnel or training officer and any other relevant executives. The design should allow for additional material, whether new or amendments, to be inserted. In ideal conditions, one of the best ways of introducing a new assistant to the right and wrong ways of serving is by film, filmstrip, or by a slide presentation using a linked commentary.

Of course, film production may well prove beyond the resources available, but then it is well worth investigating the services available from the appropriate industry training board or relevant trade associate, and checking with film libraries to see what can be hired. In any event, it should be remembered that every assistant is also a customer at other shops and should thus be able to relate mistakes made by others to his or her own experience. Humour, too, is a powerful teacher.

Training courses, both on arrival and as refreshers, must also exist for managerial staff. It is largely their responsibility to keep their staff, and to act as a buffer against which the occasional irate customer can vent his spleen. In certain circumstances, managers (as in banks) must do much more than this by becoming leaders in their communities. They must join local societies, or become identified with their aims, and should become involved in community problems and topics. However, when they do this, it must be with a proper sense of service and not in any cynical or hypocritical manner. In the context of customer relations, involvement like this can be important. It allows customers (and, better still, potential customers) to personalize the store in their minds. In a small way, it can help to avoid anonymity that goes with large units.

Within a large store especially, there is much that can be done to simplify life for the customer. An enquiry desk near each entrance makes good sense. Signposting is vital, as are easily identifiable assistants (in many stores, staff look like customers). Simple procedures are needed for wrapping purchases, handling deliveries, and arranging hire-purchase terms. Strictly speaking these are not the duty of the public relations man, but he needs to run his own private checks from time to time to see that they are indeed working properly and being remembered as part of a deliberate customer relations policy.

Apart from the direct contact with the customer, there is indirect contact, through the issue of monthly accounts, catalogues, special offers and so on. All of these contribute to the attitude the customer acquires towards an organization with which he is doing business. Often they will be the direct job of the advertising department, but the public relations man should keep an eye on their format.

He may find possibilities for conducting research and attitude surveys through this regular material. For example, checking the response to special offers can indicate customers' feelings. Any openings for surveying customer attitudes should be explored.

Customer relations in operations where the buyer does not come into a building but buys through the mail present special problems. A mail order company must establish and then maintain a reputation for fast and efficient handling of orders. Secure packing is vital and replacement procedures are most important. If the buying is handled through local agents, their role in helping to promote the company needs to be carefully spelled out. This can suggest a monthly magazine or newsletter, or regular meetings with groups of agents. It can be the job of the public relations man to organize these activities.

In fact, the differences between one kind of customer relations and another are only matters of emphasis. The housewife in a shop, the company buying from another company, and the mail order buyer have one thing in common. They want satisfaction, and they expect the seller to provide it. They can deal remotely or closely with the seller, they can become heavily involved in activities like owner-drivers' clubs, co-operative movements, or even the collection of limited editions, and they can be regular customers or occasional customer. The exact ways in which a manufacturer, distributor or service company handles its customers can only be dictated by its particular circumstances. If a company does not sell its products or its service it goes out of business. If its customers or prospective customers think ill of it, they will go elsewhere. They are therefore of immense importance to the public relations man, and he should make constant efforts to see that they are treated as the key public they are.

A manufacturer can be vitally affected by the distributors of his products, whether they are wholesalers or retailers. Assessing and influencing their attitudes is thus of prime importance in a public relations campaign.

In the process, due attention must be paid to the legal requirements, which are much stricter than they used to be.

There are many instances when the goodwill of the dealer can make the difference between success and failure for a manufacturer. Sometimes the dealer pushes the product towards the eventual customer, as in a supermarket handling manufacturer's branded lines. At others, the customer comes to the dealer and asks for the product, as in the mail order selling of nationally advertised lines. Whether the dealer pushes, or the customer asks, the effect on the transaction of the manufacturer's reputation is a key factor. If the manufacturer enjoys a reputation for turning out good products at fair prices, the rate of acceptance of a new product, even one unconnected with what he normally makes, is likely to be higher.

At the same time, the dealer's view of that reputation is crucial. Broadly speaking, the dealer builds up an attitude towards a manufacturer as a result of various pressures, they include: what he reads about the manufacturer in the press, whether national, trade or local; how he is treated or served by the manufacturer's representatives; how simple or difficult are the procedures through which he has to go to re-order or get service; how his own customers view the manufacturer; how much promotional backing he gets from the manufacturer; what discount rates or other preferential treatment he receives; and how many complaints he makes or his customers make. The order of priority of these varies in each trade. It is the first duty of the public relations man, once he has discovered his employer's or client's distribution patterns and problems, to sort out that order. This is a situation in which some from of research may be necessary. It is a common failing among manufacturers to believe that they know what dealers think of them. They often fall into the error of complacency. Apart from professional research, a personal study can often be rewarding. Going on the road with a manufacturer's representative, or just going and calling on dealers can be highly revealing.

This is a public relations area on which it is worth spending a good deal of effort. Much activity on advertising, sales promotion, general editorial publicity, packaging, and the like can be wasted if the wrong relationships exist at the point of sale. The retailer who says to a customer: 'Don't have that product, madam, they've got trouble at the factory' can ruin the work of months in a moment. At the same time, finding the reason why he made the remark can be either complicated or easy. His last order may have been late in arriving and he may have thus lost sales. He may have been badly handled by a representative.

A sales promotion drive may have meant too much work for him to do. Or he may have been building up a resentment towards the manufacturer for many months. The smaller the distribution point—the corner grocer's shop is a good example—the more difficult it is to maintain good relationships. The public relation man's job is threefold : firstly he must find out the distribution method and study it; secondly he must look at the whole trade in which he is involved, learn the history of distribution in it, and see how his company or client compares; and thirdly he must evolve the particular mixture of communications methods he needs to use to achieve his public relations objectives.

The communications methods present no special difficulties and have no special mysteries, but their application does call for constant study. This is more true if the point of sale is a store or bar counter, if only because competition is more keen and account needs to be taken of the intangible but constant pressure of public attitudes and demands.

A traditional method of keeping in touch is a dealer publication. They come in various forms. Some are cheaply produced, some are expensive. The expensive method is not necessarily better than the cheap. It must be conditioned by the type of recipient, by budget, and possibly by the quantities involved. The format can be either that of a simple bulletin, a newspaper or a magazine. If there is relatively little information to pass on but a need to pass it on frequently then the bulletin might be the best method.

This can be duplicated or printed. If it is to be duplicated then some consideration should be given not only to the method but also the paper used. It is usually wise to use the best quality paper to give the bulletin a clean appearance. If it is to be printed, perhaps with illustrations and colour on a coated paper, time will have to be spent on layout. This needs a professionals touch.

Producing a dealer publication as a newspaper or magazine inevitably means the services of an experienced editor. The decision on which format to use will be made after working out the frequency needed; the ease with which information becomes available for dissemination; the type of information being disseminated; its urgency; the need for quality of illustration; the level of intelligence, awareness, or perception of the readers; and the quantity of the publication needed.

If the written material comes over better with high-quality illustration, a magazine format may be better.

Despite the attempts of many people, a newspaper format only really succeeds on newsprint. At the same time, of course, merely using newsprint will not turn a bad layout and advertising-type headlines into a good newspaper. It is arguable that a dealer publication should not pretend to be a newspaper.

A commercial publication appears regularly at traditional intervals: daily, weekly, monthly, quarterly or whatever. A sponsored publication need not follow this pattern. There is no reason why a magazine should not appear only three times a year, or eight times a year - both of them slightly curious frequencies. There are times of the year in all industries when the dealers are frantically busy; at such moments they will probably not be anxious to read more than is absolutely essential.

This should emerge from the initial study of the distribution pattern in an industry. However, if it is decided to establish an unorthodox publishing frequency it is wise to say so at the outset. It is in any event necessary to publish on time. A magazine format has certain advantages. For one thing, it allows for depth or feature treatment which in some circumstances is the most effective way of putting over a point. The high-quality picture reproduction which is possible may be essential in telling the company's story.

The one major disadvantage in that more time must be spent in reading a magazine and if the dealers involved are busy the may well not what to put in that time. Careful attention to design can, of course, help the dealer to read the paper quickly yet absorb its content. Even after the method has been decided, there still remain several questions and further decisions. There is the policy of the publication. Is its to be a communication form the company to distributors, telling them what is happening in the company, the company's attitude to trade issues, giving news of new products, processes or services? Or it to be a publication which tells dealers what other dealers are doing and carries only occasional company notices? should it carry advertisements, whether form the company itself or form non-competing outside companies? should it be hard-sell or soft-sell? Light-hearted or serious? should it contain regular or occasional pull-outs or display pages that a dealer can put up on his wall? should it aim to inform the dealer, or educate him, or amuse him, or enthuse him? Should it include material that is nothing to do with the company? these questions must be studied and talked out before a publication is launched. There should be a periodic check on the acceptance of the publication. It is possible to do this through sales representatives, but it is almost certainly better to hand it over to a research organization.

A sales force can take round a questionnaire, or it can be included, with a reply-paid envelope or label, in the paper itself. The danger of this method is that those few readers who take the trouble to reply are almost bound to provide the answers they thing are wanted and the survey results will thus be biased. However budget may come into this decision. A properly conducted survey which gives statistically correct and truly impartial answers is fairly expensive, since it takes time to carry out and time to evaluate.

Readers should always be encouraged to write letter to the editor and their opinions on new features should always be solicited, but do not expect too much.

In many ways the most important decisions are the twins of writing and editing. There is a fairly powerful case to be made out in certain types of dealer publication for copy written in an advertising style, with brash headlines and hard over-selling. The more logical style of a journalist may fail to impart the manufacturer's message.

The editor must also remember to demonstrate to the reader the value and desirability of the publication. Even commercial publications-which one must presume are bought because people actively want to read them-find it necessary to boast about themselves form time to time. A dealer publication usually comes free. In a sense it is thus suspect since it is obviously pleading a special case. To reduce its possible credibility gap, it is wise to take space occasionally to remind the dealers that they may miss some commercial advantage by not reading it. In any event, the editing-in the sense of implementing policy, deciding on contributors, rewriting copy, writing headlines, handling layout, and so-is a professional job. The second major method of establishing and maintaining a relationship with dealers is the face-to-face meeting, conference, seminar or exhibition.

In this area, it is the task of the public relations man to recommend whether one or more of these is right or wrong. It may then be his task to set them up. The point to remember is that dealers will ask certain kinds of questions and have certain kinds of attitudes, neither of them to be compared with the questions and attitudes adopted by eventual customers. Whoever form this company or client is on duty at a meeting, large or small, it is absolutely essential that they are properly briefed and have done their homework. Dealers cannot be fobbed off with half-answers or promises to get the information later.

Dealer meetings often have to be arranged in the evenings, since the people are working by day. They must therefore be made interesting-the promise of value form a visit must be kept-or dealers will leave with a feeling of anger at having given up their spare time. It is seldom necessary to be lavish with hospitality, but even if the food and wine does flow it must be supported with useful information.

It is not, of course, and inviolable rule that meetings with dealers have to be in the evening. If the only way of showing dealers the story is to do it during the day, then that is the way that must be used. And it is wise to remember hat dealers often have staffs of their own who may be involved in meeting or handling the final customer. Travel agents, for instance, sell tours, airline services, shipping services, and so on.

The producers of the tours, as well as the airlines and shipping companies, replay to a large degree on the selling done by counter clerks. They, therefore, must not only inform the owners of the travel agencies, but also their staffs. In this particular industry, much time and effort is devoted to educational trips which mean staff being away from their offices for several days. No other method is equally effective. Conferences or seminar for dealers are subject to the same basic rules as those for any other group. One difference, of course, is that a dealer will not usually be expected to pay to attend a conference arrange by a company.

Any expenses he incurs must be paid to him. And since to is an unavailable truth about human nature that people are often less interested in something they get for nothing than is something for which they pay, it is vital that the organization and administration of a dealer meeting are first-class.

The public relations man may find that the professional or trade body of his dealers is arranging a conference. This can present a possibility: a special minor event set up alongside the main conference. This could be a reception, a lunch, an exhibition or a film show, to name a few examples. Only one useful generalization can be made on this: the professional or trade body acting as main sponsor must give its approval tacit or declared to anything an individual company does. Not to also them or inform them is not just discourteous, it is bad public relations. Further, to go ahead with any private plan in the face of their disapproval is to court disaster.

A trade exhibition attended by dealers is yet a further opportunity. Its exploitation may be in the form of a stand. Or it may be a private exhibition in a company's showroom or in a hotel quite nearby. All that is needed is a good mailing list so that all dealers are aware that the company is not in the main exhibition hall. The public relations man will naturally be closely involved in the arranging of any special lunches or receptions for groups of dealers, and in any advertising companion used to bring them to the show or the stand. It is normal practice to try to create some special event in the opening day or press preview day to attract journalists. It is important not to do anything that prevents dealers frame getting to the stand. The purpose of a trade exhibition, and a stand at it, is to sell to dealers. Creating a publicity-seeking event may help that selling, but not if it means turning away potential customers.

After these two main methods, there is a third. It is in the distribution of material which will aid the distributor to do his job better, to do it more easily or to turn his selling point-be it shop, bar counter, cash-and carry warehouse or whatever-into an extension of the manufacturer's own premises.

This activity is in the field of sales promotion, and is one more where the public relations man does not have the dominant role. He can and should advise on the minds of Recipients will naturally study any such material going out in bulk and will see if it should be shown to the press.

Relationships with distributors can often be the key to success for a manufacturer. They constitute one of his prime publics. As such the job of creating and maintaining the right relationships is very much the public relations man's province. In some parts he will be the leader, in others the follower. As in so many aspects of this complex business, he must know when to lead and when to follow. He must not commit the error of always trying to impose his roles, his disciplines, in others.

Shareholder relations

Shareholders are more than a specialized audience: they are different in character from other audiences. They have a unique relationship to a company: they own it, however often this fact appears to be forgotten by executive management. And this simple fact means that they have a right to be told what is going on. Employees, too, have a right to know, but that is a moral right, whereas shareholders have a legal entitlement to information about how their money is being used.

The Companies Act, 1980, widened the range of information which companies must provide. The board of directors, through the company secretary, is responsible for giving the facts and figures which are statutorily required, but the public relations man must always consider if this is enough to meet the shareholder needs of the organization.

As with every other area of public relations, he must begin by a study of the nature of the audience. As shareholders, they are already clearly identifiable and accessible, but as an audience they need further examination. Are they many or few? Are they mainly ordinary individuals with small holdings or wealthy persons with large holdings or institutions managed by professional investors? The approach to a mass of small shareholders in a large company which is in the public eye and is active in the market will be basically different from that required for an equally powerful concern which, by the nature of a its activities, is not financially active or well known and which is controller mainly by institutions or family interest holding large blocks of shares. In the first case there is a need to generate interest, enthusiasm and a feeling among shareholders that the company is a successfully run concern worthy of their investment. In the second case it is likely that no among of skillful presented information will after views based exclusively upon a hard view of the current results, the recent record of profit, and the prospects for the future. It is up to the public relations man to insure that proper trust is fostered in those who are running the company.

The ability of the audience to appreciate the complexities of finance and industry has to be taken into account. The professional audience of the institutional shareholders may be as well qualified to run a company as the board of directors an is quite capable of showing that it believes it knows better.. The audience of small shareholders is virtually obliged to put it trust in the board, although often voiceferous members of this audience are prepared to express their opinions.

Attitudes towards shareholder relations have changed in recent years and are changing still. The are when those who held shares were automatically regarded as top hatred capitalists is long past; today shareholding and the game of playing the market are widespread throughout all start of society. Equally, the growth of the class of professional managers has led to a great increase in the number of executive directors on company boards, with no significant personal shareholding. The old concept that the board should immediately and almost wholly represent the largest shareholders has faded in the face of the need for directors who can provide expert management. This is not to say that major financial interest are not and should not be represented on company boards: their shown expertise may be just as necessary. Attitudes among directors and company secretaries are changing, too, although more slowly. It is pat of the discipline of the company secretary to adopt a cautious approach to change; his responsibilities are grave and he should not lightly accept new ideas.

A sound relationship of trust between the public relation ideas. A sound relationship of trust between the public relations man and the company secretary and his staff is essential. In many companies. The shareholders have long been regarded as exclusively the concern of the company secretary and the PR man has intervened at his peril. Provoked by those companies with a need for popular communication with a mass of small shareholders, the though is spreading that the public relations department has the skills to tackle the problem.

Always it must be remembered that the shareholder has entrusted his money perhaps his whole saving to the company and that if the company fails him he may lose it. It is therefore his right, even beyond the requirements of the law, to be told how the company have used, is using, and propose to use his money. The other side of the coin, of course, is that the company will never lose by gaining the understanding of its threatened with a take-over.

Two statutory requirements are that the company must hold an annual meeting and that it must prepare an annual report and statement of accounts. These two activities usually form the center of a year's programme of shareholder activities. Often they are the only activities, and this may be enough for some companies. Whatever the nature of the organization and of its shareholder audience, the most should be made of these, opportunities to present the company's achievements.

An annual report may be a simple, formal document, soberly presented and containing only the minimum legal requirement of information. Or it may be a lavish brochure, filled with colored illustrations and diagrams, written in lively way, and with the year's figures set out so that they are readily understandable by the most unsophisticated reader.

The choice of which course to follow or, more likely, what line to take between these two extremes is based largely on the firm's need to inform the shareholders although some large concerns with only limited public shareholding make use of attractive annual reports as prestige or background documents, particularly to inform that, amorphous mass of financial interest known as the city, for recruiting, for press reference, and customer or other general enquiries.

The annual report usually includes the statutory notice of the annual meeting and the agenda, although this may be circulated to shareholder separately. The timing of this notice is governed by law. The accounts customarily include, in addition to the balance sheet and the year's profit and loss account, a report by the chairman on the year's working and a forecast of prospects for the future. This report is capable of being expanded for information purposes not only into a review of twelve months work but also a survey for the company's plants and facilities, its place in the market, its significance in the national economy, and its plans for short and long term development. What shareholders want to know extends beyond the financial results for one year into a comparison with past performance and a realistic assessment of how the business stands and how it will be in the year to come.

The ways of expressing this information are many and varies, and chairmen usually have a strong view on what they want to say and the best way to say it. This brigs up the familiar public relations problem of the vital need to ensure the message is expressed in a way that the audience will be able to compared. The language of chairmen and financial experts is not often the language of the small shareholder and usually the skill of the public relations man needs to be brought to bear in support of clarity, simplicity, and avoidance of jargon. There are many editorial and graphic design units capable of advising on and handling the production of annual reports.

Company secretaries can sometimes be stimulated to consider a fresh visual approach by a study of the entries for the annual award sponsored by the accountant for the best presentation of accounts. The annual meeting, at which the shareholder are entitled to ask questions about the report and accounts and generally express their opinions, is often no more than a morality. In a great many companies, the meeting is regarded as an unavoidable nuisance and if more than a handful of shareholders appear the board is surprised. If a company is doing well or just proceeding one steady course, it is understandable that a small shareholder in cheltenham should not take the trouble to visit London for meeting which may only last for a few minutes.

If the company is in trouble of some sort, the shareholders are more likely to turn not in force, but large meetings are the exception, apart from those relatively few organizations which deliberately set out to attract shareholders to them. The company meeting, if the trouble is taken to great it to the information needs of the concern, may be a potent means of dissipating the ivory tower feeling that the small shareholder may have about the directors. In the first place, a meeting that is only a formality will never attract many shareholders even if food and drink is offered. It is necessary to generate some interest that will bring them from distance. This may be done by livening up the meeting or by taking the meeting to somewhere more interesting than a hotel room. For a company with a wide public shareholding, an exhibition of product, particularly new ones, can be an attraction, especially if they are consumer good.

A display of photographs of impressive new production facilities or a film out a great overseas investment can also offer an enlivening interest. A large and diverse company could make an annual newsreel of activities and achievements. None of these ideas need to be an expense slowly set against shareholder relations, for they have an obvious potential for information customers and employees as well. Something to take away should always be provided at a major shareholder event, whether it is an attractive booklet to remind the audience of the main facts or a collection of samples of consumer goods to show to their neighbors.

When a new plant or laboratory has been built it is worth considering holding the annual meeting on the spot. If a layout or a process is involved which would make it dangerous or uncomfortable for visitors, some of whom may be elderly of infirm to walk round, closed circuit television might be the answer. The sense of involvement with the company in one of its own locations is not the only value, as there may also be an opportunity for the shareholders to meteor at least be seen the by the employees.

The though that the ordinary shareholder is no different from the ordinary employee can still be new to a man brought up with a black and white concept of capital and labour. A company which has slowly developed and it is a slow process an interest among shareholders in its annual meeting as an event not to be missed, will find that it has created a major administration and budget item if it enters into visits to locations. Hiring of trains, ships, and aircraft is not known and large-scale disruption of production may have to be accepted. But even the smaller concern with a likely attendance numbered in tens rather than hundreds of shareholders can gain a great deal if appreciation of what it is doing by the use of the open day, not necessarily associated with the annual meetings.

Whatever the occasion, from a mass visit to a formal meetings, the policy should be to meet the shareholders as people in as friendly a manner as possible. And that dos not only mean the public relations man and the secretary shaking hands with them at the door. It maps the chairman, the managing director, the chief engineer, and the production director available for a chat over a cup of coffee or a drink. It is never less than worthwhile to prove to a few more active shareholders, even if their holdings are not significant, that the company, as represented by its top to it. When time of comes, the faith of the ordinary shareholder may be critical.

The organization which relies heavily upon popular investment and its reputation in the market is likely to need to do more than make the most of the annual report and the annual meetings. Brief, attractive quarterly reports mailed to the shareholders can help to sustain interest and indicate the trends of business. Melange again can be useful, particularly in consumer goods companies, to introduce new product and services, but even basic industries can use direct combination to inform shareholders of major developments. An occasional shareholders news sheet is worth considering in large an varied organizations.

As in so many other cases, the press is the most effective indirect many of telling shareholders and the financial community what is going on. The financial press and the City pages of the newspapers have changed in character in the past fifteen years or so from being slowly concerned with share prices and company results to a wide ranging coverage of industry and economics. This is partly a reflection of the and to foster greater understanding of industry and commerce, and partly contribution to standing of industry and commerce, and partly contribution the great are participation of ordinary people in the capital structure of British industry. Many of these people are employees of the companies whose shares they hold, either from individual initiative or as the result of enlightened organizations own share ownership schemes. They therefore have a dual interest in knowing about progress and problems, success and failure.

They all read papers of some sort and an essential ingredient of any shareholder information programme is to ensure that financial journalists are fully informed, kept up to date and aware that their questions will be readily answered. Their friendship and understanding can be invaluable, notably in the interpretation of understanding can be invaluable, notably in the interpretation of short term poor results or in the assessment of the merits of a take over bid. The shareholders will have their own view, but they will also be influenced by what they read.

Who answers the question when a shareholder telephones the head office and says to the switchboard girl; I am a shareholder in your company and I want to know about so and so? Perhaps it should the public relations department, but there must always be a designated individual available to cope. It may be the company and concern. However it is handled, the shareholder should receiver even more courtesy and help than any other caller. He feels that he is involved with the company; he should, therefore, never be made to feel that he is less than welcome, however eccentric or irrelevant has enquiry.

This sense of participation and identification can be enhanced in various ways. If a company has a firm visual design policy and its advertising, vehicles, packaging, and so on, are all immediate recognizable because of a symbol or a chosen type style, then that visual identify should be emphatically used in every form of communication with the shareholder. At the other end of the may be worth including shareholders in the mailing list, or sending personal prints to every shareholder photographed during a meeting or visit.

The ways of creating links with shareholders are endless and many will be peculiar to individual companies, because of their structure. Some have an intimate relationship growing from a small shareholding concentrated geographically; others have to face the fact their identity to their shareholders is blurred because the company is part of a larger group.

The company secretary is often the key man in deciding what is needed, for it is he who has the legal responsibility and the executive duty to carry out both the requirements of the law and the wishes of the board in matters of shareholder relations. A sound understanding of one another's position and of the varying skills of the jobs is vital if the company secretary and the public relations man are to work together to inform this special audience which, unlike most others, has a right to be told.

Fund raising

The basic purpose of fund raising is to finance a project of one kind or another, be it long term or short term. The subject is normally associated with voluntary, charitable or non-commercial operations, where people are asked to give money for the sake of the project itself, rather than for the sake of a financial or other return. Many example spring readily to mind, such as restoring an ancient church, providing for the dependents of people who have fallen on bad times, building a new repeater theatre in a provincial town, surrounding famine stricken children. The list is endless.

As the pace of society becomes faster and faster the competition becomes fiercer and fiercer and the weak are left by the way. As modernity grips our cities, our links with tradition in the shape of historic monuments becomes weaker. One part of the world gets richer; the rest remains impoverished. When natural disasters overwhelm poor people, the rich give up a portion of their wealth to help. Causes are embraced as people seek ways of entire keeping their individually, repaying their good fortune, or buying their immortality.

Most good causes—or to use another word, charities are good The place of most is readily recognizable and recognized. They may be international, national or local in scope. Yet to succeed they must promote themselves. They must create in the minds of both donors and possible donors and awareness of the good they do, and how they do it.

All voluntary activities need finance, To get that finance they must approach their need by the same rules as a commercial company. They must advertised. They must attempt to obtain editorial comment on their activities. They must send direct mail shots to subscribers, actual and potential. All these activities will maintain a flow of money an make in easier to raise new money to keep the activity going. There is a line of distinction between professional fund raisers and public relations people.

There is an overlap between their qualifications and duties. For the purposes of this chapter it is assumed that the two are synonymous. However, there is a deference between the two. It is the function of the public relations practitioners to create the conditions in which that money is raised more easily towards the organization for which the funs have been raised, and the report how the money raised in being spent.

In the same way as advertising is used directly to sell goods, so professional find raisers use their techniques to achieve their objectives. The normal techniques of the public relations man do not have their reflect quickly enough to bring money in for deserving causes.

The two can, and should, work together. Each should recognize the place of the other and not try to supplement him or replace him.

To a degree the raising of money for charitable purposes relies on moral blackmail. It is often a deliberate policy, even if by implication only, to try to include feeling of guilt in potential donors. The recognition of this element in charity appeals does not mean that it is wrong or evil. If the object of the appeal are unquestionable to benefit people for instance, to relieve famine then it is arguable that the ends justify the means, If the only way to raise enough money to ameliorate suffering is to show pictures of children dying of starvation, then their is no reason why the pictures should not be shown. Charitable bodies are undergoing great hardship in many directions.

The need for them remains constant, but the costs of raising money and the level of spending necessary to achieve some good have rocketed. Inflation has hit them and there is more competition for less money. All these situations have PR connotations. The timing of appeals must be just right. The message and the audience must be even more clearly identified. And the charity must demonstrate its ability to keep its overheads to a minimum.

Another point the public relations man needs to remember is that charities are staffed and served by a mixture of professional paid staffs and volunteers. There are often classes between the two. The public relations man has to stay between them, serving both, and in the he process must watch his own relationship with them.

The public relations methods used in fund raising are dictated by the scope of the charitable operations being promoted. If its objective is to help the blind throughout the world the net can be thrown wide. On the other hand, if its objective is to restore a village war memorial the sources of money are strictly limited.

Thus, as in all public relations campaigns, the first job of the practitioner is to identify his publics and place them in an order of priority. One of two examples will illustrated the process. Starving children are a regrettable phenomenon of the modern world. Everybody almost without exception likes small children and wants to help the. This desire goes as far as not caring about where the children are starving. Their nationality or color. Thus in a charity appealing for funds to feed starving children, all people are a public. This is an extremes example. Restoring a village ware memorial appeals to few people. At the same time, the appeal can be stronger since the few may well be more closely identified with it.

The residents of he village; relatives of those who are commemorated by it; members of the regiments in which they served; people who used to live in the village all these are first publics. It is seldom difficult when preparing a list to pick out the groups at who to aim an appeal. It is also much better to make the list as wide as possible since it is a peculiar fact of fund raising for voluntary purposes that the most unexpected sources produce money. Given a list, the public relations man must now face his second problem; how much money is needed. If the charity is permanent as might be the case for starving children it may be sufficient to as that 'as much as possible is the total. A short term appeal will have a limit. With his list and target for the money needed, the public relations man must now decide his method of approach.

This must always be governed by another rule of fund raising. Most of the total raised for a national appeal will come from a relatively few major donations, but the publicity created to attract Honduras of small donations will make the large ones possible. This is not an inviolable rule but it almost always happens. Direct mail, editorial publicity, advertising, personal effort, and persona contact are the generally accepted methods used in fund raising. Their importance varies in each types of appeal, and it is dangerous to generalize. The direct mail will take the form of letter sand leaflets.

The letters may be individually types or produced with matched in address. It is of course, possible to produce a simple stenciled appeal which is broadcast as widely as possible, but this is seldom advisable. Remember the elements of blackmail and identification. The recipients of letter must react favorable, or with interest. A stenciled and generalized appeal is unlikely to make them do either. Who signs the letter again depends on the circumstances. It may be signed by the patron, or president, or chairman, or by a notable personality, such as a television star.

The signature may be from somebody completely unknown. This decision will be taken in relation to the recipients. For instance, appeal to housewives might produce a better reaction if it were signed by a famous film star, but the same appeal sent to the managing directors of more industrial companies might produce nothings. An appeal for a football charity would evoke immediate interest if the apparently came from a star like Pele, but his name would carry little weight in an appeal for new piece of scientific apparatus for a university. The signature should be relevant and logical; it should not look forced or out of character.

The use of leaflets produces another set of specific decision. There are dangerous in producing lavish, well illustrate brochure, since it carries the implication that money is being spend rashly. On the other hand if it is possible to obtain the services of a designer, typographer,, writer, and printer without charge and this is made clear on the leaflet, then the quality approach may be the best method. Whatever the leaflet looks like, it must at all costs be informative and emotional. It must say clearly what are the objectives of the appeal, and as far as possible show how the money is to be spend, but it must do so in emotional terms.

Remember again that the donations being solicited are spare money, that is, which could be spend on other things. There is no financial return to the donor involved. Thus put crudely the leaflet must pull at hi heart stings or stir his memories. Genuine emotion will do this and it use is justified. Editorial publicity play a key role in all fund raising. Of itself, editorial publicity seldom raises large sums of money, but it creates the conditions for direct mail, media advertising, and the other methods to work effectively. Naturally, this applies less in situations of natural disaster. An earthquake which devastates a two obtains vast editorial coverage.

The statements from the voluntary organizations which age. The statements from the voluntary organizations or which a immediately swing into action appear immediately or within a day or so. This publicity attracts donations by return. In moments of lower drama, the purpose of editorial publicity is to keep attention focused on the charity. Obtaining it calls for constant vigilance a on the part of the public elections man, so that he can exploit any work of the charity by bringing it to the attention of journalists. It also calls for considerable initiative in creating events which will merit editorial reporting. There is nothing immoral in deliberately building storms to keep the charity in the public eye. It is all a part of the public relations man's amount.

The amount and type of advertising that can be involved again depends on the charity itself an its targets. National charity for starving children will look to national appear advertising; an appeal for permanent home for aged accountant would concentrate on business and trade appears. Whatever the media schedule, the advertising must follow certain rule, It must have a dramatic headline that instantly catches the eye. It is almost always better that this is supported by an equally dramatic picture.

A photograph is better than a drawing. The copy must be explicit. It should demonstrate what the charity it trying to do, what it has done up to now, and what it want to do in the future. Above all it must me it possible for the reader to take action by including a coupon. If the combination of the headlines, picture, and cop has done its job that is, produced an emotional response in the reader it must immediately capitalize on that success by providing the means for the reader to send a donation, or enter into a convenient, or request more information. One purpose of this is obvious. The advertisement in inserted to raised money. If it fails to do that its cost is wasted. The second purpose is lightly less obvious, but almost as important. It provide the charity with its own mailing list.

Some charities use this to issue regular reminders to previous donors. The reminders can be specific appeals, or copies of a magazine, of the annual report. The regular magazine has a certain value, but it should not be produced unless the public relation man i clear about it objective sand its contribution to fund raising. There is a tendency to keep people on a mailing list of this type for too long. The list should be compared with donations so that people who have not respond for some times are removed from it. Any national charity relies heavily on the keenness, enthusiasm, and effort to of local honorary groups. An early job for the public relations man is to draw up a paper to guide these local groups on obtaining publicity.

This must how newspaper work, what sort of information the want to receiver, the days and times at which it is best for them to recipe, to how to invite them to function, how to rewrite nationally issued press release to give theme local slant, and so on. This move is absolutely essential and should be taken right at the start. This guide should go further than dealings with the press. It should show local enthusiasts how to set up a group in their district, and how to keep it going. It should also cover local methods of maintaining interest in the charity, such as coffee morning, bring-and-buy sales, and the like.

It is most difficult to maintain the enthusiasm of local groups. To do so means that the public relations man must keep feeding them with ideas and with reports on what the charity is doing. They must be made to feel closely involved. Equally, of course, they should never feel that the money spent on keeping them informed is being wasted in expensive-looking brochures. The secret lies more in the frequency with which they are told than the method.

The amount of personal contact needs in fund raising varied with each charity. Many charities have a list of patrons, vice-presidents, or honorary advisers. It is often the function of these people to set up individual or collective events at the which the work of the charity can be explained face-to-face. Exactly how this is done is a matter for individual decision.

A growing feature of fund raising is the production of Christmas cards. This has an obvious value in that it allows people to do something which they would do anyway while also incorporating a donation to the charity through the profits it takes from the sale of the cards. These still represent a small proportion of the total number of Christmas cards sold, and have been badly affected by higher printing and postal costs.

Nevertheless, they are now an established idea. A number of printers now handle the design, printing and bulk distribution of cards. This entails a good deal of work, especially if the buyer can order individual overprinting of his own name and address. In any event, cards must be planned ahead, usually not less than eighteen months before the Christmas for which they are needed. It is impossible to do the job properly in a shorter time. The question for the public relations man to ponder is the relevance of Christmas cards to his particular appeal.

The public relations man should be aware of bodies such as the Charity Commissioners, National Council of Social Service and the Charities Aid Fund. All can help him in a job in which he often has to exercise a more constant flow of initiative and skill over a broader front than many of his commercial counterparts.

International public relations

The role that a public relations man can play in handling or supervising campaigns overseas can be crucial. The proper support for overseas offices or representatives, whether gained by full-scale programs of activity, or whether by simple press relations, can do a great deal in helping a company to maintain its overseas business or to penetrate new markets. Language apart, many shares and obstacles face the public relations man who starts to operate outside his own country. They include the level of literacy, local customs and traditions, especially religious, and different methods of working. In the end, there is no real substitute for local knowledge, supplied by someone on the spot or with genuine and up-to-date experience.

If the campaign is to be continues it will almost certainly pay dividends to have a full-time local operator or the services of a local consultancy. Clearly this is costly and can only be entertained as a working method by the largest of companies. If it does arise, it is probably sensible for the overseas man or consultant to have a period of familiarization with head office. Equally, it will be necessary for the public relations man to pay regular visits to the country concerned to discuss progress and review the programme of activity, even if the visits take place only twice a year. Of course, standards and methods vary in all countries.

While it is reasonable to expect that the developed countries of the world will share many standards and methods, experience will show shades of variation that can be critical. It is wrong to try arbitrarily to impose the exact pattern of operation in one country on to another. The public relations man will learn to look for result and not be too diverted by the way in which they are achieved. This does not imply any under hand practices. It merely recognizes that countries differ and the people in them differ, too. A journalist may be the same throughout the world in wanting a good story, but the way in which he gets it and reports it cannot be the same everywhere.

Advertising-editorial links are much more common than in Britain. Business methods-such as the notorious 'tomorrow will do' philosophy in many Latin countries—may be intensely irritating to an executive accustomed to tight schedules and instant decisions, but he must learn to accept them and work within them. How far the public relations man needs to take his involvement—even to the extent of learning the language of the country—must be controlled by how much he wants or needs to achieve. For most people international work often means no more than publicizing a visit by a sales director, or an important order, or participation in an international exhibition.

From the moment that a need or an opportunity arises, the public relations man has two courses open to him. He can follow either or both. One of them is issuing information from this country to other countries; the other is contact on the spot with journalists or businessmen or whatever. Issuing press material to overseas publications and agencies is a relatively simple task.

The press attached of the relevant embassy or legation can supply a list of publications, or will allow the public relations man to go in and consult a reference book. This is on the assumption that the material is to be issued direct. If it is, it must be translated into the language concerned. Translation is full of pitfalls. It should always be done by nationals of the country. There are within easy reach agencies which handle translations, but it is sensible to check their staffing and methods beforehand. The Institute of translators can advise. Technical subjects should be dealt with by technical experts.

The importance of having the translation handled by a national lies in the knowledge of doing that only a national can have, although not if he has been out of his native country for many years and is thus out of touch with current idiomatic phrases. Over the years, press release, leaflets, and other literature in foreign languages have been littered with mistakes. Some of them will merely raise loud laughs, but there is always the danger that they will either cause offense or be inaccurate. It can be wise to send the original copy to an overseas branch office or representative for translation, especially if the material is technical. It all takes time, but it is always time well spent.

If the written material has to be accompanied by charts or drawings, captions and any labels on the charts must also be translated. The name and address of both the issuing source and a local representative or agent should be included to facilitate press enquiries. Obviously, copies should be sent to the representative or agent. A possible variation is to mail copies in bulk to the local man with a press list and allow him to send the release himself. It is usually unwise to let him make his own copies, since they will look unprofessional, but this is not a hard and fast rule.

An alternative, when the story is for lay newspapers rather than for trade publications, is to issue it—in English—to the London representatives of the country's press. Major countries' news-papers have representation in Britain. The names and addresses can be found in the list of members of the Foreign press Association. When this is done, it should be made clear that it is being sent to them and not also direct to their head offices. Obviously, if the story is tied to a date, such as a visit by an important businessman, they must be allowed time to cable or write to their offices.

There are a number of international news agencies which will handle material for overseas. They apply the same rule as any domestic news agency: the story must be good enough to merit them spending the money it costs to issue it. An effective organization is EIBIS International, based in London.

This commercial agency prepares, translated and issues material in bulk or on an exclusive basis to publications selected from its lists of more than 20,000 titles in 325 categories. Its fees include monitoring the results. BBC overseas services cover almost every country in the world. Material can be sent to individual producers, or channeled through the BBC Future Events Unit, who normally take six copies and circulated them to any producers likely to be interested.

There are export and other periodicals published which circulated overseas and which may sometimes afford a good opportunity, particularly for feature material.

Lastly, there is the Central Office of Information, a government organization which has the dual role of projecting official British policy overseas, and of carrying out information and publicity work in the UK for government departments and other publicly financed bodies. It operates through specialists divisions, with a research unit which evaluates their work. The home publicity services include arranging press, cinema, TV, radio and poster advertising; producing booklets, leaflets, films, radio and TV material, exhibition, photographs and other visual material; and distributing department press notices. Departments are also served by a network of COI regional offices.

The overseas press and radio division sends abroad more than 6,500,000 words of export news items and feature articles and is responsible for more than 3,500 recorded programme a year. The industrial service provides stories about new products, processes and services; publicity for UK trade fairs and British participation in overseas exhibition; news of developments in electronics and transport; and a programme covering aspects of China trade.

The photographic services section handles approximately 850,000 prints and about 14,000 printing blocks annually. The films and television divisions cover more than 1,000 industrial stories a year for inclusion in television and newsreel services. The exhibition division designs, produces and supervises the building of exhibition overseas sponsored by the Foreign and Commonwealth Office, British participation in trade fairs now being usually the responsibility of the Department of Trade. The reference division produces a documentation service primarily for use and distribution by British Information Services offices abroad.

The tours and facilities section arrange conducted tours within the UK for more than 1,500 visitors annually, at the request of the Foreign and Commonwealth Office. It is also responsible for the distribution and shipping section which includes among its services the regular supply of newspapers and periodicals to about 260 posts throughout the world.

Taking part in an exhibition, trade fair, conference or convention overseas—which is becoming more and more common as selling becomes mere international—presents a different situation. To achieve success, both in public relations and publicity terms, requires a good deal of planning, hard work, and visits to the location. The first visit should be made well in advance.

If the public relations man needs a local consultant he will find the national public relations association or society helpful in giving him a list of names. He can check it against the membership list of the International Public Relations Association, which includes biographical notes and the experience of most of the members. However, even if he does use a local man this does not absolve him from the duty of being on the spot at least twice beforehand and for the preview and opening.

The local consultant may be efficient, and he will have the added value of understanding local conditions and methods, but the cannot be expected to understand all the public relations problems of the client, especially when he is,involved for only a comparatively short time. He needs guidance, and it is the duty of the public relations man to provide it. The major problems encountered in publicity and public relations work of this type are mostly connected with the language.

The public relations man will therefore find it sensible to retail the services of an interpreter who can be with him as he travels about. Alongside this there are problems of the handling of material. In some countries, for instance, printed matter can be held up for several weeks before it is cleared by customs. The purpose of the advance visits is to find out as early as possible what mechanical and procedural flag have to be overcomes, and thus what planning must take place from head office.

In any event, close liaison should be maintained with the Department of Trade and Industry, British Overseas Trade Board, and specialized bodies for particular industries, such as the British Agricultural export Council. Their services can be helpful over stand design and whether it can be carried out in Britain or whether it should be handed over to a local contractor. There are many points to watch. For instance, the use of some form of visual presentation to overcomes language difficulties may have merit, but not unless it is made for the market concerned. A re-hash of existing material is seldom good enough. The object of taking part in an overseas trade show may be simply to sell more goods. It may then be found that local laws or attitudes are a stumbling block in front of those hoped-for greater sales. This will then turn the public relations man's job away from simple publicity operations and into other aspects of public relations.

He may find it necessary to mount a continuing press campaign, make and distribute films, conduct a series of conferences, or enter into negotiations with government departments. If that turns out to be the case, it is then the duty of the public relations man to make recommendation designed to solve the problems. It is for his management to decide whether the effort and expense are worthwhile. It will certainly involved retaining the best local services available.

Any overseas trip should include a visit to the British embassy or consulate. There, the staff, whether specialized or not, are usually knowledgeable and helpful. Even if the reason for going abroad is to seek publicity in the country visited, the public relations man must not neglect the opportunity it presents for publicity in his own country. A successful selling tour in, say Zambia may produce good publicity in Zambia. It is also a publicity opportunity in Britain. Methods by which material can be funneled back here should be established; a trade press news conference can be arrange for the day of the salesman's return; stories and pictures should appear in the he organization's external or internal magazine. Equally possible is arranging a visit to an overseas exhibition for trade journalists from Britain who are interested in the subject and may not otherwise have the opportunity to go. For an important exhibition in which they may only be interested in a small part the investment should be imply repair by the goodwill it creates for the future.

Overseas operations are not confined to press relations. In certain circumstances the public relations man may find that direct mail can play a useful part. He must then study the postal regulations and see that his material conforms to them. The basic rule to remember is that when a public relations man goes to another country it is he who is the foreigner. He must therefore adapt himself to the ways of his hosts. The least he can do is to spend some time studying facts about the country he is to visits; often a visit to the Stationery Office and a discussion with officials of the country's embassy or legation will provide enough background for him.

Political public relations, that is promotional and informational work on behalf of political parties and pressure groups, is an area of the business in which relatively few people are employed. Naturally, these tend to be individuals whose personal beliefs accord with the causes they are pleading. On the other hand, the average staff or consultancy public relations man, whatever his political views, is likely from time to time to handle issues which will involves the need to work with government departments and to inform Members of Parliament and other representative of political parties. To tackle this aspect of public relations successfully, it is necessary to learn how the machinery of government works, to appreciate the attitudes of civil servants and politicians, and, most important, to understand the rules which must not be infringed. The structure of the civil service departments dealing with various aspects of national and international affairs is set out in an official list and in standard reference books. It is not immutable and reorganizations for political or practical reasons take place as the government of the day requires. Responsible for each department or ministry is a minister supported by the ministers of state, parliamentary secretaries and under-secretaries, the precise titles, posts, and numbers varying according to the size and complexity of the department.

Ministers and their sub-ordinates are almost all members of the House of Commons, though some may be in the Lords. Some ministers will be members of the Cabinet, itself a variable body, and others will not. Ministers come and go as the government reshuffles its talents and manpower. So do representatives of what is popularly known as the Shadow Cabinet. This is the Opposition group of potential ministers who study the activities and ideas of their opposite numbers in the government and speak on their chosen subjects in debates. It is important not to forget that Members of the House of Commons are elected, while Peers sit in the Lords by right. The ministries are run by civil servants.

Most departments are headed by a permanent secretary, who does not change with internal government moves nor with alteration in the party in power. Beneath the permanent secretary is a staff of under secretaries, assistants, principals, and officers in a complex structure that varies according to the needs of the department. Some ministries are much larger than others. All have their specialists, knowledgeable in the financial or technical aspects of trade, industry, and agriculture, the trends in overseas affairs, the requirements of the armed forces, or whatever may be applicable. In recent years, government has been re-arrange from a large number of small ministries into a smaller number of 'super' departments with subsidiaries.

Thus the Department of the Environment now covers transport, housing, sport and so on. Most of them have regional offices. The Welsh Office in cardiff and the Scottish Office in Edinburgh have a degree of autonomy, which was considerably increased as a result of the agitation in the 1970s for devolution. Northern Ireland is a special case. Provided the public relations man keeps himself abreast of changes he can soon learn his way around. When faced with the need to obtain information from a government department, or to offer information about a project, the public relations man has both ethical and practical problems.

The civil servants with whom he may have to deal will be working within the broad policies laid down by the government and within the precise terms of the legislation governing the activities for which their department is responsible. Yet the senior officials still exercise a considerable degree of personal discretion in their judgments and recommendation. They must preserve an absolute impartiality and it is an offensive error of judgment, to say the least, to endeavor to mislead them or persuade them beyond the presentation of facts, figures, and logical argument. To take an example, if a company has to close a factory, it is necessary to inform the regional officials of the Department of Trade and Industry and the Department of Employment. The effects of the company's action may, for instance, lead to questions in the House of Commons upon which the departments will be called to advise their monazites. More positively, prior notice of the situation to these departments would enable them to offer advice on the best way to go about it and to take action to cushion the effects on labour and industry in the area.

Consultation and presentation of the situation in a frank and factual form is what is needed. It would be a grievous error to attempt to minimize the adverse effects of the closure by, any, trying to deceive ministry officials about the number of employees the company proposed to absorb elsewhere. The practical problem for the public relations man is that sometimes he simply does not know where to start or whom to ask. Often the simple answer to this is to seek the guidance of his collages in the public relations, press or information department of the ministry concerned.

All ministries and government offices have information staffs who are prepared to help public relations people in industry and commerce find the answers to question or to direct their approaches to the right officials. In the more specialized departments, like those dealing with consumers, energy, a and agriculture, for instance, there are experts who need to be kept up to date in their own subjects in order to be able to do their jobs properly. They may welcome the provision of information, whether in the form of literature or are interested only in facts and not in persuasion. It is as well, therefore, to make individual contact before offering material. Casual or employer's mailing of sales material and invitations in useless to busy civil servants.

There is an attitude of helpfulness and willingness to learn in government departments that is entirely the opposite of what an outsider might suppose from the cartoonist's or playwright's version of the typical civil servant. The public relations man must discover how he an his client or employer can help and be helped and then respect the civil service tradition of impartiality, discretion, and confidentiality. There is a great deal of misunderstanding about the relationship of public relations people and Members of Parliament.

This stems partly from the abuse by some PR men of their freedom to communicate with MPs in the hope of persuading them of the brightness or value of some project, and partly from an excessive suspicion on the parts of some Members of any endeavor to inform them on topics in which they might, or perhaps should, be interested. The duty of an MP is to represent his constituents and to support his party's policies. Many members also have specific interests in subject, possibly stemming from their own backgrounds or the geographical regions they represent.

A number of specialists subject such as television, transports, and the film industry are discussed in partly committees, the members of which often develop detailed knowledge. On the government side, these committees are composed of backbenchers, since minister' responsibilities preclude them from taking part, nut the opposition committees also include front bench members. These committees each have a chairman and sometimes a vice chairman and secretary, and these are the Members to be contacted. The two major party offices, the conservative Central Office and Transport House, should be able to supply the names of committee officers.

The interest of MPs in receiving information and its acceptability to them when received both depend on a discriminating approach to what is sent to whom. For example, a member of the film industry committee would probably be glad to have a copy of a market survey on cinema attendance.

All Scottish Mps might conceivably be interested in a pamphlet proposing a new approach to rail transport north of the border. Members who began their careers as journalist might be expected to be approachable on the subject of control of newspaper mergers. Nut a member who is farmer and represent a constituency in North Wales is most unlikely to be interested in any of these. It might impress an unsophisticated management to say that the company's annual report has been mailed to all Members of Parliament, but it is not likely o do any good.

All MPs, and most Peers, receiver such a weight of small that only the most relevant material has any hope of being studied. The quickest way to learn about MPs, an Peers for that matter, is to buy Vacher's Parliamentary Companion, a pocketsized book published each quarter which lists all member of but Houses of Parliament, part affiliations, MPs' constituencies, and frequently private addresses. If also list the ministers and officers of the House, and outlines the department of the government and the more important officials n each. Whitaker's Almanack and the list of Members published by the Time at each general election are also valuable reference material.

If a company has factories employing many people, the MPs in whose constituencies they are situated might be interested from time to time in being kept in touch with events. It depends on how large a factor the company issue in the life of the community and therefore, in the life of the MP. The more employer in a amount may well rate a slice of the MPs' over filled time. A visit once a year, a copy of the annual report, even copies of the magazine if i is not too parochial, and certainly an invitation to the dinner for the fiftieth anniversary these are worthwhile. Putting the poet man not he mailing list for everything the company issues would be lubricators and would be rightly presented. If a major development is proposed, where positive like starting a new plant in a development are a or negative like making many employees redundant, it is helpful to inform the Member in advance.

His ability to speak from knowledge on subjects raised in the House may be more than useful, especially on emotional issues. His ability to speak privately to ministers may have a beneficial effect. His ability to dell authoritatively with the queries and worried of has constituents on the basis of accurate information may be a cardinal point in the company's favour. If he knows something of the background of the organization and its philosophy, he will be able to make his own judgment and speak his mind publicity and privately.

But he must be let to make his own judgment. Member rightly guard their independence and the public relations man who tries to sway an MPs' interpretation of a situation is court in disaster. There is great integrity in the House of Commons and the Member who is less than honest, or though to be over susceptible to persuasion, will have no useful influence on issues. The rules of the Parliamentary game have to be played straight. The public relations man must learn those rules most of which are unwritten. There are books describing the procedure so the House of Commons, the functions of the Lord, the duties of he various Parliamentary officials, the way in which Bulls are dated, debated, and become Acts, and all the time hallowed paraphernalia of Parliament. These will help, but a reading of the debates in Hansard and the entertaining reports of the parliamentary sketch writers in the serious dailies can do more to establish an appreciation of the atmosphere of the House and the ways in who it thinks.

The PR man should also attend and listen to debates and questions time. Apart from bills and debates of particular relevance to him, it is question time that may prove to be of the greatest interest to the PR man. During this period at the start of the day's proceedings and those questions which are not reached may be answered in writing. Non urgent or non contentious questions are also put in writing for written answers. Both are recorded in Hansard. By custom, various ministers answer questions on specified days.

The members who has put down a question, and others who are interested, may ask supplementary questions and the insuring exchange may produce more information than the responsible minister originally proposed to give or may serve as an opportunity for a Member to express a point of view. Question time is the liveliest part of the proceedings on most days. Every MP is entitled to put own any question he likes although he may not get an answer that satisfied him or even an answer at all.

The may wish to seek information; he may be prodding a government department about some action he thinks should be taken; or he may be using the form of question to air a topics in which he is interests. There is nothing wrong in asking Member if he would are to put a question on a specific issue. For example, the PR man for a trade association might approach a Member known to be interested in that trade and suggest that he might put a question on some current problem. Whether the MP agrees to do so and, if he does in what form he puts the question is a matter entirely for his discretion.

The desirability and manner of making the suggestion in a matter of discretion on the part of the public relations man; he should be sure of his facts an the propriety of the situation before he acts. Often, a direct approach to the right department would have elicited the answer anyway. The PR man's interest may be reversed if the organization for which he is working is the subject of a question. In that case, forethough should have ensured that both the appropriate government departments and the Members like to be interested will have been informed of the facts as fully as possible.

The parliamentary service of the Press Association will provide advance notice of question that have been put down the Members. There is no better guide through the thorny paths of Parliamentary procedure and the sensitivities of Members than a Member himself. Contact with a sympathetic MP, or on how is particularly interested in the subject with which the public relations man is concerned, can lead to contact with other Members, some of whom are almost certain to have an opposing outlook.

A member can also be the host at receptions and dinner parties in private rooms in the place of Westminster. He can arrange, for example, for film shows for Members. He can bring Members and Non -Members together more or less formally in committee rooms and informally in the public rooms. He can explain the complexities of what is and is not allowed in dealings with MPs; how a petition is presented, for example, or how bulk delivery of letters for hand distribution for MPs is not permitted. There is no single book which explains exactly what is permitted and what is not, what might be acceptable, and what would probably be presented. What might be acceptable, and what of someone fully experienced in the ways of House is the only safe course.

In any event, the member of the Institute of Public Relations must observe clause 12 of the IPR Code of Conduct dealing with business relationships between Mps and PR men, while on their part Members now have to declare publicly their outside interests. In local issues, there is not only sitting Member to consider. The opposition party, and perhaps the Liberals and other parties, such as the as the Social Democratic Party, will almost certainly have nominated candidates ready to fight the seat a the next election.

Frequently it is worthwhile for an organization, or its local manager, to be in touch with these candidates, their agents and the chairmen of the constituency parties. Often, any case, these people are significant members of the community in their own right. Recent events have spot lighted a growing concern about the standards of conduct of those in public life. The public relations profession has laid down rules so that reptile practitioners shall be seen to exercise great care in their approaches to MPs. Strict observance of those rules, coupled with the traditions of Parliament itself, will avoid any danger that the PR man is thought to be attempting to compromise a public servant.

Employee communication

In any organization too large for every employee to be known by name to the top man there is bound to be a problem of communication. Conveying a message ceases to be a straightforward process. In concerns of any size there may be as many as four channels of communication: the normal management chain of command, the established relationship with a trade union or staff association, the joint works council or other consultative body, and the grapevine. These means of conveying information cannot be controlled fully, nor should they be.

The managers and supervisors may not be good and conscientious communicators, their relationship with those under their command may be yours, or they may be lacking in clear guidance from the top on what to communicate and how. Communication to member of unions and staff associations lies with the shop stewards or other elected representatives. They may not be skilled at this, however well they represent their members' interests, or they may be troubled by having to face a sharply divided membership, or they may not believe what the management has told them.

Even those consultative groups that have progressed beyond discussion of the price of tea in the canteen and the lack of soap in the washrooms are liable to cease to be effective at the point at which further communication by the employees' representatives becomes necessary. The good committee man is not automatically ale to pass on clearly and interestingly to decisions of the works council and the reasons behind them. Quite likely the management does nothing to help him do so.

The grapevine is totally uncontrollable. Sometimes it carries a true story, usually a distorted one, often a wholly inaccurate one. Anything can start a rumor going, from newspaper speculation about a take-over bid to a messenger misunderstanding a half-seen memo on a secretary's desk. Natural curiosity, the desire to be first with the news, concern about job security, fear of change—all these help the grapevine to flourish. There is no easy answer to the multifarious problems of communication within an organization, and no two organizations are the same in their needs.

Their individual histories, the nature and distribution of their operations, the inside and outside pressure that may affect morale, all these and more are influences on the situation. Yet there are certain factors which are common. Increasingly, internal communication is changing from being an 'optional extra' in management to a positive requirement in the employer/employee relationship. Indeed, legislation is making the disclosure of far more information to employees a requirement rather than a matter of choice. At the same time, the growing demand for participation in the world of work, as much as anywhere else in society, is leading to more broadly based management structures, advisory boards, employee directors and a wider range of consultative groupings of varying effectiveness. This in turn is leading to a growing need for more realistic information services inside companies, although the techniques employed must be condition by the size of the enterprise.

Equally, there is much wider media coverage of industry and commerce than even a few years ago. This, combined with slowly improving communication within trade unions and the publicized pressures of environmentalists and consumer groups, leads to the danger that in adequate internal communication may result in a one-sided debate and a poorly informed work force with a lowered morale.

All this, plus higher standards of education and unthinking acceptance of the professionalism of the news media, means that companies have to try harder to communicate fairly and intelligibly to their employees, not only in the cause of improving internal relationships but also so that the members of the organization can play their part in communicating outside in the community at large.

A studied programme of employee relations based on a carefully thought-out management attitude can help.

The objective should be to ensure that management policies and actions are defined and explained to employees to gain their understanding and acceptance. If they understand, they are more likely to respond sympathetically to management initiative. Employee relations is a loosely used term that often cover a wide range of activities spreading beyond the normal remit of the public relations man. It is usually taken to exclude labour relations—the area of wages and working conditions—but it can include virtually every other topic that is of common concern to management and employs. The precise meaning of the phrase can only be determined within the context of a particular organization; similarly, the role of the PR man in employee relations will vary widely from one organization to another.

It is possible, however, to make two generalizations. In most instances, the public relations function is concerned primarily with the communication problems of employee relations. And it the company PR executive, with his more intimate knowledge of people and operations, who is likely to be deeply involved in employee affairs rather than the agency or consultancy executive. This is not to say that the outside view on what needs to be done is not sometimes clearer.

Just as the meaning of employee relations is open to definition a fresh in every organization, so the relationship of the public relations man and his personnel colleagues will differ. In a large and englightened firm the personnel department may have the staff, the budget, and the skills to handle the internal magazine or newspaper, write and publish factory handbooks, produce safety and suggestion scheme posters, sponsor films, and tackle all the other techniques of direct employee communication. But in many companies the personnel manger is likely to look to his PR colleague to suggest the means and provide the techniques to put across the messages that they will discuss together.

There can be no clear dividing line. Consultation and co-operation between the specialist functions of personnel and public relations is the only sensible way to meet the employee communication needs of an organization. However the two functions may be defined by managements, together they share a responsibility for the communications link and for emphasizing the need for a policy of planned communication.

The basic principle of knowing one's audience and appreciating its capacity to accept a message applies in employee relations as in any other form of communication. A complicating factor is that a relationship will already exist that may hinder rather than help communication. For example, the chairman may be regarded by employees as so remote from any understanding of their way of life that a message from his is liable to be rejected as irrelevant. Or a factory manager may be looked upon as weak because he condones indiscipline and his genuine attempts to communicate may therefore be derided. Or a warning of hard times ahead from a manage who has previously painted a false rosy picture to employees to try to keep them happy may either note be believed or lead to disillusion. Problems of this kind, which can only be recognized and understood after careful investigation, add to the initial difficulties of communicating in the right way. For instance, if it is necessary to communicate some basic change to all employees, then the Daily Mirror language that might be effective for the bulk of shop-floor people is likely to be looked upon a condescending by the graduates in the laboratory.

As another example, an explanation for employees of why the company has made a loss needs not only to be spelled out so that all can understand it, but to be put before them at the same time as they read the City editors' structures. When the house magazine comes out a month later the damage has been done. Even if the public relations man, with the help of the personnel an, can thoroughly appreciate the attitudes of those to whom the message must be passed and can devise a way of putting it clearly and at their right time, there are still further difficulties. Perhaps the largest of these is the failure of top management to accept the difficulties the PR man is facing; this is particularly so with long-term senior managers who sincerely believe that they know the organization and its people inside out and cannot conceive that they are out of touch. Another problem is that the audience reaction inside one company cannot be relied upon to be the same in every place and at every time. What goes over well in the Welsh valleys will not necessarily be acceptable on Tyneside and what succeeds in the Home Counties may well fail in Cornwall. Likewise, news of a redundancy danger will be even worse received if given just before Christmas, and an announcement of a drastic reorganization will be even less welcome immediately after a pay claim has failed. There can be no substitute for knowing the management and the employees, the locations and the histories, the attitudes and the relationships when planning employee communication.

There can be no blueprint for success; the problems are never the same in any two companies or in any two factories or offices. The techniques used to try to sale the problems may be common to them all, but only study and experience will show the right way to apply them. In the face of all this, is it worth attempting to communicate to employees? The answer is that neglect of communication is a management failure, allowing false ideas and distorted concepts to form and gain currency by default.

Lack of communication, or inability to communicate clearly, is at the heart of a great deal of industrial unrest, job dissatisfaction, and operational inefficiency. Good communication can contribute to more harmonious working relationships, understanding of commercial conditions, the acceptance of change, and the improvement of productivity. It is not a panacea, but it is a vital part of good management. Employee communication can, of course, have a general or a specific aim. The need may be to create a sense of belonging to a worthwhile organization or to explain the working of knew pension scheme; to improve safety standard throughout twenty factories or to revive a suggestion scheme in one.

The choice of techniques, apart from deciding upon the most suitable for the subject and the audience, will depend upon the money, time, and skilled staff available. Often these are scarce commodities, for many managements still place a low priority on their personnel work, and upon their internal public relations activities, as opposed to the external publicity which appears to offer more tangible results. While the choice is almost unlimited, certain means of communication have proved themselves effective in employee relations. Of these, the internal magazine or newspaper is both the most common and the most misunderstood.

At its best, a successful internal publication can help employees to feel that they know how the company is doing, that there are others like themselves in different locations, and that the organization is being run by competent people who are human too. At its worst, it can be a medium for numerous pictures of the chairman, for senior executives to pontificate about their holidays and their hobbies, and for exhortations to 'the workers' to pull together for the good of the shareholders, particularly at Christmas. Where internal publications succeed it is usually as a result of management's genuine desire to communicate, as opposed to the lip service to the concept of communication which is paid by those who say, 'Of course, nowadays you have to tell them,' while thinking, 'Why can't they just do as they're told?' It is frequently easy to gain acceptance for the idea that an employee publication should aim to bring employees news of the organization and an understanding of its affairs that they will not obtain from other sources. It is not usually so simple to establish that for this to be done adequately the editor needs to be fully informed.

And those two words do not mean the kind of information that comes in an occasional memo from top management telling the editor about an action that has already been taken. An editor must be in constant and free contact with all levels of management and given advance knowledge of policy and action decisions.

It is a mistake to think that an efficient news-gathering system that brings the editor information from all parts of the organization is enough. It is vital to ensure that there is a flow of information downwards from the top as well, if he is to interpret and present the organization successfully to the people who make it run. Many employee publications are started for the sole reason that it seems a popular idea. In fact, there are many practical questions to be asked before a sound beginning can be made.

Format and frequency will depend upon a number of actors: the nature of the readership, the budget available, the time and skill of the staff, the character of the organization and therefore of the flow of information that can be expected. To take an extreme example, there is little point in deciding to have a monthly tabloid newspaper for an organization with only a few hundred employees where major news stories occur infrequently and only the part-time services of an amateur editor are available. If the best story for an issue is yet another clutch of gold watch presentations, it is patently absurd to attempt to give it front page splash treatment. Not every organization can be expected to provide enough suitable copy and pictures for a tabloid newspaper once a month, however desirable this form of publication may be because of its acceptability to most readers and its ability to imbue stories with impact and immediacy.

The smaller and less event full concern might do better to consider a two-monthly magazine, when more mundane material can be made attractive through skilled editorial presentation. On the other hand, in a major concern much in the newspapers and often on radio and television, the speed of industrial or commercial coverage read or seen outside the organization by employees throws into question the worth of a monthly or even fortnightly internal newspaper or magazine, for the handling of topical issues as opposed to background material. Newspaper writing, sub-editing, and layout is a job for the professional. Magazine editing can, if necessary, be tackled at a less skilled editorial level, since graphic design can be given to an outside expert.

The relationship of content and visual presentation in a magazine is less close and less demanding than in a newspaper, where copy and layout go hand in hand. The magazine approach also offers easy means to group minor items into collective features, to balance content evenly without the newspaper's demand for a story or picture to dominate each page, and to establish a pattern for the presentation of regular items. The employees of any organization form a community of sorts; they have in common at least the fact that they all earn their living from the same source.

They have many other things in common, too, such as an interest in the births, marriages, and deaths, the retirements and anniversaries, the sporting achievements, and the social events of the community within which they work. However much an employee publication acts as a means of management communication and information, the parochial nest of each location is as important a part of its content as it is in every local newspaper in the land.

People want to read about people. The paper which is all management pill unsugared by stories about the readers themselves will fail even quicker than the magazine which is mainly head office news with little from the factories.

From the extreme of the multi-edition tabloids of the nationalized industries to the simple duplicated news-sheet serving one location, the need for a combination of management information and employee news is more or less the same. Also the same is the pattern of news-gathering, which must rely not only upon what the editor finds out for himself and learns from management sources, but upon a network of contacts around the factory, or correspondents in every store in the chain, or whatever is applicable. The duplicated news-sheer, if well written and neatly laid out, should not be despised.

In small organizations, or in separate locations where it can fill the gap between issues of a company publication, it can serve a useful purpose. Reliability of publication is another cardinal factor. Readers are used to commercial publications appearing on time, so the employee paper that is persistently late or misses an issue because the editor is busy on something else damages its acceptability and depreciates the value of its content.

If there is genuinely not enough material to fill a monthly magazine, then it should be a two-monthly or even a quarterly. If a quarterly cannot be sustained, then the publication should be forgotten and the money and effort applied to some other means of communication. In recent years there has been an increasing move towards the production of supplements to employee newspapers and magazines to deal with special events: the annual financial results, a relocation of offices, a new factory project, the purchase of an overseas subsidiary, anything of exceptional interest and importance. In many ways this is a healthy and reasonable technique, but perhaps it sometimes indicates that the management feel that major issues need more than the regular news service can provide. Does a national newspaper publish a supplement on the Budget or on a huge air crash? It usually copes with news of whatever magnitude within its normal structure. Should this not be the internal editor's aim too? Whatever the type and frequency of an employee publication, the first qualification for an editor is enthusiasm.

The second is often thought to be a comprehensive knowledge of the organization, but this is by no means correct. If the publication is to be lively, vital, interest-rousing, attractive, and able to compete successfully for readers' attention, then a professional editor is more likely to succeed than a long-term employee lacking in journalistic skills. One of the attributes of a journalist is that he can rapidly get under the skin of a community and discover what makes it tick. For the competent journalist, tackling a house journal is no different from moving from a local weekly to a specialist magazine.

An industrial editor should ideally be able to handle every aspect of news-gathering, feature writing, sub-editing, design and production—and often photography too—and also to be capable of interpreting and sustaining a clear editorial policy. Without a firm policy no employee publication can hope to succeed, but what that policy will be depends entirely upon the communication needs of the organization. This is a matter for study and decision by the editor and his management. When a publication has been running for some time, it is feasible to seek reader reactions to what they are being given, but a readership survey of any size and complexity is an occasion for seeking professional research advice. Experience has shown that it is pointless just asking employees what they would like: worthwhile answers cannot be expected from people with no concept of what is involved in creating a paper. The best employee publication possible will fail in its endeavors if satisfactory methods are not devised to get it to its readers. The decision on whether it should be distributed free to every employee or have some value put upon it by making a small charge is not one to be taken lightly.

The way in which each issue is sold or handed out needs careful consideration and endless policing; it is no use having the printers send a parcel to each location unless it is established that it is someone's duty to handle distribution and that adequate means are at his disposal. There is always a temptation to try to extend the use of an employee publication by sending it to an outside audience. There is some merit in considering distribution of a few copies selectively in the community surrounding a factory, or to trade union officials, or to the relevant specialist press, but no attempt should be made to use a publication with a strictly internal content for sales promotion purposes by sending it to customs.

They may be interested in the company, but they are not likely to care much about its employees. If there is a demand for a sales promotion or prestige magazine, then this should be handled separately. Here, as elsewhere in communication, it is a mistake to try to make one medium carry more than one message to more than one audience. There is no doubt industrial editing is now recognized as a highly specialized branch of journalism and of management, largely due to the efforts of the British Association of Industrial Editors. Its education courses provide detailed instruction in every facet of this area of employee communication and there are also several sound British books on the subject.

The periodical employee publication may be the center-piece of a organization's communication programme, but it cannot be expected to do everything by itself. There are always instances where a message needs to be conveyed more urgently and there are many long-term forms of communication for which a newspaper or magazine is not the most suitable medium.

Immediancy of communication can of course, most readily be achieved through the spoken word, but there are two problems, about calling general meetings of employees to pass on information and answer questions.

Firstly, work has to cease, or the meeting has to be called out of working hours when people may not want to stay; also with shift working it is difficult to get everyone together at once. Secondly, mass meetings will be seen as a means of by-passing the established union machinery or works council unless this is sorted out first with the officials concerned and explained to employees at the meeting itself. In general, a meeting called by the management to explain something should be reserved for emergencies, like a impending merger, and even then a carefully planned programme of informating senior staff, supervisors, and union officials in advance needs to be worked out. The public address system is theoretically a means of communication, but one better forgotten for general use.

For fire and imbalance calls, paging of individuals, and 'wallpaper' music it may be acceptable. As a method of covering anything more complex it is too impersonal and usually too inaudible. More recently, internal telephone systems have been used to communicate, maybe background information or maybe up-to-date news on a dispute, by pre-recorded messages played to employees who dial a pre-determined number. Limited experience has shown this to be a popular experiment. Closed-circuit television is a valuable aid for special occasions. If there is royal personage touring the plant, monitor sets in the departments not being visited can bring every employee into the event. If the company has contributed something vital to a new ocean liner, a land line link could involve every employee in the launching when only a few official representatives could attend in person. This is expensive but worth considering for its beneficial effect on morale.

Videotape, slide-tape presentations, film cassettes all offer alternate means of taking information to employee locations with all the impact that the moving picture can bring to the communication of information. For many companies the investment in equipment that is necessary is the barrier.

Because of expense, films can seldom be made slowly for internal communication purposes, except in the largest organizations. Sometimes they can share a use, as for example a yearly newsreel of company activities which could be shown to share-holders at the annual meeting, sent to overseas agents, and also distributed to every location for employees to see. Many general and sales films also have sufficient interest to be shown to employees who generally like to know what the organization is doing.

A quarterly bulletin sent from the managing director to all senior management with confidential information on how the company is doing; a monthly report in concise, pungent form from the plant manager to all foremen; a twice-yearly open letter from the top man to everyone in the company, written informally and with a facsimile signature—these simple forms of direct communication, if skillfully written and presented, can help solve problems both of short-term and long-term communications. If the company wins an export award or gains a massive order or is taking over a competitor, there is cause to consider explaining the facts through an open letter for urgent issue to everyone. Otherwise they will get the story—late, incomplete or inaccurate—from the press, from superiors only half aware of it themselves, or from the rumor mill.

If a company appears in the newspapers, there is usually interest in press-cutting displays to demonstrate that the world outside knows and, apparently, cars about hat has been achieved. The local press itself is an indirect means of communication with employees: they like to see evidence that the company is notable as part of the community and that its people and affairs are worth publication. One or two companies, deeply identified with their own communities, have even organized their own columns in the local press, although this is a somewhat artificial approach.

There is usually an interest, too, in seeing what the company does or what customers make from its products. If the factory makes the gearbox for a new motor scooter, then a local dealer will probably be willing to arrange an exhibition and demonstration of the machine and perhaps offer special purchase terms. If a company has both raw material an manufacturing plants, the employees in the former will like to see what the others make from their output; conversely, those in the manufacturing works may like to learn how the raw material is produced.

Expensively, but effectively, some companies provide touring shows of their products, either by display caravans or by display cases at each location with an exhibit changed monthly. With consumer goods, it is only common sense to make the most of enthusing the internal audience for the products, but with any type of business there is value in showing—in addition to telling—employees what happens and how. Within any office, shop or factory, there as a variety of items of information to be conveyed, some of them statutory, such as fire and health regulations. This is information which must be given to employees. There is also information which a management feels employees should have: the social club programme, the price of safety shoes, National Saving campaigns, the availability of mass X-ray facilities, and so on.

Usually these extremely variable pieces of information appear on a notice board, the most neglected means of communication in any organization. Torn posters for last autumn's cricket club dance, unread and voluminous minutes of the safety committee, a fire drill notice that is so faded it is unreadable, an ill-worded and badly duplicated announcement about the summer outing—these an similar failure to communicate murder uselessly together.

Organization, control, and the hand of the professional communicator can, with not a little trouble, convert a nasty mess into a modestly effective way of keeping the wheels of information turning.

Firstly, it is vital to establish responsibility for the design, maintenance, and siting of notice boards. Secondly, it is necessary to establish control over authorization to use the boards to display items, the size and nature of those items, and the length of time they remain. These are the tasks of the public relations man, with the assistance of whatever allies he can find in the personnel department, among the maintenance staff and the trade union or staff association officers. The potential content of a noticeboard is vast, so it is as well to try to define the various relevant categories and divide boards into sections. These might include union branch; works council; sports and social; safety and welfare; suggestion scheme; official; publicity; sales and wants, if personal use of the boards is allowed; and so on.

Design is a matter of taste and of suiting the information requirements of the situation. The rule for display is to be sure that everything is neat and bright, that all lettering is large enough to be read easily, and that the total effect is attention-getting. Commonsense and imagination should do the rest.

Messages to be read by people passing by should not contain more than a few words. A press release about an export order might run to 300 words; fifty words would be the right length for the noticeboard. The full minutes of the works council are too long to go on the noticeboard, and a digest of the main decisions should be all that is posted.

Constant change keeps attention alive and prevents material from agencies visibly. Permanent notices should be covered by glass or plastic to preserve them. The basic principle remains to convey information briefly and quickly. If the notices fail to meet this criterion, they should be altered, or the information conveyed in some other way.

A wall newspaper has different function. As its name implies, it is set in type and laid out like a newspaper, although one to be read by people standing before it at a distance of several feet.

This limits its uses, as the number of occasion on which people will stop to read something in which they have no inherent interest are relatively few. However, with skillful adaption of newspaper writing and layout techniques, using bold headlines, big pictures, short, crisp stories set in readily legible tyefaces, and predominantly dateless material, it is possible to create an eye-catching sheet which will cause some passers-by to stop and read.

The wall newspaper has been used effectively as a poster, too, by charities, religious bodies, and political organizations whose public audience could be expected to pass by only once. In an office or factory, the audience can be relied upon to pass by several times during the life of each issue and it may therefore be hoped that different items may be read on different occasions.

In most organizations there is a need to put information into the hands of employees in some more permanent form, perhaps for reference or training. There may be a welcome booklet as part of the introduction course, or factory hand book containing a variety of facts and figures of value in the working day, or a book of guidance on office produce for secretaries and clerks, or a safety manual, or a leaflet expanding the suggestion scheme and encouraging employees to participate, or a booklet issued to each man as he becomes eligible for the pension fund.

Responsibility for such material will probably lie with the personnel department, either at head office or in each location, but the public relations executive has a contribution to make. He is likely to have, or know how to obtain, the creative skills to make such publications more effective, Lively writing, clarity of explanation, bright illustrations, and attractive cover designs help to get the necessary messages across and are vital when it is remembered that personnel publications have to be intelligible to the lowest common denominator among employees. A further aspect which should not be ignored is that there may be special needs for part of the employee audience. Few people who are deaf admit it at first; many who are color-blind do not even know it.

The illiterate conceal the fact that they can barely read or write. Immigrant workers, whatever their educational level, find a new language difficult to comprehend, particularly when spoken in a regional accent or larded with slang phrases, or when written in technical terms or unthinking jargon. When a programme of internal communication is being devised and carried out their particular needs have to be borne in mind. As in so many areas of employee communication, this is a matter for consultation and co-operation with the personnel staff. In fact, they share not only the duty of trying to communicate effectively and to make the importance of good communication understood through all levels of management, but also the difficult task of trying to make communication a two-way affair.

Management needs to communicate to get work done and ought to communicate to ensure that employees understand what must be achieved, how and why. But employees can communicate too, not only through the official channels of the unions and joint consultative machinery, but directly as individuals through their immediate superiors and indirectly through formalized means such as suggestion schemes.

Nowadays, new techniques of information consultant, discussion and reporting back are being evolved. Briefing groups, in which small meetings of employees are held regularly for their manages to keep them up-to-date on developments, and similar systems which create the opportunity for face-to-face communication, asking questing and receiving answers, offer something physical impossible in a house publication and most other means of communication. For that matter, normal training programme provide a convenient means of direct communication and a chance to learn employee attitudes at first hand; sadly their potential in this way is usually neglected. An atmosphere in which upward communication is fostered can any arise in an organization in which there is a genuine desire on the part of the management to hear as well as to speak.

The personnel manager and the public relations man have listening posts; they are almost invariably the sort of people to whom others talk and their duties mean that they have contacts in every part of an organization and at every level. They need to retain their objectivity—no 'organization man' can ever be expected to present an unbiased view of the organization he works for—and to be able to face up to the difficult task of telling top management what employees think about them and the organization.

Their subjective judgment can from time to time be reinforced by scientific investigation and measurement of employees' attitudes and reactions. To persuade a management to undertake the expensive and troublesome task of endeavoring to determine employees' attitudes is not easy but the result can be rewarding, particularly in organizations with labour difficulties, poor productivity, heavy absenteeism or similar troubles. Such research is a subject for expert advice and execution.

The scope for employee relations activities is almost limitless. The problems of all organizations have certain elements in common—particularly inadequate communication—but no two are exa.tly the same, so the priorities and the methods to be used can only be decided after study of an individual situation and the character an atmosphere of a concern. The public relations man could do worse, however, than keep the subject constantly alive in the mind of management by sharing with them his nightmares brought on by bad communication. Most managers have their own chamber of horrors on this subject, like the case of the thousands of workers at a Midlands car factory who first learned of their impending redundancy from the local evening paper as they came out of the gates! Unbelievably, this was in the second half to he twentieth century.

8

Corporate Planning

Planning activities represent an expenditure or investment of company resources. Such an expenditure can be justified only if the benefits attained sufficiently out weight the costs incurred. Although some of the benefits of planning are hard to quantify, they are nonetheless or a new opportunity uncovered can easily offset the costs of planning. Furthermore, the costs of planning can be compared to the costs of insuring against serious strategic errors or missed opportunities in the marketplace. Being first down the road is of little advantage if one is on the wrong road. Planning helps to choose the right roads to achieving company goals. The need for planning is thus twofold: first, to avoid errors in the market, and second, to recognize opportunities and challenges in order to meet them effectively. Other "fringe benefits" of planning are the following:

1. It encourages systematic forward-thinking by management.
2. It results in a better international coordination of company efforts.

3. It leads to better preparation for emergencies and obviates the likelihood of costly improvisation.
4. It provides for continuity of effort and direction.
5. It gives participating executives a stronger sense of their integration with the rest of the company activities, that is, between subsidiary and parent, or between the different corporate functions.
6. It provides for a continuing review of operations and a continuing education for participating management.

The planning *process* is similar in both domestic and international operations. Our discussion therefore will merely highlight the ways in which planning is modified in the multinational company.

Short-range planning for corporate management we will define as the establishment of corporate targets and the preparation of operating programs to meet those targets. The time span will usually be one operating year, whether a fiscal or a calendar year. IBM World Trade Corporation uses a two-year operating plan but revises it annually. Although the corporate management plan is just part of the firm's overall plan for international business, it is the only part that concerns us here. The overall short-range plan for corporate management can be composed of several elements, including, for example, a corporate plan for each foreign market, plans for individual product lines, and a plan for international product development. The amount of planning and the complexity of the plan will depend on the size and complexity of the firm's international business.

The company must analyse its current situation as to the controllable and uncontrollable variables in each of its markets. What are the important characteristics of demand, competition, distribution, law, and so on? What problems and opportunities are evident in the current situation?

Given a good understanding of where the firm is in its different markets around the world, management can propose realistic objectives that are appropriate for each market. These objectives should be challenging, but they should also be reachable in terms of the analysis of the firm's position in the market. The objectives must also be specific and spelled out in meaningful terms if they are to be operational.

Once the manager has identified concrete objectives for his foreign markets, the must prepare a plan of action to reach these objectives. His approach will include arranging the various elements of the marketing mix and assigning specific responsibilities to marketing personnel and to the marketing functions. The marketing plan could be broken down in more detail, but these three basic elements are sufficient for our purpose. They provide an adequate frame-work for discussing the planning problems of the manager. The short-range planning task of the international marketer has two basic parts: (1) developing the plan for each foreign market and (2) integrating the national plans into a coherent international plan.

Although some planning must be done for each of the firm's foreign markets, the amount and nature of the planning will depend on the firm's volume of business and level of involvement in each market. In markets where the firm does a small volume of business, the amount of planning it can afford to do will be small also, unless, of course, the firm has a goal of greatly expanding its business in such a market. Thus the amount of planning may be related to the potential volume of business in a country as well as to the present volume. The second major constraint on national market planning is the nature of the firm's commitment to the market. We will examine this constraint before discussing the planning process itself.

Exporting: When the firm sells to an importer or distributor in a market, it is not physically present to do a situation analysis or to design an appropriate strategy for the market. Although the firm can compensate partially for this limitation by visiting export markets, the planning process is seriously hindered if the firm does not have a continuing personal company presence in the market. In its export markets, the firm must rely on its local representative for most of the data for all three parts of the plan. The representative's interest in cooperating as well as his ability to do so may leave much to be desired. A good reporting and information system will help to make the best of a weak situation, especially when the distributor can be induced to operate.

Licensing: In markets where its only representation is through licensees, the firm is in about the same position as with exporting: It has no personal company presence in the market, and its licensee will cooperate in the planning process only to the degree that it is to his own interest. One factor, however, probably places the licenser in a stronger planning position than the exporter. The licenser's business is usually more important to the licensee than the exporter's is to the importer. This may be reflected in a stronger contract as well as more rigid information reporting requirements in a licensing agreement. Furthermore, the sales of a particular licensee may be related to the sales of other products of the company, 'making him more dependent on the licensor.

Joint ventures: Joint Ventures offer more favorable circumstances for planning; the firm does have its own personal representation in the foreign market, enabling it to make a better situation analysis. The joint venture arrangement can present serious difficulties for the planner, however, the local partner may have objectives and strategies different from those of the international firm.

He also will want the situation analysis conducted from the viewpoint of the joint venture rather than fro that of the international corporation. Therefore, even the joint venture operation cannot be integrated easily into the international planning process. Joint ventures tend to take on a separate life of their own. The problem diminishes as the percent of the international firm's ownership increases, which is a partial explanation for many international firms' preference for wholly owned ventures.

Wholly owned subsidiaries: A wholly owned subsidiary, whether for marketing along or for both production and marketing, elements the problems encountered in the other kinds of involvement. The corporate management planner can count on company personnel to participate in the planning process. The international planner and those working in the various national subsidiaries will probably have a line relationship. The focus of our discussion here will be the planning process when wholly owned subsidiaries are involved; the treatment will not be complete, of course, because the international company must plan also for those markets where it has a lesser degree of involvement. However, a discussion of planning with wholly owned operations will gives an adequate picture of the planning process. Then the appropriate limitations and modifications can be noted for those countries where the firm has a lesser involvement. Besides degree of involvement, another variable to consider in the international planning process is that the firm's product line also may vary from market to market requiring the planning to be modified accordingly.

As the international firm develops planning expertise, it can make this expertise available to all its subsidiaries, thereby cnabling the subsidiaries to save the time and money involved in developing the expertise on their own. In each of its markets the firm examines the same variables-for example, demand, competition, law, and so on-and uses a standard analytical and reporting format. Then when the international planner receives the national plans he is better able to interpret and evaluate them. In addition to the relevant variables in the local situation, the national analysis should identify the problems and opportunities expected to arise during the period of the plan. These problems and opportunities expected to arise during the period of the plan. These problems and opportunities will trigger and guide the strategic planning. The actual conduct of the situation analysis is primarily a marketing research job. The format used is derived from that employed in the firm's domestic market. Undoubtedly international and local market modifications of the domestic approach would be necessary, but it provides a useful starting point.

The more carry over from the domestic to the foreign planning approach, the better comparisons the firm can make of opportunities in the two areas. Such comparisons are necessary for a firm that wants to optimize its performance on an international basis. The techniques used for national planning also probably will derive from domestic practice. These techniques usually are most highly developed in the firm's domestic operations. The firm should assure that the best planning tools and models are used in each of its markets.

Having determined its current situation, each national subsidiary must set objectives to be attained during the period of the plan. Traditionally, objectives have been set by extrapolation or by some manager's rule-of thumb or whim. The purpose of the situation analysis is to enable objectives to be set more realistically. The objectives should relate the resources of the firm to the problems and opportunities in the local market; in addition, they should be spelled our specifically for the various products of the firm and for the different marketing functions. The national subsidiary should play a major role in setting its own market targets. Its participation will help to keep the targets related to the market and assure the firm of the subsidiary's cooperation in reaching them. The actual objectives in the national plan should be quite detailed and specific. Some items that could be included are the following:

1. Target sales of each product, in units and dollars
2. Target market share by product
3. Target number of new distribution outlets
4. Target percent of brand awareness
5. A new product introduction with a specified sales or distribution tin level
6. Local market test of new product by target date
7. Export target of some dollar or percent-of-sales level
8. Specific marketing research activities to be completed

The analysis of the company's situation in a particular foreign market leads to the formulation of specific objectives or performance targets. The role of strategy is to determine the firm's general approach to reaching its goals. Tactics indicate the specific tools and programs that will be used to implement the strategy. For example, a firm might have an objective of reaching a certain sales volume or market share in a country. Its strategy might be to compete on a nonprice basis by emphasizing product quality, by introducing new and improved products, and by making a strong promotional effort.

Its operating plan would then spell out in detail the particular tools and techniques to implement the strategy, including an appropriate budget. For instance, the plan would identify the product development activities for the year; the specific new product to be introduced, its timing and marketing program; the advertising program, including appeals, amount and timing, and media schedules; and so on.

The operating plan that spells out the firm's tactics is usually the most comprehensive and lengthy part of the short-range plan. It includes a calendar of events; the assignment of responsibility to the marketing people in the firm and to those working with the firm, such as distributors, advertising agencies, and marketing research groups; and the budget allocations to facilitate the fulfillment of these responsibilities.

Large companies may even use PERT or some other critical-path scheduling technique as part of their operating plan. The corporate manager's responsibility is to oversee the development of such short-range operating plans for each of this foreign markets. To keep his task manageable and to operate efficiently, however, he must realize some synergism or economies of scale in his planning effort. His efficiency can be improved by the proper division of labor in the organization and by the use of comparative analysis.

The firm's overall organization for planning is a topic best pursued elsewhere. Our interest here is in the organizational relationships in corporate management planning. *Who* contributes what to national operating plans? What are the respective roles of corporate headquarters and the national subsidiaries?We are assuming that neither completely centralized nor completely decentralized planning is desirable. Instead, some kind of interactive planning is most effective, drawing on the best capabilities of each part of the company. From the center, the manager and corporate headquarters should contribute planning know-how. Based on its domestic and international experience, the firm should have developed planning expertise which it can pass on to all its foreign operations so their planning effectiveness is improved. This transfer includes planning guidelines and outlines, a planning schedule, and perhaps the training of subsidiary personnel in planning.

If the national subsidiary is not a self-contained operation, corporate head-quarters can provide information inputs for the situation analysis as to how the subsidiary's operations are related on the supply and/or demand side to the rest of the firm's international operations. The international marketer will, of course, also have his own ideas as to appropriate objectives for each market. Because of his international experience, he will have valuable ideas about effective strategies and tactics too. Thus the international marketer contributes to all three aspects of the national operating plan: (1) he give guidance and information to the situation analysis; (2) he gives a corporate viewpoint as to the desirability and appropriateness of various subsidiary objectives; and (3) he transfers corporate international know-how about strategies and tactics.

The national subsidiary obviously must do the major part of the actual planning, but in this planning, it has an advantage over its strictly national competitors. Because of help and know-how received from its corporate parent, the subsidiary of the multinational firm should be a more effective, sophisticated planner. The major contributions of the local subsidiary are (1) the actual work of preparing the plan and (2) local knowledge. Whereas the international parent has planning expertise, only the subsidiary has the intimate local knowledge needed for a realistic plan. Most of the hard data for the plan, therefore, must be supplied locally. The plan resulting from the data is more effective because of the complementary contributions of the two parts of the multinational firm.

The actual planning process will often work as follows:

1. The subsidiary receives planning guidelines and schedules from the parent.
2. The subsidiary prepares an operating plan and submits it to the parent.
3. Parents and subsidiary negotiate to reconcile differences about the plan.
4. A compromise results in an agreed upon plan and budget which become the operating program for the next year.

Then final role of the corporate planner is to coordinate the national plans into an effective international plan for all the firm's markets. This coordination is not done after all of the national plans have been completed; rather, it must start at the beginning of the planning process and continue with it. Otherwise, the national plans will come up with conflicting claims on company resources and require expensive and time-consuming revision. Therefore the coordination begins with guidelines sent to each national operation at the beginning of the planning period. National plans may be modified during the planning process, but the communications between subsidiary and parent must be such that these changes can be coordinated within the overall international plan.

Comparative analysis is not a new topic but rather a continuation of our discussion of the role of corporate headquarters in the international planning process. The ability of the manager to contribute to the subsidiary's planning derives from two sources, the firm's domestic experience and its international experience. If the manager has analyzed carefully the company's operations in all of its markets, certain patterns, groupings, and observations probably have emerged. He will begin to understand in what ways these markets are alike and in what ways they are different. At the simplest level, he might note a difference between industrialized and nonindustrialized countries. At a more sophisticated level, he might find that his foreign markets fall into three, four, or five categories or groupings according to their behavior on the sale and use of his firm's products. He can begin to classify countries on the basis of characteristics that are relevant for his marketing activities. Comparative analysis is an attempt by the firm to maximize the value of its multinational experience.

Comparative analysis in international marketing involves three steps. First, the relevant variables or dimensions of national markets must be identified. Here these variables are those that affect the firm's markets and the similarities, differences, and patterns or groupings that emerge must be noted. Third, the collected data must be classified and analyzed.

The first step, identifying the relevant variables, is a form of model building whereby the firm gains an understanding of its interactions with the market. Although such a model need not be, and probably is not, a complex mathematical formulation, still every firm has some model or picture of how it relates to its markets. This model may be implicit, but it is more useful if made explicit. The second step, measuring markets on these dimensions, is part of the marketing research and information system activity of the firm. The third step, analysis and classification, is the task of the manager and his staff, requiring both experience and analytical skill.

The contribution of comparative analysis to international planning lies in setting objectives and determining strategies. The tendency and temptation in setting objectives is to consider each national market as unique. The national subsidiary likes to see itself that way because its power is enhanced vis-a-vis the parent. If the subsidiary is indeed one of a kind, it plays a bigger role in setting its own objectives and evaluating its own performance. If instead the international manager, through careful analysis of the firm's multinational experience, can determine that a particular subsidiary or market bears similarities to others he an then play a greater role in setting objectives.

He can perhaps raise subsidiary objectives and ask for greater performance if his comparative analysis has shown that this is reasonable for subsidiaries unpopular with subsidiary management precisely because it claims its situation is different from that in countries with which it is being unfavorably compared. A well-done comparative analysis and classification, however, assures that the subsidiary is being compared with others in a similar situation.

In determining strategies and tactics for particular markets, comparative analysis is also useful. If markets have been identified and grouped according to their similarity on the strategic and tactical variables, the international marketer can help to plan strategy for a particular market based on his firm's experience in these other similar markets.

A pharmaceutical firm used A, B, C, D rating or classification system to guide its detail men in scheduling call frequencies for doctors. The doctors who had the greatest influence on adoption and use of an ethical drug had an a rating, and so on. This system was used in the firm's domestic operations. The international division of the company adopted a similar rating or classification system for foreign markets. It was used to prepare the promotional strategies and budgets for these markets. An electronics company was studying sales and performance data of one of its major product lines in foreign markets. The various analyses showed clearly three distinct market groupings for this product line. This led to a change in the firm's international planning. Instead of preparing individual planning guidance for each of the foreign markets, planners began preparing guidance for three groups of countries, they added just one page of individual material for each country to handle anything that was peculiar to it.

We have been looking at planning especially in terms of countries where the firm has subsidiaries. Comparative analysis can help the exporter too. The exporter's planning is handicapped by his lack of continuing first-hand contact with his markets. As he accumulates experience in a large number of markets over a period of years, however, he an partially overcome this handicap. An analogy might be useful here. The parent of a ten-year-old child has some understanding of ten-year-olds and can make some predictions about their behavior; but a person who has taught ten-year-old children for a number of years should have a better understanding and be able to make better predictions. The company that has only domestic operations is like the parent; its understanding of other country markets is limited. The experienced exporter is like the teacher; and if he has organized and analyzed his multinational experience, he should overcome, at least partially, the handicap of a lack of personal presence in his export markets.

For present purposes, we will define international long-range planning as the analysis of the future international environment of company operations, the establishment of company goals for that environment, and the determination of overall strategy to reach those goals. As in short-range planning, the firm is concerned with expected change and what it means for the firm. However, several distinctions separate short-range and long-range planning.

One is the time span: short-range plans usually are for one year, which means a one-year horizon and planning cycle; long-range plans more commonly encompass five or more years. The long-range planning process is more an ongoing than a recurring activity, and it is often relatively independent of the annual short-range planning cycle. Actual company practice varies as to the time horizon of the various plans.

For example, CPC International plans on a one, five, and ten-year basis. The five-year plan is considered an extension of the one-year plan and is therefore more operational than long range. The ten-year plan for them is the true long-range plan where new environments and markets are considered.

A more important distinction between the short-range and long-range plans is in the environmental assumptions each makes. Parameters considered fixed in the short run become variables in the long run. In fact, one of the major purposes of long-range planning is to identify and evaluate the potential, but distant, changes in the environment so as to prepare to respond to them effectively.

The following items are among those that are probably constant for the short-run but not for the long-run plan: the level of technology, or state of the art; the nature of the demand for the firm's products; the company's product line; the number of countries in which the firm is operating; the firm's level of involvement in foreign markets.

For example, the traditional concern of long-range planning was merely to determine what facilities and financing might be needed to meet future demand for the firm's existing products. Today, long-range planning is more concerned about what the firm's future products and markets should be. On the international side, these additional questions might arise; Should we be selling products or services abroad? What new markets should we be in? What should we be doing in East-West trade? What kind of involvement should we have in foreign markets?

Another difference in long-range planning is the amount of detail or specificity required. As noted above, the short-range plan must be very specific, as it is a sort of job description by which individuals and subsidiaries will be evaluated. By contrast, the long-range plan gives no marching orders but merely alerts the company to approaching change and gives general guidelines as to further investigation. Long-range planning is a kind of early warning system for possibilities of approaching change. However, until the exact nature of the change can be identified-that is, until it comes closer in time -no specific directions can be given.

In contrast to the detailed operating plan and budget resulting from short-range planning, the result of long-range planning is usually general memoranda given to key individuals or committees for their further consideration. Of course, the shorter the plan's time span, more specific its coverage must be.

The *personnel* needs in long-range planning are also different from those in short-range planning. Operating personnel in the subsidiaries and in the international division are involved in short-range planning, but long-range planning concerns staff people removed from day-to-day operations.

For instance, long-range planning requires a higher level or executive involvement; a special long-range planning committee or similar arrangement is likely to include key executives on a regular even though infrequent basis. TRW, for example, has an annual retreat where its top executives take such a look into the future.

Long-range planning further requires a much greater input of outside expertise. Because the firm is concerned about long-run changes in the economic, social, political, and technological area, the necessary expertise usually will be well beyond the capability of the in-house staff. For example, Business International has published research reports on long-ranges international planning in which a large part of the material is supplied by scholars in political science, sociology, economics, and engineering.

Now that we have distinguished between long-range and short-range planning, we should not the link between them. At some point in time, the changes and strategies identified in a long-range plan must become part of a short range plan. That is, the early warnings eventually must take shape and become specific marching orders. In this way, the long-range plan provides a frame-work within which to design the short-range plan. As the long-range planners point out changes in the environment and develop broad strategies appropriate to meet these changes, the short-range planners see that the required adjustments in products, technology, markets, organization, and level of involvement are made gradually through a series of short-range operating plans.

For example, if the company's long-range plan indicates a seven-year target entry into a particular new market with certain kinds of products and levels of involvement, short-range plans will be patterned in such a way that each one leads the company progressively closer to meeting these long-range goals. Thus the two kinds of planning stand in an important relationship to one another, the long range dominant over the short. This link, however, does not require that the two planning activities be closely related within the organization but only that appropriate communication exist between them.

Although the long-range and short-range planning processes include the same steps, these steps are carried our differently. The first step in long-range planning is again analysis of the situation, but here the situation has yet to take place, and in an environment well hidden from the planner. The rationale for long-range planning is that if the firm can get a picture of future developments, it can avoid being overtaken by events. Perhaps it can even gain a competitive advantage by being prepared for these events. Therefore, management must try to peer through the clouds that veil the future. Dimensions of the future are not difficult to define in general terms: they include every factor or variable that can have a significant influence on the firm's success.

1. Population-global and in individual markets
2. Demography-education, literacy, health
3. Income-size and growth of foreign markets
4. World trade -growth and patterns
5. International relations-Cold War, regionalism, commercial policy
6. Technology-relating to the firm's products and operations
7. Political environment-nationalism, relations with host governments
8. International business-foreign operations and international competition

Extrapolation: How can the planner identify and evaluate the future environment? One common way to look ahead is through extrapolation of past trends. This is the easiest and most convenient method. but it has severe limitations. It requires the assumption that the future will be like the past. Only more so, thereby eliminating possible forecast of breakthroughs and new developments. Nevertheless, extrapolation may well be one useful input to the planner's view of the future. Any projection of the future involves uncertainty, and the planner needs inputs, from all possible sources in order to make the most informed prediction. Thus he may want to have extrapolations to compare against other kinds of estimates. Of course, extrapolation works better for some kinds of variables than for others, being probably more useful for determining population or world-trade trends than political or technological developments. If extrapolating population growth rates, the planner can look at the factors determining population changes. In a given country, he would look not only at birth rates and death rates but also at government population policies, family planning programs, and religious and cultural influences.

Such an approach taken to each of the important parameters of the future environment can yield a range of estimates for each parameter. Although this method is more satisfying from a logical point of view, it is not guaranteed to be more accurate than an extrapolation. For this reason, the planner will find it helpful to use both methods and compare the results. Such a dual approach will offer better understanding and insights. Mathematical and computer models can be build around this approach, but much of the data are hard to quantify, and the amount of conjecture and uncertainty increases, the farther one looks into the future, if such models are to be operational, they may have to wait for advances in the state of the art.

Outside expertise: We have assumed that the first two approaches to divining the future are conducted by the planning manager or his staff, if he has one. In many cases of long-range planning, the use of outside expertise to supplement these efforts will be desirable. For many parameters of the external environment, the people most knowledgeable about the future are likely to be outside the firm, in academic or research organizations. For other parameters, executives from various company departments and from foreign operations will have the greatest expertise. In every instance, the best inputs should be obtained, assuming the cost in reasonable. One special technique is available for getting the best guess about the future of a given parameter from a group of experts. It is called the "Delphi technique."

Although named after the Oracle of Delphi in ancient Greece, the Delphi technique was developed by the Rand Corporation in about 1950. Many hundreds of corporations are considering its use today for their long-range planning, and in view of this growing acceptance, we will give a brief description of the steps involved: First, a panel of experts on the particular problem at hand is drawn from both inside and outside the company. Second, each expert makes a forecast, anonymously. Third, each panelist gets a composite feedback of the other panelists' gets a composite feedback of the other panelists' answers. Fourth, a second round of forecasting begins. From then on the cycle is repeated, perhaps continuing for several more rounds. Because the forecasts are anonymous, each panelist feels more free to change his mind and less committed to defending his original idea. Successive iterations are considered to improve the individual answers and to add up to a better group judgment. It is basically a form of consensus forecasting. One American company using the Delphi technique is TRW, which has fourteen panels at work with an average of seventeen experts each. Such a sizable effort would be impossible in smaller companies, but a similar approach could be used.

Once the best possible estimate of the future environment has been made, setting company objectives is a much simpler task, and one that does not require complex approaches or outside expertise. In deciding on the company's international posture, management must consider not only its international involvement but also the desired relation or integration between its domestic and international operations. It must set long-range goals for finance, production, personnel, and R & D, as well as for marketing. We will confine our discussion to such long-range corporate management goals as the firm's international product line, the number of foreign markets, and the nature of the firm's involvement in them. Goals must be set for the whole company, as well as for product lines or divisions and for country subsidiaries.

In setting long-range international marketing objectives, comparative analysis again can be useful. Let us consider first the case of planning for new market entry. As a firm expands its international business, it will want to enter new markets. How should it choose these new markets. One way is to screen the potential markets, to rank them according to the relevant criteria for selection, and then to make a more detailed study of the better candidate markets. In this latter area, comparative analysis can help the evaluation.

Let us assume that the firm has been operating over the years in many different countries at different levels of development. A level of development in this context does not necessarily refer to economic development but rather to whatever market development or classification scheme is meaningful in terms of the company's experience. These countries are classified, for example, as A, B C, or D countries according to criteria important to the firm. In the list of new market candidates, the countries probably also can be classified on an A, B, C, D basis.

As the planner analyzes the reasons for the firm's success or failure in present A, B, C and D markets, he has a higher probability of success in identifying the better markets among the new candidates. They would be those most like successful existing markets. Of course, the comparisons between present and potential markets are never perfect because each country is unique in some respects. Nevertheless, a comparative analysis that organizes the experience of the firm in a meaningful way should yield a more complete evaluation than will an analysis based only on an *ad hoc* evaluation of individual countries.

A second situation where comparative analysis can help the planner is in setting objective for changing the firm's posture in a market. This can mean changing from exports to local production, expanding or changing the product line, or changing the ownership pattern (expanding or contracting equity). Too often, a firm's change of posture results from government action or competitive pressure rather than from its own planning. A firm with experience in countries at different levels of development-says, A, B, C, and D countries again—should be better prepared. As it analyzes this experience, it should discover patterns in its own development. Countries moving from a D level to a C level may be ripe for the introduction of a new product or line ahead of competition.

For example, an executive with a large American food company developed just such an approach for planning his international product line. Countries moving from a C level to a B level might be ready for local production in place of exports, or a joint venture rather than a licensing operation. The point is that by studying its historical development in all of its markets, the firm should be able to formulate some "model" or understanding of its market development which will in turn enable its planners to predict important turning points when a change of posture is appropriate.

The long-range plan is quite vague compared to the great detail of the short-range plan. This difference is especially evident in the area of strategy formulation. Long-range corporate management strategy includes plans for the variables in the marketing mix plus other company activities that relate to the marketing program. Among the major elements are the following: (1) the design of the product development activity that leads to the international product line of the future; (2) the laying out of steps for entering the new markets where the firm will change its level of involvement in present markets to that which it feels will be appropriate in some future period; (4) the design of the firm's international logistics to meet its future international market situation as well as the future level of technology and trade restrictions.

We will not go into the many other aspects of long-range strategy except to mention the corporate management intelligence operation. Long-range plans are made on the basis of data that are very "old" in terms of the seven or ten-year target of the plan.

To allow for appropriate mid-course adjustments and corrections (as in space exploration), a good monitoring system is necessary. With the growth of the firm's international involvement and a steadily changing environment, most companies need to improve their information system as part of their long-range strategy. Many firms have invested much in their information system for domestic operations. As their international business grows, the same kind of sophistication will be needed for international intelligence.

Comparative analysis again: Formulation of long-range strategies is another area where comparative analysis can help the planner. In preparing strategy for a foreign market, or group of markets, the planner can again draw on his multinational experience. International marketers frequently have observed patterns or stages of market development insofar as their firm's products are concerned.

Thus it may be that European distribution patterns are following American developments of one or more decades ago. This knowledge can be of great help in planning company distribution strategy for European markets. One manager found that his firm's experience with the disappearance of resale price maintenance (*rpm*) in the United States was very helpful to him in planning his European strategy, because the same trend away from rpm was occurring in Europe. To the extent that American marketing practices are precursors of developments elsewhere, this kind of comparison gives the American firm an edge in planning foreign market strategy.

Not only in comparing foreign operations with those in the United States can lead-lag relationships be found. Often the more fruitful comparisons will be between the firm's experience in foreign markets at different levels of development. Experience in France might be useful in planning strategies for former French colonies, for example.

One firm found that consumption of some of its synthetic-fiber products in Argentina followed the pattern observed in its Italian operations, but with a several-year lag. This information obviously would aid planning product and marketing strategy for Argentina. Another firm, in its production planning for less developed countries, found that the best model was not the United States operation but the Brazilian. The operation in Brazil was not at an intermediate level, and its current or recent experience was much closer to the kinds of problems encountered in countries lower on the development scale. These examples show that, in order to be most useful, comparative analysis must be truly multinational or global. If comparisons are made only on the basis of United States experience, or only within a geographic region—say, Latin American—the value of the analysis is lessened.

Long-range planning generally requires less participation by the national subsidiaries and more by the international division and corporate headquarters than does short-range planning. Three reasons for this are that long-range planning requires much less of a commitment by the national subsidiary, the kind of information required for long-range planning is of a different and broader nature than that ordinarily available to local operations, and that the long-range plan is strategic, not operational, and therefore requires centralization.

Decisions must be made at the overall corporate level on certain basic questions: (1) What business should we be in tomorrow? (2) What markets should we be in? (3) What should be the division of our efforts between international and domestic? Once the corporation has answered these questions, the international division can plan within the guidelines given by the answers. The next step is to get some inputs from the regional headquarters and/or the national subsidiaries. Even though country operations play the lesser role in long-range planning, they still should participate to some extent. By their participation they will not only add viewpoints from different environments, but they also may contribute valuable insights not forthcoming from the corporate level, where a certain intellectual conformity may exist. Furthermore, the firm will benefit from improved subsidiary morale if they have a voice in shaping their own future.

At an early stage is his investigation of foreign market possibilities, the manager must make tentative regarding the place of foreign operations in the firm's total picture and the general form that such operations will take within the corporate organizational structure.

The basic decision relates to the firm's commitment to international operations: Is the company planning to operate internationally on the basis primarily of export, licensing, or perhaps manufacturing, or is it aiming to go all the way to multinational or true international operations? Having made some tentative policy decisions along these lines, management may then proceed to determine where within the corporate structure the international operations will fit: whether as a department reporting to sales, an international division, a separate international corporation, or an international holding or management company, for example. The factors influencing these decisions are many and complex, and there are no ready answers to the questions management asks.

The manufacturing firm may very well decide that, initially at least, the best way to enter a particular market is to ship the finished goods through an importer, agent, distributor, or company sales office to customers in the market. This system has obvious advantages in terms of minimizing investment in fixed facilities and hence hedging risks; on the other hand, it usually means payment of tariffs and a less favorable reception in the market. The agency arrangement was for many years the most common means of entering an overseas market. Gradually agencies have been replaced in many markets with sales or marketing subsidiaries, but the agency remains an important channel of international distribution.

Although the agency arrangement is relatively inexpensive and requires little or no effort on the part of the manufacturer. It does limit his ability to control the market. The advantage of not being faced with the problem of organizing and maintaining an organization of one's own carries with it the drawback of having to be satisfied with limited coverage. Middlemen frequently cannot handle large-volume orders.

Their financial resources may not permit the maintenance of minimum inventories and their staff may not include the technical men that are needed. The agent would, however, be more knowledgeable of local market conditions. Moreover, as in Egypt, tariff changes, exchange restrictions, and import curbs may result in the virtual exclusion of the manufacturer from certain markets except through agents.

Historically, companies that entered the export field were concerned primarily with the selection of distributor organizations in the local market to handle their products. As a rule, these distributors were assumed to have adequate merchandising facilities to stock, sell, and advertise the products, develop the markets, secure selling prices to reimburse them for their costs, and leave them a reasonable profit.

An occasional visit by the exporting company's sales representative and a return visit by the distributor were deemed sufficient personal and business contacts. Letters and cables were expected to do the rest, particularly when the volume of sales did not justify extensive traveling abroad. As both local and foreign competition became more intensive, more sales help, such as systematic visits by sales representatives, arrangements for them to call on leading customers with the distributor, increased advertising assistance, and training of distributor personnel, might be offered.

Between the two world wars, exchange limitations and import restrictions led to widespread building abroad of manufacturing facilities in the principal markets. Such plants served the market in the country and in some instances, the natural markets served by other manufacturers located in that country. Usually, the former distributors were unable to handle the new sales, and therefore new marketing organizations often patterned after the sales organization of the parent were built.

During and after World War II, many countries producing raw material has tried some makeshift arrangements for local manufacture moreover, nationalist sentiments were leading to a desire for industrial self-sufficiency in most countries. Traditional manufacturing countries that had their economies ravaged during the war were making desperate attempts to get back on their feet. These conditions resulted in a series of currency restrictions and trade barriers.

New equipment and technical assistance under the United States aid programs, coupled with the restrictions referred to above, helped most of these countries get back into the world markets or, in some instance, keep traditional exporters out of their markets. By the 1950s, overseas distribution activity was undergoing dynamic changes. Many companies could no longer think of overseas markets in terms of outlets for their surplus production. No longer could a company passively wait for orders from abroad; it had to seek out sales aggressively. Proposals to establish overseas operations were measured no longer in terms of effort required but in terms of the potential profit.

Because of these changing conditions, there was a tendency to move away from a system of manufacturers' agents or distributors. "Should we shift from the agency system? What from should our organization abroad take? How much would be tied up in it; and above all, would it be a safe investment?" These questions began to trouble many exporters when they reexamined the markets to which they had been exporting.

The answer to the first question was, in many instances, in the affirmative: either the market was growing so that an agent could no longer handle it, or it was getting smaller because of restrictions from local governments and competition from local manufacturers. The answers to the other questions were more difficulty. For many, the answer lay in increased investment in, and attention to, overseas markets.

Under a branch sales operation the manufacturer, through active instead of passive market exploitation, typically has greater control over the markets and the sales effort. Such control may prove expensive and time-consuming. The sales force may have to be built with men unfamiliar with the market or with nationals unfamiliar with the product and marketing techniques.

A certain volume of sales would be necessary before such an organization would prove profitable. From a tax point of view, as long as the branch makes losses, such losses can be charged to the parent company. If it makes profits, the parent usually pays the maximum taxes payable. In addition, as a company operating in a foreign country, the parent company is liable to legal action in the foreign country.

The United States government's antitrust action against Massey-Ferguson, reported in the *Financial Post* of May 23, 1964, would appear to indicate that the parent company may come under litigation abroad even if the overseas operation is through a subsidiary.

When operating through a subsidiary, a lower overall tax is normally paid; and even the impact of this can be shifted by changing the date on which the subsidiary pays its dividends. Funds saved from such tax advantages will be available for investment overseas. Such an arrangement also allows for complete control over the markets, greater economies due to (usually) lower labor costs, and greater proximity of management to markets, etc. Perhaps the most important advantage is that all facets of the business-product, pricing, selling, and advertising-are under unified control.

On the other hand, establishing a subsidiary may be expensive and may thus require a larger volume of business to justify itself. Foreign governments may not take very kindly to organizations owned outside their borders and may enact legislation unfavorable to the foreign company. Public opinion may also be unfavorable if local personnel are not employed in key positions, even if it should prove difficult to obtain qualified personnel in the country. What is the advantage of setting up a wholly owned subsidiary rather than a branch operation? There are a number of tax and financial considerations that must be examined, such as:

1. The nature of the business. Does the company make more money from sales or manufacturing?
2. The company's general investment policy and relation of foreign to domestic assets. Does it desire to start with little capital and grow with earnings? Does it desire to keep foreign and domestic assets and or liabilities separate?
3. The pattern of earnings. If the foreign operation is going to be operated at a loss for some time, or if some of many foreign units are going to be losers while the others are profitable, it would probably be best to operate them as branches.
4. The future local capitalization. If it is proposed to admit local capital later on, or if it is possible that stocks of other local companies are to be purchased at some future data, it be advisable to start as a subsidiary.

Licensing is used as "... a generic term covering ... patent license contracts, trade mark and copyright contracts, know how contracts, technical assistance contracts, franchise contracts... and combinations of the above."The licensing device may be used to enter a market that is closed to a manufacturer because of import or exchange restrictions or prohibitive tariffs.

Other reasons for entering into licensing agreements are diversification of methods of foreign income remittance; protection of foreign trade sales of licensor's subsidiaries; protection of foreign trade sales and local manufacturing of licensor; minimum involvement in foreign problems for parent companies not equipped to cope with such overseas problems; development of foreign markets for particular products in this line only; obtaining of foreign licensees' special know-how; fears of seasonal or continuing decline of domestic sales and threat of possible general recession at home; priority demands by domestic parent and domestic subsidiaries for limited investment capital and personnel; and, generally, insufficient capital or insufficient economic justification for any other type of international operation. For instance, it is claimed that for small companies licensing may be the best way, if not the only way, to enter foreign markets.

Licensing is less expensive (and no capital investment is necessary), but at the same time it is usually less profitable to the licensing firm than are other potential forms of international operations. Special care is necessary in investigating taxes applicable to royalties and local laws governing remittance of royalty funds. In view of the possibility of the country's acquiring technological advances, the usual practice has been a minimum of restrictions on royalty payment remittances.

Where trademarks or manufacturing rights have been licensed, exclusively, to a majority-or minority-controlled manufacturing subsidiary (or a foreign company in which the manufacturer has no interest), provision is generally also made for quality control and maintenance of standards. It is common to include a minimum sales volume clause in the agreement. Under a know-how agreement such controls are not necessary, because one's own trademark is not "on the block."

Although licensing is a flexible arrangement with minimum financial risk, which helps to spread costs-particularly high research and development costs—over a wider base, the large company with sufficient financial and personnel resources would as a rule be better off setting up its own plant. Patent or trademark protection for licensed products may be an allusion. Patents are enforceable over limited time periods, and in any case, acquiring of skills takes time; therefore, the manufacturer may be helping build his own competitor.

A joint venture-for marketing only, or for manufacturing and marketing may often be the only way (other than licensing) over restrictive tariff, import, or exchange hurdles. It may be necessary to go into partnership with local capital for several reasons: business, legal, tax, and political. Among the business reasons may be (1) to utilize a franchise, license, or other special concession held by the foreigner; (2) to obtain local partners whose influence or knowledge of local conditions is of great importance; (3) to take advantage of the manufacturing facilities or the distribution organization of an existing foreign company; (4) to obtain local capital to finance the venture-particularly if it is desired to share the risk with local investors because of special economic or political considerations which may exist; and (5) to meet the statutory requirements with regard to foreign capital in the country of operation.

Although there maybe definite legal requirements concerning the amount of local participation, it may be more important that income tax concessions and import duty concessions are available only if local participation is envisaged. Particularly in the field of import licenses and exchange quotas, more favorable treatment would generally be extended to a joint venture than to a totally foreign-owned company. Politically, it may be prudent to obtain official and public goodwill by going into partnership.The most important disadvantage of local capital participation lies in the matter of control of the decision-making machinery. The group that has the controlling interest should be able to make decisions-say, about the percentage of profits to be declared as a dividend—without any undue influence from nonbusiness considerations. If foreign and local capital is evenly divided and closely held, there are dangers of deadlock. If the local interests hold majority stock, there is the possibility of the foreign interests-being frozen out. If the local group is the minority, it could become obstructionist. Apart from the local company law that could be used to safeguard the interests of the foreign group, special provisions—e.g., quorum requirements for shareholder and directors' meetings, specifications about reserves, and assurances about representation on the board of directors for all groups-could be written into the articles of association of the company.

However, as Joseph S. Cardinale reported to the International Management Association: "Legal safeguards are important and necessary, but they cannot replace a satisfactory relationship with the local associates. Every effort should be made to secure maximum protection, but care should be taken that trust and confidence are not impaired at the outset by unduly pressing for and insisting upon every possible safeguard."Ownership of producing company may take the form of a virtually independent, fully integrated manufacturing and marketing operation in the foreign market at one extreme or simply the establishment of a partial assembly or service organization at the other. Between these extremes are many possible levels of operation, such as the importation of components or semifinished items and the finishing or assembly of these items in the foreign country. Ownership of the operating company may obviously be on a 100 per cent basis or on some other basis of control.

A wholly owned manufacturing subsidiary is a common approach to overseas markets. Historically, wholly owned operations have bee favored for the following reasons: ease of administration and quality control: maximum security for business methods and know-how; maximum financial flexibility with respect to dividend policy, reinvestment of earnings, intercompany transactions, etc.; unwillingness to share profits with outsiders; and, absence of any problems or relationships with any local stockholders. Nevertheless, a too strong emphasis on complete ownership carries with it problems as well. In 1957 an International Management Association report said: "There is define risk of loss of many present and future markets in following the restrictive and potentially dangerous policy of not undertaking overseas operations unless sole ownership or complete control are possible."

A wholly owned manufacturing subsidiary is most useful for the establishment of a manufacturing enterprise in which foreign know-how or capital investment is of overriding importance to the host country, or in operations in backward countries in which local capital and know-how have not yet developed. The foreign holding company is sometimes used in conjunction with the kinds of structural organization listed above, generally for tax or financial reasons. A foreign holding company is a subsidiary organized under the laws of another country for the purpose of conducting business in the country of organization and or in other areas of the world outside the country of the parent. There re four classes of countries in which such a company may profitably be sited: those that do not levy an income tax of any kind; those that do not levy income taxes on holding companies; those that do not levy taxes on income derived outside their borders;

and those that do not tax the income of foreign corporations when such income meets the special requirements of their tax law.The foreign holding company may take part in (1) buying and selling in the country of operation; (2) promoting and handling sales of the parent's products in third countries; (3) providing technical and managerial services in the country of organization; (4) licensing patents and trademarks in third countries; (5) holding stock of its own subsidiaries in third countries-subsidiaries that otherwise would have been subsidiaries of the parent; and (6) investing in the country of organization or third countries. The "internationalization" of a company has often been described as a three-stage evolutionary process along roughly the following lines:

Export: The company receives orders from foreign buyers and begins to export. Based on its early experience with such sales, it may appoint an importer or agent abroad to handle sales in a foreign country or countries. Export sales are often marginal business, pushed when domestic business is slow, but deemphasized when the domestic economy is booming. Under these circumstances, risk is usually minimal, returns are high, and investment is very small. As domestic conditions become quite competitive, the firm may decide to play a more active part in soliciting international business, appointing agents and establishing an export department, and perhaps even a sales branch or warehouse, overseas. Two dangers have to be watches for during this stage of the operations. Firstly, if the product is gaining consumer acceptance and the exporter continues to treat the market only as an outlet for surplus domestic production, and therefore does not try to meet the full potential, a competitor with more long-range intentions may step in very quickly and succeed in capturing the market. Secondly, the market may be unnecessarily restricted if the exporter prices his product on a full-cost basis, and therefore higher than he needs to, though the overseas market is helping him to run his plant at a higher level of output.

Foreign manufacturing: The decision to manufacture abroad usually marks a decisive step in the company's thinking; it is usually at this stage that large investments must be put on the line, people must be selected and trained for overseas operations, and management must devote a significant amount of time and attention to supervision and control of its overseas investments.It is at this stage that the company must normally make a long-range decision regarding its policies toward international operation. Investments may be minimized and international expansion facilitated by licensing arrangements with foreign-based firms, or a percentage ownership may be established, at least initially. These and other moves enable the company to acquire local market know-how and operating experience without a fullscale commitment of funds, facilities, and manpower, such as is implied in a wholly owned foreign manufacturing subsidiary.

The international corporation: The final stage, one reached as yet by a relatively few corporations, is the truly international company. Here there is no real domestic operation: ownership, management, production, marketing, and financing all flow from many countries. Some form of top-level management organization or holding company usually coordinates the activities of may subsidiaries of all types. While it is theoretically feasible, there are many practical difficulties blocking the attainment of such a corporate structure.

Index